D1708624

BAHIṆĀ BĀĪ

BAHIṆĀ BĀĪ

A TRANSLATION OF
HER AUTOBIOGRAPHY AND VERSES

by
JUSTIN E. ABBOTT

Foreword by
ANNE FELDHAUS

MOTILAL BANARSIDASS
Delhi Varanasi Patna Madras

©MOTILAL BANARSIDASS
Head Office: Bungalow Road, Delhi 110 007
Branches: Chowk, Varanasi 221 001
Ashok Rajpath, Patna 800 004
6 Appar Swamy Koil Street, Mylapore,
Madras 600 004

First Edition : Poona, 1929
[Published by the Scottish Mission Industries Co.
in Poet-Saints of Maharashtra Series as No. 5]

Reprint : Delhi, 1985

ISBN : 0–89581–822–1

Printed in India by Shantilal Jain at Shri Jainendra Press,
A-45 Naraina, Phase I, New Delhi 110 028 and published by
Narendra Prakash Jain for Motilal Banarsidass, Delhi 110 007.

FOREWORD

The writings of women are a rarity in Indian literature; this makes Abbott's translations of Bahiṇā Bāī's poems welcome from the outset. Moreover, the fact that a significant portion of Bahiṇā Bāī's work is autobiographical makes the translations all the more valuable. For they provide readers of English with a Hindu woman's own account of her experiences and aspirations, as well as her own interpretation of her tradition. Finally, Bahiṇā Bāī's particular experiences, as well as her particular interpretation of her tradition, are important in themselves, for they document an important reconciliation of competing ideals in the Hindu tradition.

Bahiṇā Bāī's greatest significance is the reconciliation that she achieves between duty and devotion, *dharma* and *bhakti*, marriage and love of God.[1] Such a reconciliation is rare among the medieval Indian women saints whose writings or life stories are known to us: for Āṇṭāḷ, Mahādevī, Lallā, Mīrā, and others, the love of God made impossible a stable married life. They rejected human suitors and husbands, and sometimes even dispensed with conventional modesty; they thus dramatized their *bhakti*, but they failed to fulfil the *dharma* of a woman. Bahiṇā's autobiography (2-78), by contrast, though it reveals the conflict in her marriage between her God and her husband, also portrays a resolution of the conflict: in the end, Bahiṇā is able to have both her marriage and her love for God.

The series of Bahiṇā's poems describing her former lives indicates that this state of things is the culmination of a long progression: in the first three of her twelve previous lives, she reports, she

1. I have discussed this theme in greater detail in "Bahiṇā Bāī: Wife and Saint," *The Journal of the American Academy of Religion*, L (1982), 591-604.

was not married (90-92); about the next four lives she implies, though she does not state clearly, that she was unmarried (93); in her eighth life, she says, she became a young widow, and, in the ninth, she died at the age of nine (94); whereas in her tenth, eleventh, and twelfth lives (94-96), as well as in the life during which she is writing, she was a married woman devoted both to her God and to her husband.

The superiority of this combination is further indicated in the "Verses on Wifely Duties" which close the present volume. While some of the poems (468, 471, 472, and part of 470) praise a love of God which defies convention and overrides worldly concerns, others (most clearly, 469 and 473) prescribe dutiful wifeliness without referring to any god but the husband. But a few of the verses seem to indicate that, for a woman, marriage and devotion are necessary to each other. On the one hand, Bahiṇā states, "Without a husband one does not keep God in mind" (467.2), and on the other hand, "she whose mind constantly contemplates God, she is recognized in the three worlds as the dutiful wife" (267.6).

In Bahiṇā's own life, the conflict between loving God and being a good wife is resolved somewhat arbitrarily—by chance, one might say, or by grace. Her husband stops opposing her devotional life, and comes to share her love for God, but this occurs only after her husband has threatened to leave her, and she has chosen him over God ("My duty," she writes, "is to serve my husband, for he is God to me." 35.4). These events may seem unique, irreproducible in others' lives, but Bahiṇā Bāī nevertheless provides an example for other Hindu women, a promise that they too can remain faithful to their wifely duties and still participate fully in the *bhakti* tradition. The writings and life of Bahiṇā Bāī thus contribute to what might be called the domestication of medieval *bhakti*, its reconciliation with the world and with the orthodox tradition.

In other areas, too, Bahiṇā's writings exhibit a tendency to hold on to elements of orthodoxy which a more radical *bhakti* might reject. On the question of caste, for instance, Bahiṇā reinterprets the qualifications for becoming a Brāhman without fundamentally questioning the superiority of her own Brāhman caste (404-435). And in the realm of philosophy, Bahiṇā seems to find no tension between her devotional religion and the prestigious non-dualist metaphysics which she so often mouths (e.g., in 162-171, 186.2, 435). In both these areas, Bahiṇā Bāī is heir to a long tradition of compromise and syncretism.[2] Bahiṇā's original contribution is to be found in her life and in her teachings on marriage.

Here, too, is to be found her importance for subsequent generations of women. Bahiṇā's is not a radical *bhakti* like that of Āṇṭāḷ, Mahādevī, Lallā, or Mīrā, but it is a *bhakti* much better suited than theirs to the life of the average Indian woman.

One wonders whether the poems ascribed to Bahiṇā Bāī had in fact all a single author, the opinions they express are so diverse. But it hardly matters whether Bahiṇā Bāī was a single person or the composite product of a scribal and editorial tradition. For Bahiṇā is important, not for the particularity of her life story, but because its outcome is universal. Bahiṇā's name, which means simply "Sister," might best be translated, "Everywoman."

Arizona State University Anne Feldhaus

2. For caste, see Thomas Hopkins, "The Social Teaching of the *Bhāgavata Purāṇa*," in *Krishna: Myths, Rites, and Attitudes*, ed. by Milton Singer (Chicago: University of Chicago Press, 1966). In philosophy, the "qualified non-dualism" (*viśiṣṭādvaita*) of Rāmānuja is the most famous of numerous attempts to reconcile *bhakti* and non-dualism, but Bahiṇā Bāī is more likely to have been directly exposed to the attempt in the *Jñāneśvarī*, Jñāneśvar's thirteenth-century Marāṭhī commentary on the *Bhagavadgītā*.

PREFACE

I take special pleasure in introducing to English readers the Saint and Poetess, Bahiṇā Bāī, for, until recently, her autobiography and verses have been known to but a few. A few manuscript copies of her works exist. The first printed edition, edited by Dhondo V. Umarkhāne, appeared in 1914, and was soon out of print. Another edition, printed from another manuscript, edited by V. N. Kolhārkar, was issued in 1926. It is probably true that there are not many Marathi readers of her poetry. To introduce Bahiṇā Bāī to a larger circle of readers in India, and to introduce to the West a name there absolutely unknown, but worthy of being known, I consider a privilege of no mean order.

I have not attempted to translate all her verses, for the translation of the whole, with the text, would make too bulky a volume. I have, therefore, chosen such portions as seemed best adapted to give to the English reader the thoughts of this Indian woman that found expression in her verses nearly three hundred years ago.

I do not hesitate to acknowledge many unusual difficulties in translating her language and thought. Her style is exceedingly elliptical. Her vocabulary and grammatical constructions, belonging to the Marathi of three hundred years ago, create many difficulties for me, a foreigner. Her allusions to customs and traditional stories require a wide reading to prevent those mistranslations that would bring a smile to the Marathi reader. I acknowledge my debt therefore to Pandit Narhar R. Godbole for information and suggestions that have enabled me to avoid many a pitfall.

Copyists of Marathi manuscripts were not always careful copyists. There are differences, therefore, between the two printed texts mentioned above. I have in the main followed Kolhārkar's text, because it is now the only text available. I have gone into the question of the respective merits of these texts.

I may also add here that Bahiṇā Bāī's verses require considerable illumination for the Western reader. Her allusions to Puranic stories, customs, to philosophic thought, to religious observances and the like, are outside the Westerner's ken. But to make the necessary explanations in notes and footnotes would take so much space and lead me so far afield, that I have limited myself to the most necessary explanations in footnotes and glossary, and have left it to the Western reader to gain further information as best as he can, if he feels an interest in doing so.

To the Rev. J. F. Edwards of Bombay, I owe a debt of gratitude for his assistance in seeing this volume through the Press.

JUSTIN E. ABBOTT.

SUMMIT, NEW JERSEY, U.S.A.

INTRODUCTION

ON THE POET-SAINT BAHIṆĀ BĀĪ

The Marāthā people can point with pride to many of their poet-saints who were women of literary ability, wise in philosophy and godly in character. Such have been Muktā Bāī, Janā Bāī, Veṇu Bāī, Bayā Bāī, Ambā Bāī, Chimā Bāī, and Bahiṇā Bāī. But poetry is natural to Indian women. As in the early morning they grind the flour for the day's meals, they sing aloud, often composing words to fit the metres they enjoy. The subjects of their song may be philosophy, religion, personal sad or happy experiences, a prayer, or words that have little sense, but please the ear. All through the centuries the women have sung at their handmills, before the sun has risen, and while their men folk were fast asleep. They were too modest to record their own verses, the men folk too indifferent to do so, but all the same all through the centuries Indian women have composed verses and sung them down to the present day.

Bahiṇī, is believed by Marāthā scholars, to have been born in 1628 and died in 1700, at the age of 72. Her autobiography, unique in Marathi literature, supplies all that is known of her. Her name is mentioned with respect by later poets, but she alone has furnished the details of her life.* Her autobiography covers only the details of the early years

*Niloba, a disciple of Tukarām, gives a few details.

of her life. For her later years with their mental struggles, temptations, perplexities, and thoughts of approaching death, one has to gather from her verses such details as she has made possible.

While Bahiṇī was a girl of tender age, living in Kolhapur, she became deeply interested in the poems of Tukārām. *Tukārām was then a young man of about 30 years of age, but his fame had already spread far and wide. Bahiṇī became very desirous to go to Dehu, a village not far from Poona, where Tukārām lived, and was performing his inspiring *kīrtans*. Her husband opposed her in this desire as he was a Brāhman, and Tukārām was a Shudra. In a dream, however, Tukārām placed his hand on her head and gave into her ear the *mantra* that had come down to him from the past ages, the six syllable *mantra* "Rāma-Krishṇa-Hari." From that moment Bahiṇī regarded herself as Tukārām's disciple, and her whole life came under his influence and inspiration, as her *guru*.

Her verses show her to have been a most thoughtful woman. By tradition and by her own thinking she was a believer in the Vedāntic philosophy, but she was not without doubts, and she passed through such mental strains that she even contemplated suicide. She felt the handicap of being a woman, and not allowed the freedom of study and speech that men enjoyed. As she approached the end of her life, at the age of seventy-two, her bark floated on

---

*For "Life of Tukaram" see Edwards' *Life and Teaching of Tukaram.*

For Verses of Tukaram see *Translation of Tukaram's Verses* by Fraser and Marathe.

peaceful waters, and she was ready to face the hour of death, that would take her to the great Beyond.

One is impressed by Bahiṇī's high moral ideas, and one cannot but think that she lived as she thought. Living and dying in her little distant village of Devgāv, where her town still stands, there was, however, no poet there to sing her praises. If there had been, one may be sure his imagination would have supplied the Chariot-of-Light [*vimān*] that the gods were accustomed to send to take to heaven the souls of the specially godly. The Chariot-of-Light would surely have had its load of flowers also, to shower on this saint, as she took her seat, to pass from this life into the next.

CONTENTS

CHAPTER I.

Ādiparampara.

CHAPTER II.

Ātmanivedan Autobiography.

CHAPTER III.

Niryāṇpar Abhangs

CHAPTER IV.

Manahpar Abhangs

CHAPTER V.

Bhaktipar Abhangs

CHAPTER VI

Sadguruchī Thoravī

CHAPTER VII.

Anutāpapar Abhaṅgs PAGE.

CHAPTER VIII.

Santavarṇanapar Abhaṅgs

CHAPTER IX.

Bodhapar Abhaṅgs

CHAPTER X.

Nāmamāhātmyapar

CHAPTER XI.

Brahmakarmapar Abhangs

CHAPTER XII.

Paṇdhari Māhātmya

CHAPTER XIII.

Puṇdalīkmāhātmya

CHAPTER XIV.

Pativratādharmapar Abhaṅgs

CHAPTER I.

A TRANSLATION FROM THE SANT BAHINABAICHA GATHA

Adiparampara.

HER GURU ANCESTRY

1 (1) Adināth [Shiva] taught a mantra to Pārvati [His wife]. Matsyendra heard it from within the belly of a fish. (2) Thus through him the supreme *mantra*, that Shiva held in His mind, became effective through *bhakti*. (3) He [Matsyendra] showed his favour by passing the *mantra* on to Goraksha [Gorakhnāth]. Through him it became known to Gahini. (4) Gahini bestowed his favour on Nivrittināth, even while he was a child, but yet a Yogi. (5) From him Dnyāneshvara received the favour of the *mantra*, and this made him famous at Alandi, the home of Siddhas. (6) Dnyāneshvara gave his blessing to Satchidānanda, the home of *bhakti*. (7) Further on Vishvambhara, in the beauty of his Shiva form, gave the *mantra* to Rāghava [Chaitanya]. (8) He gave it to Keshava Chaitanya, and he to Bābāji Chaitanya, who gave it to Tukobā [Tukārām]. (9) Because Bahiṇi placed her undivided devotion at the feet of Tukobā, she received (the *mantra* through him).

CHAPTER II.

ATMANIVEDAN
HER AUTOBIOGRAPHY AND VERSES

BAHINĪ'S BIRTHPLACE

2 (1) Devgāv was my own beautiful parental home. To the East of this place lies the town of Verul*. (2) At

*Ellora Road, Ry. Station 219 miles from Bombay, or 57 miles from Manmad Junction, for the famous Ellora caves.

Devgāv may be noticed a crowd of gods gathered together. (3) Here it was that the Rishi Agasti, coming from the Himalayas, spent four months. (4) To the west of the town the river Shiva flows. Among all holy bathing places this one is unsurpassed. (5) The equivalent of a hundred thousand *tīrthas* are there, to be bathed in. A hundred thousand of them for ever exist there. (6) Agasti saw this holy spot, and at the rising of the sun used to come here to perform his austerities. (7) The Rishi Agasti gave a boon that at Lākshāgrāma a hundred thousand *tirthas* would reside; (8) and that he who might bathe here, make gifts, repeat God's names or perform austerities, would realize his desires. (9) Agasti made his abode at Devgāv, but came regularly to the river Shiva for his bath. (10) Says Bahiṇī, "It was at such a place, Devgāv, that I was born."

BAHINĪ'S BIRTH AND GIRLHOOD

3. (1) The scribe of the town was Aujī Kulkarni. I was born into his family. (2) My mother's name was Jānakī; my father's name was Audev [Aujī]; and Devgāv was the name of their home. (3) The family was childless; to have a child they did all manner of things. (4) They were for ever bathing in the Laksha *tīrtha*, and adopted Shiva austerities. (5) For some days my father Aujī continued having a dream. (6) In it a holy Brāhman old him he would have a daughter and two sons. (7) Says Bahiṇī, "Within a year after that I was born as a daughter fter nine full months."

4 (1) Brahmans assisted at the festival of my welfth day. The Brāhmans, after the feast, returned to their homes. (2) My father soon after happened to go

into the forest. Suddenly he made a happy discovery. (3) On the Verul road he found a gold mohar tied in a yellow robe. (4) Returning home he cried out with joy: 'This daughter of ours is bringing us good luck!' (5) The excellent Brahman astrologer, Vireshvara, made out my horoscope. (6) 'You will be blessed through her,' was the horoscope which he read from the paper before him. (7) The astrologer declared, 'She will be one to possess good fortune. The cord of her life shows great strength.' (8) Says Bahiṇī, "So said the Brahman, and he was given presents of garments and a cow."

BAHIṆĪ'S MARRIAGE.

5 (1) Deciding to give me in marriage, they began early planning to bring it about. (2) Just then, unexpectedly, as if directed by Fate, a near relative from Shiur turned up. (3) To begin with, he was a relative, and moreover, he wished to get married. He was an intelligent *purāṇik,* an excellent jewel of a man. (4) The request for me was made, and the word of promise was given. The marriage day was fixed, and the wedding took place. (5) A brother was now born after me, as the former austerities had been performed. (6) They all exclaimed, 'This good fortune that a son should be born after her, is undoubtedly due to her. (7) Says Bahiṇī, "Three years now passed. I will relate now what happened thereafter."

6 (1) My father's noble family line was that of Maunas. My husband was of the high Gautam *Gotra.* (2) He was the astrologer of Shivapura. My father and mother gave me to him. (3) It was his second marriage.

He was thirty years of age. My husband was one whom fortune favoured. He was a wise man. (4) Says Bahiṇī, "To such an one I was given in marriage, together with many marriage gifts."

FAMILY QUARRELS LEAD TO EMIGRATION

7 (1) Four years after my marriage our relatives became hostile to my father. (2) The quarrel arose in connection with his office. He, therefore, sent for my husband. (3) 'Settle all my debts to my family. Give deeds for fields and gardens. (4) We must go from here to some foreign country.' (5) He said, 'Only thus shall we have peace.' (6) You are closely related to us, of our own kin, a son-in-law and friend. (7) Do not see us in such extremity. If we should be thrown into prison, who will deliver us. Be a friend to us and deliver us.' My, husband, therefore, in the middle, in the dead of night, took us away. (8) With my father, my mother, my brother and myself he went by night, arriving at length at the bank of the Gaṅgā river [Godāvari]. (9) We had our Gaṅgā-bath at Pravarā Saṅgam where the Pravarā joins the Gaṅgā and paid our homage to Siddhanāth. (10) Says Bahiṇī, "From there we set out on foot for Mahādev."

8 (1) But having seen the Gaṅgā, and the God Siddheshvara, one knew not how to leave the place. (2) The reasons for our affection for the place were past influences. There was also our reverence for the *kïrtans* we heard. (3) There was our love for listening to the *Purāṇs*. There were the worship, the temple, and the worship of

Brahmans. (4) We felt our hearts clinging to the feet of the *sannyāsīs*, the holy men, and the great souled saints. (5) We were exceedingly sorry to leave the place What is this that wretched Fate has done to us? (6) Says Bahiṇī, "We started for the Mahādeva forest, my husband taking us along in an honoured way."

9 (1) We journeyed, begging as we went along. We had to suffer many hard experiences. (2) As we, mother, father, brother, and husband, journeyed with the purpose of visiting the Mahādeva forest, (3) we had a satisfying sight of Narasimha, and then visited the temple of Paṇḍuraṅg. (4) We saw the Bhīmā river, the Chandrabhāgā, and the shrine of the saint Puṇḍalīka. At Veṇunād mankind finds deliverance (from birth and death). (5) We bathed in Padmālaya pool. We went to see the god [Pāṇḍuraṅg]. We listened to the praises of God's name. (6) We saw the images of Rāhī, Rakhumāī, and Satyabhāmā; and all the rest of them, together with the eastern entrance (of the temple). (7) As we entered through the main door our hearts felt exceeding joy. (8) When we saw the holy image of Pāṇḍuraṅg our eyes, with the other organs of sense, were delighted. (9) We made *pradakshiṇā* around the god, in joyous ecstasy, with minds free of all worldly thoughts. (10) We felt in our hearts that we wanted to stay right there, but that was not in the thought of Fate. (11) Even though it might mean death to us, yet Paṇḍharī was the place we would be in. We felt as though we could not leave its river-water. (12) Says Bahiṇī, "Because of good deeds in a former birth, we had the privilege of staying in Paṇḍharī for five days and nights."

10 (1) At the time of the full moon, in the month of Chaitra, we arrived at the Mahādeva forest. We saw here the god and the gathering of his worshippers. (2) In seeing Shaṅkara we were comforted, and through our *bhakti* we asked that his hand of assurance might rest upon us. (3) After remaining here five nights we came to Siṅgaṇāpur. (4) Here in our begging we easily obtained uncooked grain, and my mind was made happy thereby. (5) The food made of it tasted to me like nectar, for in the eating of it one's sins seemed burnt away. (6) Says Bahiṇī, "I was then nine years of age, and I have revealed my heart's emotions."

11 (1) My husband consulted every one of us, and the thought of all was that it was not a safe place to stay. (2) It seemed better to our thinking to go and live in some Brāhman city. (3) We said, 'At Rahimatpur there are a great number of Brāhmans. Let us make our place and abide there.' (4) Says Bahiṇī, "This was the arrangement of Fate, for otherwise one could not have left the place, even if one had sought to do so."

THE FAMILY SETTLES AT RAHIMATPUR.

12 (1) Thus we all went and settled down at Rahimatpur, where we all began to beg. (2) My husband was of noble character. He performed his baths and prayers regularly, and God was gracious to him. (3) It now happened that the priest of the town who lived there was preparing to go away to Benāres. (4) He made my husband his successor in carrying on the religious services of

the town. (5) And seeing that he was honest, wise, and learned, all the citizens brought their problems to him. (6) 'I am now going to Benāres,' the priest said, 'and I leave to you this priest and astrologer.' (7) My husband agreed (to the proposal), and we remained there, supporting ourselves, for a whole year. (8) After that time the priest returned to the town, but he took care of us for still another year. (9) I was now eleven years of age, and felt a strong desire to be associated with the saints. (10) I wanted to listen to the stories that were heard in the reading of the *Purāṇs* and I delighted in the worship of Brāhmans. (11) But Fate pulled us away from there; so leaving that town we again journeyed on, (12) sad in heart, pleased with nothing. There is, however, no means of withstanding Fate. (13) Says Bahiṇī, "We arrived at length at Kolhāpur, that exceeding holy city."

THE FAMILY MOVES TO KOLHAPUR.

13 (1) There was here a Brāhman named Bahirambhat, a *Vedāntī*, versed in the two *Shāstras*, a *Yajurvedi*, (2) noble in character, favoured of fortune, holy, a keeper of the holy fire, to whom many pupils came to learn. (3) Obtaining a place in his house we remained there where undisturbed, we were able to listen to his readings. (4) We used to listen also to the frequent *Hari-kīrtans* by Jayarām Gosāvī of stories out of the *Bhāgavat Purāṇa*. (5) Says Bahiṇī, "While living here we gave ourselves constantly to contemplation and meditation on the soul."

THE FAMILY IS GIVEN A BLACK COW.

14 (1) Now it happened on a certain occasion, when I was in my eleventh year, that there was a great festal event on a Monday. (2) During this festival a cow was given to Hirambhat [Bahirambhat], the donor having found a cow, about to calve. (3) This one-coloured cow was wholly black. He made a *pradakshiṇā,* waved the tail over himself, and gave the cow away. (4) Her horns were gilded with gold leaf, her hoofs were silvered, and she was covered with a yellow robe. (5) The cow was given with all the proper ceremonies, and everybody came to see her. (6) A calf was born to the cow, and Hirambhat took her to his house. The calf drank the milk that was milked from the cow. (7) Ten days passed, and on the eleventh day a Brāhman appeared to Bahirambhat in a dream and said: (8) "Offer this one-coloured cow to the Brāhman who is occupying your veranda." (9) Bahirambhat made the dream come true, and gave the cow with sincere good wishes to my husband. (10) The hearts of us all rejoiced in this gift, and the care of the cow fell to us. (11) My father and mother went every day to get grass. She was cared for carefully, and it was done with joy.

Bahini had a little calf

It's hair was black as coal.

(12) The calf of the cow was also of one colour, and it had a great affection for me. (13) Only if I unfastened it, would it go to get its milk, and as I milked the cow it was with me. (14) I was the only one to give

it water, and the only one to feed it with grass. Without me it was unhappy. When I went out to draw water, the calf would bawl aloud, and with tail erect would follow me. (16) The people watched us and thought all this a strange thing while the calf and the cow looked casually at us. (17) When the calf was loosened, it would not even go to the cow. (18) Only when I gave it grass, would it eat. Only when I gave it water, would it drink. (19) At night it slept on my bedding. As it listened to the reading of the Purāṇa it would sob with emotion.

And everywhere that Bahini went

The calf was sure to go.

(20) When I went to a *Kīrtan,* it would come along with me and stand quietly listening. (21) The cow would be in her stall at home, but the calf would be at the *kīrtan.* When I went to my bath the calf would follow me. (22) People would remark to me in various terms, 'The calf acts most extraordinarily with you.' (23) Some remarked "The calf must be a *yogabhrashta.*" Some said of me, 'Its habits are bad.' (24) Others said, 'The calf is her debtor and only when the debt is paid will she be rid of it.' (25) The calf, however, would not leave me, and I loved to be with it. (26) If the calf was not in sight, I was troubled; I felt like a fish out of water. (27) Whether I was grinding, or pounding grain or carrying water, I was unhappy, though with others, without the calf. (28) My husband was of a fiery temper, and he did not like this, but finally his heart yielded to pity. (29) Said he, 'Let it be. You

have no child, and this calf is a plaything for your heart. (30) You enjoy listening to the Purāṇic stories and *kīrtans*, and the calf costs you nothing.'

It followed her to church one day.

Which was against the rule.

(31) It was at this time that Jayarām Gosāvī happened to come there. (32) He conducted *kīrtans* from house to house where the worship of Brāhmans took place, and he began to feed the twice-born. (33) He conducted his *kīrtans* both at night and during the day. My father and mother attended them with much pleasure. (34) I also went with them to these *kīrtans,* and the calf used to go with me also. (35) Where my mother sat, there I sat also, and the calf would rush in and stand beside me. (36) Inoffensive in its actions, it stood listening to the *kīrtan* and the loud acclaim of God's names. (37) After the verses of praise, when all bowed to the ground, the calf also placed its head on the floor.

It made the people laugh and say:

'To think! A calf can pray!'

(38) Everybody laughed when they saw this, but they were kindly and happy over it. (39) They said, 'It is a *yogabhrashta,* a worshipper of Hari in a former birth. In the form of a calf see how it acts as one indifferent to the things of this world.'

11

THE CALF BRINGS TROUBLE TO BAHIṆI

(40) It now happened on a certain day that Moropant invited the *bhaktas* to the performance of a *kīrtan*. (41) The day was the eleventh of the month, and at noon with great rejoicing the *Hari-kīrtan* was begun. (42) Jayarām Gosāvī, with his multitude of disciples, sat in the assembly on special seats. (43) There was singing accompanied with cymbals and drums. A large crowd had gathered there. (44) Among them were myself, my parents and my brother, and we listened with exceeding joy to the recitation of the *Purāṇic* stories. (45) The calf seated itself by me, but some people dragged it away to the door. (46) They said, 'There is no sufficient seating space for the people. Is a beast a proper creature to be a listener?' (47) I began to weep for my calf, and the Gosāvī heard me. (48) And as the calf cried, I fell to weeping. Someone explained the matter to the Gosāvī. (49) They said, "This is a little girl living at the house of Hirambhat. She has come to this *Shrī Hari-kīrtan*. (50) She has a calf with her, which she has always following her. (51) The calf has been taken outside, because of the seating difficulties. For this reason the girl is sulking and crying. (52) The calf is outside crying out, and she is crying here inside, hence this commotion.' (53) Jayarām Svāmī was a discerner of the soul. He recognized the soul of the calf. (54) 'Bring the calf here,' he said. 'Can Hari, the knower of the soul, not be in the soul of a calf? (55) It is overcome with desire to listen to the *kïrtan*. One should not call it a beast.' (56) So he had the calf brought in, and had it stand by him.

JAYARĀM SVĀMĪ COMFORTS BAHIṆĪ

As Jayarām looked at the calf, he had a feeling of joy. (57) On account of my *prārabdha,* because of good deeds done in a former birth, the kindly man called me to him. (58) Looking intently at us, he caressed us both, though this was unacceptable to the people. (59) The *kathā* [*Purāṇic* recitation] continued with very loud refrains, for the hearts of the Vaishṇavas were full of joy. (60) Jayarām Gosāvī thought that both parties were true hearted and of good deeds. (61) He said, 'The calf stands during the *kathā,* in its actions showing intense attention. (62) This is a little girl, of tender age. It is very strange that she so loves to listen to these stories. (63) Is there any one here at the *kathā* belonging to her?' (64) One replied, 'Yes, her father and mother. She has a husband a very worthy man. But her *vairāgya* seems very great. (65) She comes to these reading of the *Purāṇas* with her father and mother, and brings the calf along with her.' (66) At this point I acted for myself. I prostrated myself at his feet. (67) The calf also fell at his feet as I did. To all the people it was extraordinary. (68) At his left and right there were two persons. They raised us up, the calf and myself. (69) When the *kathā* was ended, the people went away, remarking to themselves on the event, such as had never occurred before. (70) Hirambhat and many others also said, 'Who knows what this is a sign of.' (71) Says Bahiṇī, "This is what happened at Kolhapur, and now I will tell you what happened thereafter."

15 (1) With my father, mother, and brother, and accompanied by the calf, we then returned to our lodgings.

(2) At that time only two *ghatikās* of the night remained. The calf was fed, and the cow was milked. (3) Hirambhat performed his bath in the spirit of fire-worship, and the *kārtik* lamps twinkled in the sky. (4) I swept and cleaned the floors, performed my bath, and caressed the cow and calf. (5) My husband also performed his bath. Kolhapur is the Gayā of the South country.

BAHIṆĪ'S ANGRY HUSBAND BEATS HER

(6) It happened that at that time there was there a certain woman named Nirābāī. (7) She began relating what had happened at the *kathā*. (8) She let fall on my husband's ears a recital of all the events at the *kathā*, as being most extraordinary, the actions of the calf, and my crying. His ears were filled with her recital. (9) She added how Jayarām Gosāvī, while in an ecstatic state, had placed his hand upon her head. (10) Great was her good fortune that he should speak to her, and give her his gracious blessing. (11) My husband was a religious mendicant by profession, but a man of very angry disposition. He rushed upto the house. (12) He seized me by the braids of my hair, and beat me to his heart's content. Hirambhat was greatly distressed at this, (13) but could not restrain him from beating me. The cow mourned aloud, and the calf also was in great distress. (14) All this happened to me when in my eleventh year. In what duty to my husband had I failed? (15) My mother, father, and brother kept quiet, until my husband gradually restrained his rage. (16) When he became quiet, they asked him why he was so troubling his wife? (17) He replied, 'In last night's *kathā* what special greatness or devotion did she

notice in Jayarām! (18) Who cares for the *Purāṇ*! Who cares for the *Hari-kathā*! I'll give her a beating and nothing else.' (19) Thus talking, my husband again could not control his rage, just like a fire out of control. (20) Says Bahiṇī, "My body accepted it, who can ward off the force of Fate?"

16 (1) When it came to his mind to do so he beat me violently. He tied me (hand and foot) into a bundle and threw me aside. (2) Hirambhat cried to him, 'Get out of here! He seems like a murderous wretch!' (3) My father and mother pled with Hirambhat and soon quieted him. (4) 'Have mercy on us this day,' they said, 'tomorrow morning we will seek for another place.' (5) In the meantime the cow and the calf would eat no grass, nor drink water. (6) And my husband, seeing this refusal of the cow and calf, untied me and set me free. (7) And as I came close to the cow and the calf, they lowed just as a mother coos over her son. (8) When I saw the calf and the cow, I said to myself, it is better that I should die. (9) Says Bahiṇī, "It was their great affection for me that made them refuse the grass and water given to them."

JAYARĀM SVĀMĪ ADMONISHES BAHIṆĪ'S HUSBAND

17 (1) They would eat no grass and drink no water. I also refused all food. (2) They would not arise from the place on which they were lying. Everybody came to see what was happening. (3) Someone told Jayarām Svāmī of what was going on, and he also came to see, at

this time of my extremity. (4) My husband made him a *namaskār*, with a mind sincerely devoted to him. (5) He gave Jayarām Svāmī a special seat, and Hirambhat worshipped him. (6) People gathered to see with their own eyes what was taking place. The Svāmī also at that time experienced a sense of joy. (7) He said, 'O Brāhman, you are her husband. I am going to tell you the truth; listen with attention. (8) Your wife is a *Yogabhrashta*, and the manner of life she must adopt is of a very austere kind. Now do not distress her any more. (9) By her special wifely duties she will do you service; and you will save your soul. (10) You must possess some good deed done in a former birth. By means of it you have become associated with her. (11) The cow and the calf are her companions and one with her in her religious life. (12) The calf is her *guru;* the calf is her means of salvation, for it destroys the cord that binds it, (13) and all who live in association with her, will joyfully drink the sweet juice of *Bhakti.* (14) If you will listen to me, it will be well for you. But what authority have I here?' (15) Says Bahiṇī, "As Jayarām thus advised, he saw that all signs were favourable."

18 (1) Jayarām started to return home. A great crowd of disciples accompanied him. He remarked, 'These three [Bahiṇī, cow, and calf] were unitedly engaged in the performance of religious rites during a former birth. (2) Some hindrance prevented the completion of those rites. (3) The cow and calf have been born as such because of their former good deeds. (4) This girl, however, has fully completed the rites and possesses purity of heart.' (5) As Jayarām and others were thus talking to one another, I

listened respectfully. (6) Says Bahiṇī, "The Svāmī then returned to his lodgings. I will now tell what further happened."

THE DEATH OF BAHIṆĪ'S CALF

19 (1) The twelfth day of the fortnight had passed, and now was the thirteenth. The calf was about to die. (2) At that moment Hirambhat casually and in his usual way began to repeat a Sanskrit *shloka.** (3) *'Mukam karoti'* [He, by whose mercy the dumb speak, and the lame climb mountains]. (4) As he finished the first half of this *shloka,* the calf began to repeat the latter half of the *shloka* thus: *'Yatkrupa tamaham vande'*—'By whose favour these great achievements (mentioned in the first half of the *shloka*) are performed, to Him, [the great Mādhav, who is Supreme Joy] I bow.' (5) Everyone heard the calf repeat this latter half of the *shloka,* and began talking about it among themselves. (6) Just then the calf yielded up its life. (7) I rushed towards it. I wished my own life to accompany its life, but no effort avails against Fate. (8) The cow began to moan, with her neck upon both of us, but of course how could she speak? (9) Says Bahiṇī, "Fate preserved my body. What happened later, who could know?"

20 (1) Jayarām Svāmī heard of the event, that the calf had died; (2) and that as it was dying it had repeated the latter part of a *shloka.* It put to shame what *Yoga*

---

*Gita Dhyana 8:—मूकं करोति वाचालं पंगुं लंघयते गिरिम्
यत्कृपा तमहं वन्दे परमानन्दमाधवम् ॥

could do. (3) Then all the chief men, the saints and *sādhus,* carried the calf to its burial singing God's praise as they went along. (4) The calf was carried in a pompous procession, with musical instruments and banners, the cow accompanying. (5) Lowing, the cow followed behind the procession, overwhelmed within with exceeding grief. (6) The people buried the calf, and then after bathing returned to their homes. (7) The cow went to where the calf was buried, moaned, and then returned back to her home. (8) As the people looked at me, they saw I was unconscious. They could observe no sign of life in my body.

BAHIṆĪ HAS A VISION BY NIGHT

(9) After four days had passed, in the middle of the night of the first day of the fortnight, I had a vision of a Brāhman coming before me, and saying to me: (10) 'Awake! Bāī! Begin to think! Let your mind awake! (11) Awake! awake! awake!' As my ear listened, my body trembled. (12) Awaking, I saw not the cow, nor the calf, but the people and my mother, sitting before me. (13) So also I saw my brother, my father and my husband sitting where a lamp was burning brightly. (14) Then coming to full consciousness, my memory brought my mind back to its right state. (15) Says Bahiṇī, "My body is altogether feeble, but my soul is strong."

21 (1) As I opened my eyes and looked before me I saw God Pāṇḍuraṅg. (2) The same image came to my imagination that I had seen at Paṇḍharī, and I saw Jayarām also before my eyes. (3) And my mind preserved in its memory the appearance of the Brāhman I had seen in my

dream. (4) I saw nothing else before me. My memory retained the name of God. (5) The old stories of Hari, that I had often heard, my mind recollected. (6) The non-dualistic popular verses of Tukobā (Tukārām) touched my heart through their teachings. (7) And I felt it would be a great joy to my heart, if I could but meet the author of those verses. (8) Through listening to his verses in the *kathās,* I had already become devoted to Tokobā. (9) I felt that, if I ever met Tukobā, that moment would be like Heaven. (10) If I could only hear a *Hari-kathā* from Tukobā's lips, my mind would find its peace. (11) So keeping Tukobā pictured in my imagination I lived with it in my mind in full consciousness. (12) Says Bahiṇī, "Tukā is my good *guru,* and my brother. Could I but meet him, it would be supreme happiness."

22 (1) Just as a fish flops about when out of water, so I acted in my love for Tukobā. (2) He who can see aright the emotions of the human heart, will understand me through his own heart-experience. (3) Just as a thirsty one loves water, so was I. Without him I was like a body without soul. (4) Says Bahiṇī, "My longings were at the feet of Tukobā, as I listened to his verse with my whole being."

23 (1) Know, O my Soul, who is there aside from a *sadguru,* who can burn up the accumulated deeds of a former birth? (2) For this purpose one should have an exceedingly good *sadguru,* able to extinguish the hardships of this worldly existence. (3) Who can cool the three-fold fevers of life, if one does not attach oneself wholly to a *sadguru?* (4) And how can the fact of the succession

of births and deaths be avoided, if one does not indeed meet with a *sadguru*? (5) All my wrong desires will be absolutely taken from me whenever I meet the *sadguru*, Tukobā. (6) Says Bahiṇī, "I feel as if I would die. Why does not Tukobā feel pity for me?"

24 (1) I am unable to express in words the appeal of my heart. Tukobā does not listen. What is to be done? (2) Wretched Fate! Even God does not help me. It is the longing of my heart. What shall I do! (3) It was he who left his manuscript of verses in the water of the river for thirteen days, and then forsooth, recovered it uninjured: (4) He, in all seer, who in the Marathi language is giving to the people in verse the substance of the Vedānta. (5) My heart admits that it has a longing to listen to it, but my mind does not comprehend it. (6) Says Bahiṇī. "It is I who must be at fault. Injustice could not possibly be his."

TUKĀRĀM APPEARS IN A DREAM

25. (1) I began to experience great sorrow in my heart. Why, O Viṭṭhal, have you forsaken me. (2) I am all in a heat from the three fevers of life. What matters it, let me die! (3) But just then on the seventh day, repeating aloud the names and praises of God, Tukārām appeared in a vision before my eyes, and said: 'Remember the first lines (of the calf's *shloka*). (5) Do not be troubled, I am beside you. Take from my hand this nectar. (6) When a calf puts its mouth to the cow, a stream of milk flows. This is excellent nectar, drink it.

(7) With this he placed his hand upon my head and whispered a *mantra* * in my ear. (8) I then placed my head on his feet. He gave me a book called the Mantra *Gītā*. (9) This vision in a dream occurred through the *Guru's* favour on a Sunday, on the fifth day of the dark half of the moon in the month of Kārtika. (10) My heart rejoiced. It fixed itself on Brahma, Pure Intelligence. I sat up astonished. (11) I recollected the *mantra*. Tukobā, in the form of a vision, had manifested to me his abundant mercy in this dream. (12) He had fed me with nectar, which to the taste was unlike anything else. He only can appreciate this who experiences it. (13) Says Bahiṇī, "Such was the mercy of the *sadguru*. Tukārām had truly shown it abundantly."

26 (1) I was comforted by the Brāhman's words. And I remembered the verses which I had heard in my dream. (2) Without having actually seen Tukobā, I meditated on my mental image of him. (3) He whose verses give the mind rest, he in his bodily form is Viṭṭhal himself. (4) There seems no difference between him and Viṭṭhal. That was the witness my mind gave. (5) Pāṇḍuraṅg and Tukā, Pāṇḍuraṅg and Tukā. How could they appear different? (6) In the *Kali-yuga* Hari took the form of Buddha, and entered the body of Tukobā. (7) Tukobā's intelligence took the form of Pāṇḍuraṅg, while the mind [*mana*] was Tukobā's. (8) He who sets Tukobā's bodily organs in motion is truly Pāṇḍuraṅg. (9) Tukobā's eyes are also Pāṇḍuraṅg. His ears are Pāṇḍuraṅg in the form of the *Abhaṇg*. (10) Whatever Tukobā's hand writes, that is clearly Pāṇḍuraṅg. (11) All the actions of Tukobā

*Rama—Krishna—Hari.

are Hari, who makes him one with Himself, through the fact of non-duality. (12) Says Bahiṇī, "Tukobā pervades in visible form. I see his very form in my contemplation (of him)."

27 (1) (I have already related how) my husband had tied me up into a bundle, and beaten me, unable to endure my grief (for the calf). (2) How also on the fourth day when I was on the point of dying, Viṭṭhal performed a miracle. (3) In the form of a Brāhman, he came to me and awakened me to consciousness. (4) My soul did awake, and my thought fastened itself on Tukobā. (5) It was the seventh day after the calf had died, that Tukobā had appeared in the dream, (6) comforted me, fed me with nectar, having led the calf (me) to the cow (Tukārām). (7) After feeding me with nectar he whispered a *mantra* in my ear, which everywhere men repeat. (8) He placed his hand on my head and blessed me. The favour he bestowed on me, he alone could know its worth. (9) The greatness of such a blessing is unlimited. It was what the calf declared in substance when it repeated the latter half of the Sanskrit *shloka*. (100) On the eighth day I became physically conscious, having drunk to the full the nectar Tukobā gave me. (11) Just then I saw the cow directly before me. She looked at the point of death, because of her calf's death. (12) But Tukobā said to me, 'I have fed this nectar also to the calf. Never can death touch it. (13) The calf is here with me, immortal, its soul partaking gladly of the nectar.' (14) Says Bahiṇī "After all the above had happened, the next events to take place will now be related in detail."

JAYARĀM AGAIN AIDS BAHIṆĪ

28 (1) Jayarām, the great, the ocean-of-wisdom, who could see things through his peculiar power of vision, (2) sent for Hirambhat, and asked him about my condition. (3) Hirambhat related to him all the events that had occurred at his house; (4) how a *guru* appeared to me in a dream, in the form of Tukobā; how he had enlightened me in the dream. (5) He told him, how the little girl awoke to consciousness, how she sat up, and how she had called the cow to her, caressed her, (6) and milked her while the cow was drinking water and eating the grass. (7) But he added that the character of the girl was changed. Her heart was now overflowing with emotion. (8) He told how her heart was absorbed in Tukobā. Her parents had chided her. (9) Her husband had become crazed against her, and was gazing at her not knowing what to do. (10) She was sitting in the house, absorbed in meditation, her thoughts being concentrated on Tukobā. (11) Such were the events Hirambhat related to Jayarām. He on his part rejoiced to hear them. (12) Says Bahiṇī, "Having heard these facts, Jayarām, did me a very kindly act."

29 (1) A very kindly feeling arose in Jayarām Svāmī towards me, and he came personally to see what my mental condition was. (2) When I saw him I felt very happy, and my throat was choked with the emotion of joy. (3) In my heart I performed the *ārati* and chanted his praise. I bowed to him and, in my heart sincerely worshipped him. (4) Says Bahiṇī, "Pāṇḍuraṅg truly recognizes that love of his heart."

30 (1) He poured upon me his look of love, of affection, such as a mother would give. (2) Jayarām accepted my heart's worship, and with love for me returned to his lodging. (3) As he sat on his accustomed seat quietly, and with his mind brought to a state of peace, (4) suddenly a thing happened that had never occurred before. Tukārām appeared to him. (5) Jayarām joyfully made him a *namaskār* and embraced him. (6) To me also he gave a moment's vision of himself, and placed a morsel in my mouth. (7) He said to me, 'I have come to visit Jayarām, but I recognize your desire also. (8) Do not remain any longer in this place. Do not let pass the opportunity for attaining self-knowledge and enlightenment.' (9) Says Bahiṇī, "This is the second vision that Tukobā gave me through the working of my mind."

HER HUSBAND STILL CRUEL.

31 (1) The people thought all this as very strange, and came in crowds to see me. (2) My husband, seeing them, gave me much bodily suffering. (3) He could not endure seeing the people coming to see me. And moment by moment his hatred increased. (4) He exclaimed, 'It would be well if this woman were dead. Why do these low people come to see her? (5) I wonder what next we shall see in her of demoniac possession! How is God going to supply her bodily needs?' (6) Says Bahiṇī, "Such was the concern of my husband, but the Infinite One knew of it also."

32 (1) My husband now began to say, 'We are Brāhmans. We should spend our time in the study of the

Vedas. (2) What is all this! The *shudra* Tukā! Seeing him in a dream! My wife is ruined by all this! What am I to do? (3) Who cares for Jayarām, and who for Pāṇḍuraṅg, My home has been destroyed! (4) What care I for singing the names and praises of Hari? Even in my dreams I know not *bhakti*. (5) Who cares for saints and *sādhus*! Who cares for the feelings of *bhakti*! Let us always be found in the order of the religious mendicants.' (6) Says Bahiṇī, "Thus did my husband think and discuss the matter in his own mind."

33 (1) This is how my husband considered the subject in his own mind: 'I will abandon her, and go into a forest, (2) for people are going to bow down to her, while she regards me as worth but a straw. (3) They will discuss with this woman the meaning of the *kathās*, but she herself will consider me a low fellow. (4) The people make regardful enquiries about *her* while I, who am a Brāhman, have become a fool! (5) They are all calling her a Gosāvīn. Who will show me respect in her presence?' (6) Says Bahiṇī, "Thus my husband discussed the matter in his own mind, and gave his own mind advice."

34 (1) He said to himself, 'This is my wife's condition. Do not remain here any longer. (2) Let me rather go to some sacred river, for asceticism is now my lot.' (3) He made his *namaskār* to his mother-in-law and father-in-law saying, 'My wife is advanced three months in pregnancy. (4) I am going on a pilgrimage to sacred places; my wife has become mad after God; look after her. (5) I do not wish to see her face any longer. Who is to make up to us our loss in reputation? (6) Who is going to stay here and suffer humiliation at her hands? Who

cares to keep such a wife as she is!' (7) Says Bahiṇī. "Thus did my husband talk, and I then began to think to myself."

BAHIṆĪ THINKS OF HER WIFELY DUTIES

35 (1) What am I to do with my Fate? I must bear whatever comes to my lot. (2) I am not one who is possessed. My body is not subject to demoniac possession. (3) Therefore, holding to my own special duties, I will give my mind to listening to the Scriptures, and the winning of God. (4) My duty is to serve my husband, for he is God to me. My husband himself is the Supreme Brahma. (5) The water in which my husband's feet are washed has the value of all the sacred waters put together. Without that holy water, (all I do is) valueless. (6) If I transgress my husband's commands, all the sins of the world will be on my head. (7) The Vedas in fact say that it is the husband who has the authority in the matter of religious duties, earthly possessions, desires, and salvation. (8) This is then the determination, and the desire of my heart. I want my thought concentrated on my husband. (9) The supreme spiritual riches [*paramārtha*] are to be attained through service to my husband. I shall reach the highest purpose of my life through my husband. (10) If I have any other God but my husband, I shall have committed in my heart a sin like that of the killing of a Brāhman. (11) My husband is my *sadguru*. My husband is my means of salvation. This is indeed the true understanding and determination of my heart. (12) Says Bahiṇī, "O God, Thou hast entered into my husband's heart and given it peace."

36 (1) Supposing my husband should go away to live the ascetic's life, then, O Pāṇḍuraṅg, of what value would be my life among men? (2) Can the body attain to beauty when its life has left it? What is the night without the brightness of the moon? (3) My husband is the life; I am his body. In my husband lies all my well-being. (4) My husband is the water in which I am the fish. How can I live without him? (5) My husband is the sun, and I its brightness. How can these two be separated? (6) Says Bahiṇī, "This is the conviction of my heart, and Hari knows these my thoughts."

37 (1) If my husband gives himself to the ascetic life, I shall certainly take my own life. (2) This body of mine fell lifeless in grief over the calf, but here in this case my husband himself is the Supreme Brahma. (3) If I do not get to drink the water in which my husband's feet are washed, I might eat, but it would be to me like eating animal flesh. (4) If I do not get to eat what is left on my husband's plate, I shall carry on my head sins of the weight of the three worlds. (5) If my heart wanders from my husband, then my abode will be in hell. (6) If a day should pass without my seeing my husband, that in itself will be a great heap of sins. (7) Says Bahiṇī, "His commands are my law. My Svāmi is himself the Eternal Brahma."

38. (1) Viṭṭhal who is mere stone, and Tuka of whom I have simply dreamed, why should I for *these* give up a sure happiness? (2) I will give my body to the joy of rigorous service (for my husband), in accordance with the guidance of the Vedas. (3) A woman who serves

her husband, and is a faithful wife to him, is the means of saving both the family lines. (4) Says Bahiṇī, "I shall find my rest of soul in my husband, and the final end to my succession of births and deaths."

BAHIṆĪ'S HUSBAND IS STRICKEN ILL

39 (1) My husband had made up his mind to leave us on the morrow, when (2) suddenly he was stricken ill, and for seven days his body was burning with fever. (3) Even from those he knew, he accepted no advice. I was at his side day and night. (4) He rejected the medicines given to him. He suffered intense pain. (5) For more than a month he rejected food, and endured excruciating pain. (6) The various gods and family deities were pleaded with in special ways, (7) but there was no cessation of his sufferings. He exclaimed, 'I am about to die. (8) How I insulted Pāṇḍuraṅg and Tukobā! and it was then that this suffering came to me. (9) If this pain is due to my having insulted Tukārām, then (10) O Tukārām, you who are honoured in all the universe, perform now a miracle. (11) Says Bahiṇī, "My husband repented; Pāṇḍuraṅg is the inner witness of this change."

40 (1) An oldish Brāhman appeared and said to him, 'Why is it you are wishing to die? (2) Why did it come to your mind to take up the ascetic's life? What are your reasons for wanting to desert your wife? (3) First, think in your own heart what wrong she has committed, and then if true, give yourself into the hands of anger. (4) If you wish to live, accept her. (5) If she has conducted herself without regard to her duties, then

only you might abandon her, you idiot! (6) She is one who has no worldly desires. She is truly a *bhakta* of Hari. You should likewise be one also. (7) You will be blessed by it,' said the Brāhman, and my husband bowed down at his feet. (8) He explained all to the Brāhman and exclaimed, 'Give me now to-day the gift of life. (9) O my Svāmī, save me from this painful disease, and I will devote my life at your feet.' (10) He did not speak at all to his wife, but with all his heart he pleaded with Hari for help. (11) He then arose and made a *namaskār* to the Brāhman. The twice-born responded 'You will be blessed.' (12) I was listening to the conversation of the two, and I at once fell at the feet of my husband. (13) The Brāhman immediately vanished out of sight and my husband regained his health and well-being. (14) Says Bahiṇī, 'If God bestows His favour, all the *Siddhīs* stand at the door ready to serve."

BAHIṆĪ'S KINDNESS CONQUERS HER HUSBAND

41 (1) The immediate regaining of health and the gradual disappearance of suffering brought relief to my husband. (2) He then showed kindness to me and spoke words of comfort. He put far away the thought of anger. (3) Said he, 'Let us all go away from here, back to the place from which we came. (4) God, in the form of a Brāhman, told me what I am to expect from Fate. (5) We will do what he told us, and give ourselves to the worship of Hari. I have given up all sorrowing for the possession of rights in family property.' (6) To my father and mother he said, 'Go in peace to Devgāv'. (7) (To me he said,) 'Both of us will go into a forest to

live, obedient to the commands of God. (8) Whether it brings us good or evil, we are going to give ourselves fully to the worship of Hari,' said my husband. (9) 'We shall go to the town of Tukobā and live there. This is the determination of our hearts.' (10) Such was the change in my husband's thinking, for my Svāmī (Tukobā) is a storehouse of mercy, an internal-witness. (11) What is there that God can not do? Of this all men have a vivid experience. (12) Says Bahiṇī, "Taking all our belongings we journeyed and arrived (at Dehu) to pay our respects to Tukobā."

THE FAMILY ARRIVES AT DEHU

42 (1) The one-coloured cow, the mother of the calf, came along with us, running along attentively in front of us. (2) So I arrived where the Indrāyaṇi river flows (at Dehu), together with my mother, father, brother and husband. (3) We bathed in the river, we paid our respects to Pāṇḍuraṅg, and the whole universe rejoiced in our hearts. (4) Tukobā was conducting there a praise service. With a *namaskār* we contented our hearts. (5) The image of him that I had (back in Kolhapur) seen in a dream (when in Kolhapur), was the very form I now saw with my eyes wide open. (6) Says Bahiṇī, "My husband made him a *sāshtāṅg namaskār,* with his heart full of devotion."

KOṆḌĀJĪ'S KINDNESS, MAMBĀJĪ'S UNKINDNESS

43 (1) It was about midday and we were in need of food. My husband wandered about the town to obtain it. (2) He met a Brāhman by name of Koṇḍājī who invited

him to dine with him. (3) My husband replied, 'We are a party of five. Who would care to feed so many?' (4) The other answered, 'Come all of you to dine with me, for numbers are no concern to Nārāyaṇa. (5) Go and seek a place where you may lodge, and at noon come to my house.' (6) Says Bahiṇī, 'My husband came back and told us of the invitation to dinner.'

44. (1) There was one who lived here by name of Mambājī Gosāvī. We saw him enter his house. (2) We went to him and asked that we might be put up there. He was a fickle-minded man, and very hot-tempered. (3) He jumped up as if to strike us, and drove us outside. So we gladly had recourse to the pilgrim quarters of the temple. (4) We stayed there, and went to the Brāhman's (Koṇḍājī's) house to dine. This brought us great satisfaction. (5) He asked us our history: 'Where have you come from? What is your reason for making this journey?' (6) We told him somewhat of our happenings, and he urged us to remain until the coming festival days. (7) 'On Monday,' he said, 'will be the new moon. Remain on and enjoy the special *bhakti* services. (8) Every day there takes place in the temple a *Hari kathā* given by Tukobā. The Vaishṇavas think of him as mother. (9 Stay here, I will give you grain for your food. This also will be a good deed for me.' (10) Says Bahiṇī, "So we remained at Dehu, taking keen delight in listening to Tukobā."

TUKĀRĀM'S KATHĀS

45 (1) There was constant *kathā* going on in the temple to which we sat listening, both at daytimes and at

night. (2) In his *kathā* service Tukobā expounded the meaning of the Vedas, and through it my mind found peace. (3) The person of Tukobā, which I had before seen in a dream, when at Kolhapur, (4) now appearing in reality before my eyes, joy danced in my eyes. (5) Neither during the day nor at night (in the services) was I in the least sleepy. Tukobā took possession of my heart. (6) Says Bahiṇī, "I shook, however, with joy. This joy the wise know through experience."

MAMBĀJĪ'S OPPOSITION

46 (1) Mambājī Gosāvī said to my husband one day, 'You, together with your wife, should become my disciples, (2) I think this desirable, for both of you seem to be *bhaktas* of Hari, and free from worldly desires.' (3) We listened to him a few times, and then we told him plainly that (4) we had already received an *anugraha* (blessing). But he would not believe us. (5) Then my husband told him everything that had happened at Kolhapur. (6) Hearing our story, he was filled with rage. Said he, 'How can you find satisfaction through a dream? (7) Until you have rendered service to a *guru*, and until a *sadguru* has placed his hand on your head, (8) how can you claim to have had a true *guru*? How can the mind of a Shudra possess knowledge? (9) You have received an *anugraha* in a dream, and you have made a *Shudra* your *guru*. And he is a good-for-nothing and without knowledge. (10) You should be excommunicated from the Brāhman's community. Do not speak any more of your *bhakti* of a guru.' (11) Says Bahiṇī, "This is what Mambājī said, and from that moment he showed his spite against us."

47 (1) One day I happened to see Mambājī in the street, and with full respect (2) went towards him quickly to make him a *namaskār*. But he would not touch me. He hastened from me. (3) He exclaimed, 'I don't know what you are, who you are, nor what your caste is. I am going to call you *Shudras*. (4) Perhaps you are of the goldsmith caste, or a Brāhman half-caste. You have no share in a Brāhman's duties. (5) If you go anywhere to dine (at a Brāhman's house), I shall take you into court.' (6) Says Bahiṇī, "Having heard this from him, I told it all to my husband."

48 (1) Mahādājī, the Kulkarṇi, told all this to Koṇḍājīpant. He took us to his house, and said to us, (2) 'Why do you have anything to do with Mambājī,' (3) Mambājī, however, continued his intense hatred. He sought to beat us, thinking to kill us even. (4) Said he, 'These are Brāhmans, and yet they are making a *Shudra* their *guru*. This is where I have discovered their error.' (5) His anger increased to excess, and it became everywhere known among the people. (6) Says Bahiṇī, "God makes us suffer in many ways, but it is to test our resolutions."

APPĀJĪ GOSĀVĪ OF POONA THREATENS TUKĀRĀM

49 (1) Appājī Gosāvī lived in Poona. He was very widely known as a Rājayogī. (2) Mambājī sent a letter to him saying, 'Tukobā Gosāvī, a *shudra* and a *vāṇī* (grocer), (3) is constantly performing *kathās* in the temple, and Brāhmans are falling at his feet. (4) Even Rāmeshvara Bhatta, a

very great *yogī,* and highly honoured, even he makes a *namaskār* to him. (5) I think this is a very great wrong. It makes the teachings of the Vedas false. (6) You have the authority to punish him. You should have him bound and taken there (to Poona). (7) There is also here a woman and a man who call themselves Tukārām's disciples. (8) They call themselves Brāhmans, though they are really goldsmiths. The Kulkarṇi is also very favourable to them. (9) Seeing in this the decadence of our religious duties, I have written you this letter. (10) If you do not dishonour them, however, the (Marāthā) rule will sink to nothing. (11) They have started a course of defilement in which our caste-duties are lost sight of. These [duties] must be protected, O Chief of Svāmīs.' (12) Says Bahiṇī, "Such was the letter he secretly wrote in his house and sent to Poona."

50 (1) Appājī Gosāvī read he letter, and rolled his eyes in his intense rage. (2) 'What! A *Shudra* receiving the *namaskār*! This is a most unheard of sin! (3) One of the goldsmith caste is calling himself a Brāhman! One should not even look at such an one. (4) Brāhmans are taking *anugraha* from a *Shudra.* This is defilement of the worst type. (5) There is nothing wrong in punishing such people.' Such was his firm decision. (6) Says Bahiṇī, "He sent his written reply, and said in due time effect would be given to his decision."

MAMBĀJĪ'S ENMITY CONTINUES

51 (1) Mambājī Gosāvī, however, continued his active hatred, and told us we should go away from there. (2) We were greatly troubled by this. Why is it that this

hindrance has come in the way of our worship? (3) We have taken nothing from any one. We have not spoken against anyone. Having committed no wrong, yet his anger is against us. (4) We thought of God, and meditated on Him in our hearts. O Pāṇḍuraṅg, Thou art witness to this. (5) Thou knowest what is in my heart. I have no place for hatred in my thoughts. (6) Do Thou save us from what this Brāhman has brought upon us. And Thou art at Tukārām's head also. (7) Thou dost bring suffering to those who worship Thee, and thus Thou dost watch their devotion to Thee. (8) Says Bahiṇī, "Many kinds of joys and sorrows are our possession through deeds done in a former birth."

52 (1) We had with us the cow which we had acquired at Kolhāpur. She was still giving us a little milk. (2) (Mambājī) tied her in his house and beat her with a club. (3) We looked for our cow, and could not find her. Tukobā felt the same pain (as the cow). (4) You see the cow was in great distress, having been tied to a peg for three nights. (5) She had been given no water or grass, and was being severely beaten. She saw no way to escape. (6) When Tukobā awoke from his sleep, he found his back swollen, and could get no relief. (7) Club marks appeared on his body. He brought Vithobā to mind in various pleadings. (8) When people saw him they were sorely grieved. He told them all he had seen in his dream. (9) Then thinking of God in his heart, he cried out, 'O Mādhava, rush to the help and deliver the cow. (10) What cow can it be? Who can have tied her? O Nārāyaṇa, rush to the aid and protect the cow.' (11) Then suddenly a fire broke out in Mambājī's house, and there was a great blaze. (12)

People rushed there, and put out the fire. They saw there the cow lying down dazed, (13) the cow that we had been looking for three days. The wretch (Mambājī) had tied her up there. (14) They unloosened the cow, and brought her outside. We found she had been beaten on her back. (15) They called my husband, and said, 'You take care of this cow, O Brāhman.' (16) Tukobā came running and made a *pradakshiṇā* around the cow. He made her a *namaskār* and said to her, 'You are blessed for your goodness. (17) You caused me to dream and unknown to me, O Mother, you called on God for help. (18) Your soul and my soul are the same soul pervading our bodies. I am firmly convinced of this.' (19) When Tukobā was earnestly pleading for help, I also had suddenly felt pain. (20) I had the same feeling of sorrow as he. Viṭṭhal is my witness to this. (21) The people examined Tukobā's back, and looked at the cow, and were deeply grieved. (22) Says Bahiṇī, "This is what happened. Hari knows the cow's suffering."

53 (1) Rāmeshvara Bhatta heard of this affair and came hurriedly to the place. (2) He took note of Tukobā's condition, and also thoroughly examined the cow. (3) On the back of each there was a similar mark. All began to weep. (4) 'Who is there,' they exclaimed, 'who can adequately sing Tukobā's praises? He is the Pralhād of this Kaliyuga.' (5) In praising Tukobā as the internal-witnesser of all, they were pleased with their own joy. (6) Says Bahiṇī, "The people all exclaimed, 'Tukobā is Pāṇḍuraṅg Himself.'"

BAHIṆĀBĀĪ BECOMES A MOTHER

54 (1) We remained in the house of Mahādājī the kulkarṇi, and quietly spent our days. (2) Of course we had to endure waves of sorrow, this the Husband-of-Lakshmi well knows. (3) In times of trouble we placed our burden on God. We remained unchanged and devoted to Him. (4) It now happened that at this time I gave birth to a daughter. (5) We gave her the name of Kāshībāi. The feelings I had (towards the calf) I felt now in their fulness. (6) Says Bahiṇī, "The calf died at Kolhāpur, but it seemed to me as though it had received its birth through my womb."

BAHIṆĀBĀĪ REVIEWS HER LIFE

55 (1) Devgāv was my beautiful parental home. We belonged to the Vājesani branch and the Maunas *Gotra*. (2) In this family I received my body through birth in order that I might live the life of a woman. (3) In that family there was no direct line of *gurus*, and therefore, there was nothing to be listened to with special respect. (4) Says Bahiṇī, "The laws of birth are secret, known only to God."

56 (1) Girls of the neighbourhood used to come and play with toys, while I was thinking of repeating God's names. (2) I did not enjoy childish plays. I do not know how, but a strong faith early manifested itself. (3) I did not enjoy the games of *phugadi*, or of *tipari*. I felt I wanted my mind fixed (on God). (4) Says Bahiṇī "Whatever in a former birth was fated to be in this, manifested itself in the events of my daily life."

57 (1) My mother and father brought about my marriage. They gave me to one who belonged to the Gautam *Gotra.* (2) The marriage festivities lasted four days. I did not know what else God proposed for me. (3) My father and mother were distressed by poverty, and they were depressed by their other troubles. (4) We left that part of the country, because of (the quarrel) over family property, and in our journey crossed both banks of the Gaṅgā [Godāvari]. (5) My *Svāmī* [husband] was taken along with us. We arrived at length at the Mahādeva forest in a distant province. (6) Says Bahiṇī, "Father, mother, brother and husband and myself arriving there, we experienced a sense of rest."

58 (1) From the Mahādeva forest we journeyed to Paṇḍharpur. Here we experienced joy in meeting with the saints. (2) This meeting with the saints was a happier thing to me than life itself. But I was in constant terror of my husband. (3) I had heard of the anger of Jamadagni. My husband showed the same characteristic in his dealings with people. (4) Says Bahiṇī, "I was now eleven years of age, but I had not had one moment's joy."

59 (1) My *Svāmī* [husband] for his livelihood was a Vaidik [reciter of the *Vedas*] by profession. What use had he for God! (2) He used to repeat parts of the *Vedas,* but had no love for *bhakti* [worship and love of God]. I had no independence and my wishes had no effect. (3) I was young in years, but the popular ways seemed silly. Out of respect for the *Vedas,* I stood ready to serve. (4) Says Bahiṇī, "I was very depressed in spirits. My daily life was full of troubles."

BAHIṆĪ'S DEPRESSION

60 (1) Possessing a woman's body, and myself being subject to others, I was not able to carry out my desire to discard all worldly things [*vairāgya*]. (2) And yet a change took place through the power of right-thinking. What a wonderful thing God [Rāghobā] worked! (3) I suffered in body from the three kinds of affliction, and I was tempted to commit suicide. (4) There was not the slightest worship of God [Hari] (in our family). Both enemy and dear friends were all for worldly things. (5) I considered bodily enjoyments as enemies. Who was there now to concern himself with me? (6) Says Bahiṇī, "As vomited vomit, so my mind began to regard the illusions of this life."

61 (1) As a deer that finds itself in a net or as a blind man lost in a forest, (2) so it happened to me. Whom shall I seek for my welfare? My soul was in distress. (3) As a fish out of water, as a calf without its mother, as a deer without her young one, so was I. (4) Says Bahiṇī, "O God, in this distress of mine, look on me with the eye of mercy."

62 (1) The root of *vairāgya* [indifference to worldly things] is the putting away of worldly cares. When viewed aright, a house and a mountain are the same (in essence). (2) Distress has come upon me. (O God), quickly run to my help! Enlighten my soul through the means of Right-thinking [*viveka*]. (3) To leave a husband is against the teachings of the *Vedas*, and thereby one can never acquire the supreme spiritual riches. (4) At my door there seemed

a great serpent hissing at me. How could I live under such conditions? (5) It is the teaching of the *Vedas*, that one should not neglect one's duty, but my love was for the worship of God (Hari). (6) Says Bahiṇī, "I was in a sea of troubles. How can I describe the increasing anguish of my heart!"

63 (1) The *Vedas* cry aloud, and the *Purāṇs* shout that no good comes of a woman. (2) Now I in the natural way have a woman's body. What means then have I to acquire the supreme spiritual riches [*paramārtha*]? (3) The characteristics (of a woman) are foolishness, selfishness, seductiveness, and deception. All connection with a woman is disastrous. (Such is their opinion). (4) Says Bahiṇī, "If a woman's body brings disaster, what chance is there for her to acquire in this life the supreme spiritual riches?"

64 (1) I wonder what sin I committed in a former birth that in this birth I should be so separated from God [*Purushottam*]? (2) I am born with a human body, but in the form of a woman. It is evident that the innumerable sins (of my former birth) have now come to their fruitage. (3) (As a woman) I have no right to listen to the reading of the *Vedas*. The Brahmans have made a secret of the *Gāyatrī mantra*. (4) I am told I must not pronounce the sacred word *'OM'*. I must not listen to philosophical ideas. (5) I must not speak to any one about them. My husband was Jamadagnī himself (if I did those things). (6) Says Bahiṇī, "My soul is very downcast. God has no compassion on me."

65 (1) In our home the name of God was like a defiled thing. The *Bhagavadgītā* and *Shāstras* were considered as enemies in our family. (2) No one cared for God, for sacred bathing places, for pilgrimages, for Hari himself. It was into such a home that I was given in marriage. (3) They did not like the communion of saints, nor the *bhakti* of Rāma. They did not like the *Vedas*, nor the *Shāstras* nor the (Purānic) stories (of the gods and heroes). (4) Says Bahiṇī, "May the multitude of my sins be removed, and my heart find peace."

BAHIṆĪ CONTEMPLATES SUICIDE

66 (1) My heart has passed through the intense heat of repentance. How is it that God does not feel compassion for me? (2) I feel like throwing myself into the fire, or using this saw to sever my head. (3) I feel like throwing myself into the flowing river, or flying to some distant spot. (4) I feel like going into the jungle, there to sit until I gain my desire, and fast until I do. (5) Says Bahiṇī, "My soul is in a confused state. O God [Vanamālī], why hast Thou forsaken me!"

67 (1) Thou art causing this irritation by the hand of my husband, but my soul has made its determination. (2) I will not leave the worship of God, even if it should mean the losing of my life. Now then, O God, Brother-of-the-distressed. (3) Thou art seeking to test me? For through my husband my body is being destroyed. (4) What am I to do? I am in the midst of hardship. I have no desires for my body. (5) Let it fall in death, but O, may my longing remain to see the Infinite One with the eye of spiritual knowledge. (6) I want to render Thee worship

I want to fulfil all my special duties, and through the means of spiritual knowledge recognize Thee. (7) Will this body of mine endure for long these distressing experiences? Why dost Thou not listen to my cry? (8) I have heard that the teaching of the *Vedas* is, that, if a desire remains unfulfilled, (in one life) a rebirth takes place. (9) Now in this time of distress if I commit suicide, the fault will be on Thy head. So protect Thy child. (10) Says Bahiṇī, "O Protector of the universe. Why hast Thou become deaf and blind?"

GOD IS BAHIṆĪ'S REFUGE

68 (1) Yet, O God [Hari], Thou alone art my friend, my very own Brother, and the advocate of the lowly in heart, O Pāṇḍuraṅg. (2) In worshipping Thee I can still be true to my duty of devotion to my husband. Thou, O God [Meghashyāma], must thus think also. (3) The Supreme spiritual riches are surely not contrary to the *Vedas.* Therefore, think of this purpose of mine. (4) Says Bahiṇī, "O God [Hari], think at once of my longing, by which I can accomplish both."

69 (1) My mother, father and brother made themselves the friends of worldly things, and therefore were very grieved at my condition. (2) I could tell this to God, O Thou who knowest my heart. There is no one else to tell it to. (3) And there is no one to counsel me as to what I should do for my good. The neighbourhood is not made up of good men. (4) I am entirely alone in a forest. I have lost recollection of even hunger and thirst. (5) I do not feel like talking to any one of this. O God [Keshav].

Thou must think of this. (6) Says Bahiṇī, "I know Thy name only. Who is there to whom I could tell more (of my sad tale) O God [Hari]?"

70 (1) My soul has suffered intense anguish. I am supremely miserable, O my friend. (2) I have attempted to comfort myself by this one thought that all this suffering has come because of deeds done in a former birth. (3) Even Brahmadeva and the other gods cannot escape the same law, how much less those of humble estate. (4) Says Bahiṇī, "It is my fate to have to suffer. What can even God [Govinda] do to help me?"

71 (1) My body is responsible for my joys and woes. It is necessary that I suffer them. (2) But if this suffering means the putting far away of sin, I count it as a welcome good. (3) I wish the longing of my heart to express itself in singing God's praise, even while my body is suffering torture. (4) Says Bahiṇī, "I suffer what is in my Fate. Who is there on whom I can lay the blame?"

72 (1) The course of Fate cannot ever be avoided, why then be vainly troubled thereby. (2) My heart has made its firm resolve. Now (it is Thy opportunity) O God [Chakrapāṇi, Pāṇḍuraṅg]. (3) No one can deliver me from my bodily suffering, O God [Nārāyan], I know this. (4) Says Bahiṇī, I am now going to plead with God [Keshav]. Do not put me to a severe test, O Hari.

BAHIṆĪ'S DARK CLOUDS DISAPPEAR

73 (1) Fate's cord around me has at last been broken! My soul has become purified. (2) God has shown me his

mercy that on the banks of the Indrāyaṇi river, in this humble village of Dehu, there is a royal path to *Bhakti*. (3) Here there is a temple to God Pāṇḍuraṅg. (In its pilgrim quarters) we were given a place to lodge in. (4) Always there were three things before my eyes, Tukārām, the saints, and the kīrtans. (5) I could not make him a *namaskār*, for fear of my husband. But my mind was ever at his feet. (6) Says Bahiṇī, "Seven months passed in this way. We experienced all that Fate had for us."

74 (1) Our pilgrim quarters in the temple became a place of joy. I felt like sitting there, (2) in contemplation, to meditate with closed eyes, and bring God [Vithobā] to my remembrance. (3) As I saw Tukārām (in my imagination) he appeared to come to me in the form of Death. (4) Says Bahiṇī, "I obtained from my mother permission to remain there three nights."

75 (1) I did not know the proper *mantras* to repeat [*japa*], nor the proper rites [*tapa*] to perform. I did not know the right austerities, nor how to arrange the seat appropriate to meditation. (2) I had not been enlightened as to the method of contemplation, nor how to control my senses. (3) But I had before me the stone image of Vithobā for my contemplation, and in my heart God [Rāmchandra]. (4) It was the longing of my heart to hold a service [*kaṭhā*] in praise of Tukārām. (5) When I heared the sound of the cymbals and the *chipali*, my heart could not contain itself for joy. (6) With closed eyes, both in sleep and in waking state, I saw the form of Tukārām. (7) He placed his hand on my head, and in spoken words gave me the promise of poetic power.

(8) Says Bahiṇī, "I do not know whether this was in a dream or in my waking state, but my senses ceased their action."

76 (1) In my joy my senses were overcome with emotion. My mind contemplated Tukārām's feet. (2) When I awoke out of this state and I recollected the *mantra** of six letters (which he had whispered in my ear). (3) I fastened it in my memory. I remembered nothing else. (4) Says Bahiṇī. He placed his hands on my head, but I was not to see his body in this world."

77 (1) My joy was so great that I was driven to silence. In knowing that state, blessed will be *gurus* and *bhaktas*. (2) All my senses felt the joy. I was sitting beside God. (3) It was with me just as if a jar is dipped into a pool of deep water. Without breaking it is filled completely with water. (4) Says Bahiṇī, "So it was with my heart. And Tukārām recognized it by its signs."

78 (1) I felt that I did not wish to be aroused out of my state of contemplation, even if it meant death not to do so. For my soul was rocking with joy. (2) With my mind intensely happy I went to the Indrāyaṇi river. (3) I looked upon the image of Pāṇḍuraṅg when suddenly I felt inspired to be a poetess. (4) I made a *namaskār* there to Tukārām, and quickly came back to where we lodged. (5) Says Bahiṇī "(This inspiration to poesy) came like the tide of the ocean, or like the words of the Gods of Thunder [Indra] in the sky of my heart."

---

*Rāma – Krishna—Hari.

CHAPTER III.

NIRYANPAR

BAHIṆĪ AWAITS HER [APPROACHING DEATH]

79 (1) I saw Rukmiṇī on her way. My departure is along the same way. (2) I must send the following letter quickly to the Godāvari, for fear my son should fail me in his filial duties :— (3) You must come here leaving all business and occupations. My death is waiting for its appointed hour. (4) Therefore I hasten to write the letter, as I see the Banner of Death so clearly before me. (5) On the thirteenth day will be the Brahman feast. Hasten with the greatest possible speed. (6) There may be impediments and delays on the way. Put aside all delay, Vithobā, and hasten to come. (7) Five days from now my expecting end will come, but I am awaiting it with self control. (8) The first day of the month *Āshvin* (September), on the first day of the new moon, has been told me as the limit for my death. (9) Says Bahiṇī, "You will be able to fulfil the duties of a son, therefore hasten to come."

80 (1) *"We were all sitting around Shukleshvar. Suddenly I saw the letter.* (2) *I read it hastily. I started at once. I devised many plans in my mind.* (3) *I must go and make some plan of bringing my mother to the bank of the Godāvari.* (4) *Choosing a spot for her tomb, I rushed to see her."*

81 (1) My dear son, you heard my letter read, you gave a leap, and came with haste. (2) You have celebrated

the 13th day of Rukmiṇi. My voice is charged with sobs, your throat is choked with emotion . (3) You have fulfilled your duty to every one, in mind, body, speech and all your feelings. (4) Seeing you I am happy. My throat is choked with the emotion of love. (5) The time of my death is fixed for the first day of the full moon in the month of *Ashvin* (September). Listen, my son, I have told you this openly. (6) Do not let your heart ever sorrow over this. Do not overstep the limits I have prescribed. (7) Your sonship has come to its fruition to-day. You have arrived in time for my death.

82 (1) "*The witness of one's heart is known by one's heart alone. O my mother, you are also my guru.* (2) *I had a dream about you, mother, when I was at Kacheshvar. I saw a vimān* [*chariot-of-light*] *come for you.* (3) *Conch-shells, trumpets and many other musical instruments began to sound. With great joy the names of the gods were sung aloud.* (4) *Conch-shells, disks and clubs set with jewels bedecked them to celebrate the occasion.* (5) *Hand-drums were sounding, cymbals clanged and songs were heard. Innumerable banners were adorned by the eagle.* (6) *I also saw the pomp of the Brāhmans, the crowds of people before and behind them, all with tulsī garlands around their necks.* (7) *I saw them in my dreams accompanying the chariot-of-light in gay procession; and I had great rejoicing in my own heart.* (8) *There were also incense, fragrant powders, and saffron paste to decorate the foreheads of Brāhmans who dined in rows.* (9) *I saw these crowds of people and my mind was full of delight.* (10) *When I arose in the early dawn, I was convinced in my mind that though it was in fact a dream, it was not a false one.* (11) *Then*

as I sat with the others beside Kacheshvar, I suddenly saw your letter. (12) *I read it at once and started in haste. I was greatly disturbed in mind. I planned to go and bring my mother to the banks of the Godāvari.* (13) *I worshipped her feet and stood before her.* (14) *Mother, you know the desires of my heart.* (15) *I have asked for a place by Shukleshvar (for your tomb). All that remains now is your command."*

83 (1) I have heard your reverent words, my son, of what you have determined. (2) The place (you have chosen) is acceptable to me, but listen to a word of mine. (3) There is no time for me to go to that place. The time of my death is at hand. (4) On the first day of the next month I have to cast my body aside, and to-day is the thirteenth of this month. (5) I will, therefore, tell you a determination of mine. Praṇitā is the one place sacred to me. (6) Here it was that Rāvaṇa once performed austerities and it was here that Shaṅkar was pleased. (7) For here Rāvaṇa offered nine of his heads in worship and eighty-eight thousand *rishis* gathered there. (8) Brahmadeva and the other gods came to be near to the sacrifice. This well known sacred *tīrtha* is Shivapur. (9) During the bathing after the sacrifice, Brahmā and other gods conferred the boon that the whole multitude of *tirthas* would be included in this one. (10) Of all the established *tīrthas* there is none the equal of this on this round globe. So said Chandramouli (Shiva). (11) Considering the Benāres, Ġayā, and all the other *tīrthas* are here in this one, bathing should be done here by all people. (12) This then is truly the determination of my heart. (13) I want you to bow your head in assent to this request of

mine and rest in peace. (14) Says Bahiṇī, "Oh, my son, bear in mind all I have said, and be ready to fulfil my request."

84 (1) As we carried on our duties to holy places, gods and pilgrimages, twelve of your births and mine have taken place. (2) In this, the thirteenth birth, you are my son. You do not remember your own history; (3) but for thirteen births you and I have been associated together, united, unbroken, and devoted to one another. (4) The consciousness of wifely dutifulness to a husband is the one and only companion of us, women; to tell the whole story of this would make this book too large. (5) I intend to read the whole of the *Dyāneshvarī* (the commentary by Dnyāneshvar), but now my remaining days are few. (6) Because I gave you birth, I love you; and so, my dear boy, I have told you of our former mutual acquaintances. (7) Says Bahiṇī, "From now on I shall not have to be reborn. The passions that necessitate rebirth have ceased."

85 (1) The Godāvari, Bhāgirathi, Yamunā, Sarasvati, Tāpi, Bhogāvati and all the other sacred rivers (2) will come to Praṇitā at the time of my death. So, my son, let your heart be at rest. (3) The Krishnā, Tuṅgabhadrā, Bhimā, Phalgu, Revā, Pushkara, all these rivers of the earth, (4) together will all the gods, are to be present at that time. You will then have the experience of seeing death. (5) All the crowd of *rishis*, and even Pāṇḍuraṅg, standing upright (on his brick), will be present when my funeral services begin. (6) Says Bahiṇī, "You may think the following to be untrue, but listen now to the truth which I am going to relate."

86 (1) What other *tīrtha* is there equal to self-knowledge? The wise come to know this through the good deeds [*puṇya*] done in the former birth. (2) Where the heart has this purifying self-knowledge, *there* this *tīrtha* exists, say the *Vedas* and the *Shāstras*. (3) Bathing in this *tīrtha* of self-knowledge, twelve of my births have passed in order to cleanse my heart. (4) I have acquired this thirteenth birth by this very means. By bathing in that *tīrtha* I have no more rebirths before me. (5) I have had to work for it, and suffer the hardships due to the means for bringing this about, because I was a *Yoga-bhrashta* (one who is interrupted by death before one's good deeds were finished). (6) In that *tīrtha* (of self-knowledge) my filthy passions were made pure, and that is the real *tīrtha* to the wise. (7) At this *tīrtha* the mind becomes absorbed and that is why this *tīrtha* is superior to all others. (8) Search your heart well and look within it; there is no object in looking into the outer *tīrthas*. (9) Says Bahiṇī, "When one's soul has dipped into this *tīrtha*, the purposes of a *tīrtha* are truly fulfilled."

87 (1) At the time of my death the sky will be cloudless. In every direction there will be clear brightness, my child. (2) Keep this testimony in your mind, and remain unmoved. (3) When the chariot of the gods has started for this *tirtha*, remember that there will be a threefold movement (invisible) in the air. (4) This you can realise in your mind, Oh my son, when my body is cremated. (5) Says Bahiṇī, "Believe what I tell you; Tukārām is a witness to the truth of it."

88 (1) *"Listen, mother, to a doubt which comes into my mind. Who can drive away that doubt which I feel, but yourself?* (2) *You are my nearest kin, my mother as well as guru. You know the thoughts of my mind.* (3) *In your past twelve births you have acquired knowledge, and now my mind has become assured.* (4) *I know nothing of your twelve births, so put an end to my doubts (by telling me of them).* (5) *You know the wish of my heart. Your own heart bears witness to this.* (6) *Tell me in their order of your former births. O mother, I ask this kindness of you for this once."*

89 (1) My son, listen with attention to my words. I ought not to tell you of them. I should keep silence. (2) I ought not to tell any one; I should not reveal these secrets to others. I carry the witness of it in my own heart. (3) But if I do not tell you, you will feel badly. Your heart's wish will be unrealized. (4) Says Bahiṇī, "You should not tell of this to others, and while you listen, let your aim be realised."

BAHIṆĪ DESCRIBES HER FIRST BIRTH.

90 (1) At Betāud, on the bank of the Tāpi, there was living a man of the Vaishya caste. He was a worshipper of Shiva, Kedār by name. (2) He had no sons or daughters. To have some, he therefore, performed most rigorous austerities. (3) Gratifying Shiva by them, He appeared to him in a dream: (4) 'You will not have a son, but you will have a child, a daughter, and a very beautiful one. (5) You must give her the name of Vāruṇi, and with great care she will live thirteen years.

(6) Now Kedār of the Vaishya caste had a wife who herself had the name of Beautiful (*Rupavantī*) and among women she was the noblest in wifely dutifulness. (7) Her husband's word was her law. She had been dedicated to Shiva. (8) Rupavanti became pregnant at that time, and I was born through the favour of Great Shiva. (9) There was the influence of some past pure deeds, and at my birth this became clearly evident. (10) It became evident within a year of my birth, as they looked in my eyes and face. (11) My father, Kedār, called his *sadguru* and showed him my horoscope. (12) He would not let me be married. He easily recognized my characteristics. (13) I was initiated in Shiva-devotion and was taught the Shiva-*mantra.* I used to repeat it day and night, even when I was playing. (14) While amusing myself, I constructed a toy-temple and an idol of Shiva, and worshipped it with ardent love. (15) I did not care for anything else for my heart was filled with constant devotion. (16) When I had completed the age of thirteen, I had a sight of you there, my son. (17) You were a servant there with our *sadguru,* just like a common person working for his living. (18) But I took you as my son, so I said with my lips. It was just then that my end came. (19) After that I had another birth. To my account of it give attention. (20) Says Bahiṇī, "Thus was the beginning of my first birth. I will now tell you of the next."

BAHIṆĪ DESCRIBES HER SECOND BIRTH

91 (1) I will now tell you of my former life. Let your mind be attentive. (2) As I have told you of one

birth, now I will tell you of my next state. (3) At a place called Kumchakra, on the bank of the Phalgu, I was born into the home of a good-hearted man. (4) As regards his social duties he was of the Vaishya caste, a *bhakta* of Shaṅkar, one who had entirely discarded worldly things, and who knew the Ātma [the soul of the universe]. (5) His *sadguru* was a Brahman, named Suvarmā, who had a perfect knowledge of the Vedas. (6) He was also an expert in the science of *mantras,* and had the deepest fondness for the philosophy of the soul. (7) You, my son, were his good-hearted and simple disciple. The good-hearted man had seven sons. (8) He was in great distress of mind, because he had no daughter. His *guru* therefore said to him. (9) 'I will initiate you in the worship of Vishnu and instruct you in the observance and application of the mantra. (10) He then had a dream in which he was told: Take this lovely daughter, bringing of good fortune. (11) Through her you will find wealth, but she will leave you without being married. (12) She will live with you twenty-eight years, herself making the home of *bhakti,* (14) It was there that you, my son, was born, so that I was associated with you also there. (14) You were connected with me as a *guru*-brother (disciple of the same *guru*), and we were constantly associated together. (15) Says Bahiṇī, "Such was my second birth. I will tell you now of my third."

BAHIṆĪ DESCRIBES HER THIRD BIRTH.

92 (1) I will now tell you the story of another of my births, to which listen. It will give your heart joy.

(2) On the Godāvari, where mount Brahmagiri is to be seen, a man of the Vaishya caste lived. (3) His name was Vardhamān Shet, the most generous man among ten millions. (4) His wife, Bhāmini, a beautiful woman, made dutifulness to her husband the true law of her life. (5) She had three sons, then you, as my protector, were born as the fourth son, and you spent your infancy there. (6) Vardhamān Shet had wealth, grain, money, and many herds of cows. His household lacked nothing. (7) He was the superior of all others. On one occasion he left his home. (8) He went to Pānchāl and began his austerities there, and performed a great and complete sacrifice. (9) He did this with the desire to have a daughter. Bhāmini (his wife) was by nature a beautiful woman. (10) I was born to her, and my name was Hemakalā. (11) Just to look at me gave them joy, and they gave gifts according to custom. (12) Vardhamān now became anxious about my marriage. But Bhāmini had a dream. (13) In it she was told 'Do not give your daughter away in marriage, for Hemavanti is a model of indifference to worldly things. (14) She is distinguished in song, skillfulness, name, and service of Brahmans. She is for ever repeating the names of God [Keshava].' (15) It was here you and I again became associated together. I will make known to you the secrets of my heart. (16) Twenty-four years was the limit of my life (in that birth). When it was reached, my body passed away in joy. (17) Thus three of my lives were in the Vaishya caste, and spent with indifference to worldly things. (18) Says Bahiṇī, "Listen now to the fourth birth. Think rightly, and remain happy."

BAHIṆĪ DESCRIBES HER FOURTH, FIFTH, SIXTH AND SEVENTH BIRTHS

93 (1) I will tell you now of my fourth, fifth, sixth and seventh births as a *yogabhrashta,* (one interrupted by death from completing his religious acts.) (2) I became a daughter in the home of a milkman, and spent my time in tending his cows. (3) While doing so my time was spent in repeating the names of God, and in the company of Vaishṇavas. (4) I delighted in God, in sacred rivers, and holy pilgrimages. I always worshipped Brāhmans. (5) While tending the cows and living in the forests, I became associated with *sannyāsīs.* (6) Whenever I saw them I made them a *namaskār*, and they, knowing the different sacraments, showed their favour to me. (7) I will now tell you of the story of my seventh birth. I had left the region described above. (8) At the house of a milkman I earned my living by tending his cows and performing *kīrtans.* (9) It was here I met a *siddha* (a Knower-of-Self). Recognizing who I was, he took me away with him. (10) Said he, "This woman, indifferent to worldly things, is a *Yogabhrashta.* She has been spending her life as a slave. (11) But with singleness of devotion she gives herself day and night to the discarding of all worldly things, and to the gaining of knowledge.' (12) My seventh birth lasting sixty-six years was passed in this religious life. (13) After completing the practices of this religious life I cast off my body. I have thus described to you the details of this birth. (14) Says Bahiṇī, "There are six births left to be described. I will tell you of them as I have opportunity."

BAHIṆĪ DESCRIBES HER EIGHTH, NINTH AND TENTH BIRTHS

94 (1) I will now tell you of my eighth birth. Listen. Think rightly with determination. (2) At Verul (Ellora Caves) there is a sacred bathing place called Shivālaya, where lived one who was learned in the *shāstras*, a distinguished man, and a Knower-of-Brahma. (3) He was known in this sacred place by the name of Dharmadatta, and was highly respected by all in that place. (4) His wife, beautiful, dutiful, lovely in character, gained a great reputation through her faithfulness to her husband. (5) I was born of them, a daughter with a peaceful disposition. (6) I passed eighteen years there, listening to the *Bhāgavata Purāṇa*. (7) I was married, but my husband died. But that was an advantage to me. (8) In my ninth birth I was born in the same place, and lived there till the age of nine in the same place. (9) I had the same mother and father, the same brothers and sisters, and I was taught the same religious life. (10) My tenth birth was into the home of a Kaushik Brahman. At his house the sacred fire was kept and worshipped. (11) Here the story of Hari (Krishṇa) was regularly sung, the philosophy of the Vedānta was listened to, and he regularly bathed in the sacred Shivālaya pond. (12) Here he had the constant vision of the god, his service and the performing of rites; and because of his self-knowledge, his life was one of peace. (13) I was born to him in the form of a daughter, and lived there for a time. (14) My father gave me away in marriage, having found a Brāhman who was a follower of Shukla Yajur Veda. (15) He, living as a Brāhmān mendicant, had uncooked food given him, and he kept a cow at his house.

(16) I spent a life of forty-two years there, and I had three sons. (17) The first son was yourself, and then to be especially mentioned there were two more sons. (18) Your *Guru* and mine was the *sannyāsi* Keshav. He taught us all our knowledge. (19) After that I laid aside my body. And now I have told you the substance of the story of ten of my lives. (20) Says Bahiṇī, "Now there remain three births. I will describe and you listen."

BAHIṆĪ DESCRIBES HER ELEVENTH BIRTH

95 (1) Listen now to my eleventh birth. It took place at the junction of the Pravarā and the Godāvarī. (2) It was here that a Mādhyandin Brāhman, of noble character, made his abode on the bank of the Godāvari. (3) He lived on food that came to him unasked, and gave food to those who went to him at the proper time. (4) Gokarṇa was his name, a good man, peaceful, compassionate, religious, and of a forgiving spirit. (5) His beloved wife was of noble character, and dutiful. Her name was Saguṇā, and a very excellent woman she was. (6) I was born as a daughter to her, and they gave me the name of Saujanyā. (7) When I was seven years of age they gave me away in marriage, having found a man who was a treasure of great learning. (8) He was totally indifferent to worldly things, he practised the *yoga* in every particular; and practising his sitting postures he acquired the *yoga* powers. (9) His name was Yogeshvara, and the *Siddhis* served him heartily. (10) I pleased him greatly by the way I served him. And his life and mine became one. (11) He taught me the different postures in the practice of *yoga*, as I gave myself up to *yoga* concentration. (12) My husband was my *guru* in every respect,

and I experienced there the joy of service. (13) You were my fellow-disciple, my son, and my companion in former births, and in every birth you were the means of salvation. (14) Forty-three years I passed here. All that remained then was intense devotion for Brahma. (15) Says Bahiṇī, "Now there remains the twelfth birth to be described. Hold in your heart what I tell you of it."

BAHIṆĪ DESCRIBES HER TWELFTH BIRTH.

96 (1) Knowing the thoughts of your heart I have given you a description of my several births. (2) Listen now to the twelfth, which I shall hasten to tell you, because there is but little time left before my death. (3) Lākhanī is a place with a great expanse of water. There are a hundred thousand *tīrthas* gathered at that place. (4) The Shivanada is a part of the three and a half male personified rivers, and the place of the junction is a very terrible one. (5) There was a Brahman living here performing his religious rites. His name, as fitted him, was Rāmchandra. (6) His beloved wife was Jānaki, a woman of holy life. There were two sons in that home. (7) He was a great adept in the Brahma philosophy, and a home of peace. The father was the parental home of all the *tīrthas*. (8) I was born to him in the form of a daughter and I adopted a life of austerities. (9) I took a vow of silence, and yet lived amongst men. The people said I could not speak. (10) My father gave me in marriage to a Brāhman, who, I would have you know, was a great astronomer. (11) He experienced the direct favour of Gaṇesh, who used to talk to him. (12) At this house, abstaining from food, I enjoyed the happiness of service. (13) My mind was indifferent to

worldly things, and was irritated at every experience of sensual things. I was constantly in contemplation, and devoted to the Universal Soul. (14) My father, Rāmchandra, was a special worshipper of Rāma. He was a man of extraordinary thoughtfulness, and knowledge. (15) Understanding my inmost wishes he did what brought peace to my mind. (16) He helped me to contemplate, sitting at my side, and his enlightenment fixed itself in my mind. (17) I served my husband as if he were my *ātma-sthiti* (my own soul), giving him devotion and honour. (18) My heart did not in the least rest elsewhere. I was constantly in the act of contemplation. (19) In my thirty-sixth year my body died. I ought to have obtained final release, but there was still something remaining. (20) Says Bahiṇī, "Such was my twelfth birth. I will now tell you of my thirteenth."

BAHIṆĪ DESCRIBES HER THIRTEENTH BIRTH

97 (1) Listen now with attention while I tell you more. I have told you of my past twelve births. (2) Doubt may be entertained about certain details, but I have felt in a hurry because the time of my death is at hand. (3) He alone who is versed in the *shāstra* of Right-thinking and has personal experience can supply the true meaning. (4) I remember all my births, and at this time of my death I remember all the secrets of my lives. (5) Just as one sees one's image in a mirror, so all my births appear to my eyes. (6) Fools in their intercourse with others regard falsehoods as true. One should not talk to such. (7) Only when the crow smells the musk, then

only can a fool have the skill of understanding former births. (8) I can remember everything previous to my thirteen births, but there is no good served in stating it. (9) A tiger, though it be a very large one, cannot find the path of an ant. (10) Says Bahiṇī, "When God shows His favour, then all blessings become known to the mind."

98 (1) In my thirteenth birth this body has played its part. I will tell you of it from its begnning. (2) At Devgāv, there was one of the Vājasaniya family line, and a very skilful scribe. Listen to my account. (3) He was of the Maunas family branch, a *bhakta* of Brāhmans, simple, yet wise and highly fortunate. (4) His beloved wife was Jānaki by name, a mother who nobly performed her marital duties, (5) I was born into that home as a daughter. It was there that I was married. (6) They had chosen for my husband one from the *Gautam* clan. He was very famous as an astronomer. (7) At his home Shakti (the goddess) was worshipped. My parents made me his wife. (8) On account of some special circumstance my husband went to live at Kolhāpur in the Deccan. (9) We all, my mother, father, brother and myself the sister, went there to visit him. (10) There was there Jayarām, a saint and a disciple of Krishṇāppā Svāmi (of Vadgav). He was highly honoured, and of extraordinary accomplishments. (11) After association with him for a time this ocean-of-kindness showed himself very kind to me. (12) He told me to serve my husband, and ever live with him, drinking the water of his feet. (13) I was constantly committing to memory the *Bhagavadgītā* not trespassing into the field of the Vedas. (14) My husband now thought to return to

his original home, and he hastily started together with all the family. (15) We arrived at the Indrāyaṇi river, at the village of Dehu. Here we met Koṇḍājīpant. (16) Because we were Brāhmans, he fed us. At that time I was carrying you in my womb. (17) When he discovered my condition he said to my husband, 'Remain here in this place. (18) Your wife is pregnant. Go on your further journey after her delivery. (19) I will give you as much grain as may be necessary. After passing the time here then go on to your home.' (20) Taking counsel of our minds we remained there, and spent our time in listening to (Tukārām's) *kīrtans*. (21) With Pāṇḍuraṅg as god, Tukārām as saint, I was in perpetual joy listening to the story of Hari. (22) I used to make a *namaskār* to Tukārām, and my heart I placed at the feet of Vithobā. (23) I saw there a very pleasant room built for pilgrims, very close to where god Pāṇḍuraṅg was. (24) I felt in my soul that I would like to sit here alone for three whole days and nights. (25) My husband was simply the image of rage. How could I find a place to be alone? (26) But just then for the purpose of his business my husband hurried off to Poona. (27) So then getting my mother's permission I went to bathe in the Indrāyaṇi, and my eyes rested on Vithobā. (28) An enthusiasm for goodness flowed over my soul, and joy crowded upon me as I sat in contemplation. (29) I spent three days and nights there, and my happiness became very great. (30) The next day someone in the form of Tukārām gave me three easy *mantras*, (31) and said to me, 'You have now attained your thirteenth birth, and you have already prepared the *yoga* path. (32) From now on you will have no more births. Remain in happiness, worshipping your husband. (33) The son to be born from your womb has been associated with you during all your thirteen births. (34) He also will become a wise man devoted to spiritual knowledge. He is to have five more births.' (35) Saying this he placed his thumb between my eyebrows, and then vanished out of sight. (36) I then bathed in the open in the river, and again rested my eyes on Vithobā. (37) I wrote a hymn of praise composed of five *padas,* and offered it to Him as I worshipped Him. (38) Seventy-two years now bring me to the limit of my life. To-day my efforts to attain the accomplished life are fully completed. (39) My death is now at hand. I have told you of the thirteen births I have had. (40) Sixteen *praharas* only now remain. Give close attention, my son. (41) For you are to have five deaths. Tell your mind that at the time of your own death. (42) Says Bahiṇī, "I have told you all about my thirteen births through the favour of my *guru.*"

BAHIṆĪ FACES HER APPROACHING DEATH

99 (1) I have told you to-day of my thirteen births. They are all of them in my vision. (2) I have told you of them to-day, but I have been watching for the right opportunity to do so. I have told you of them as I am about to leave. (3) Eighteen days previous to my expected death I became aware of it, but I did not tell you. (4) As the death of Rukmiṇī took place first, you had to go to the Godāvarī for the funeral. (5) Rukmiṇī died eighteen days before me. Rukmiṇī was one who reverenced her husband and was a dutiful wife. (6) Had I told you of my approaching death, you would have hesitated to go to the Godāvarī for the funeral. (7) It was for this

reason I did not tell you of my end, keeping it carefully to myself. (8) After you had gone I told the citizens all my inner feelings, (9) that they should send you a letter thirteen days after Rukmiṇī's death. (10) From that day five days are left before I die. I have told the citizens of my desire. (11) As I remembered them I had the facts written down. I looked them over, and then later corrected them. (12) Says Bahiṇī, "He who regards as false the words which God inspires, has hell before him."

100 (1) 'At the time of death one should be alert, keeping one's mind wholly devoted to God. (2) It was this that God said in the *Bhagavadgītā** And to-day Heaven is reserved for me. (3) The power of fire is in my body, and the flame of life is burning. (4) My death will be by day, and in the bright half of the fortnight. See, I have told you after careful inquiry. (5) It is true that to-day the sun is not on its northern course, but what matters that if I have my *sadguru's* command? (6) I shall have my seat looking to the North; I will gather courage, and I will retain my life. (7) Remembering my *sadguru* in my remaining five days will be my *yoga* acts. What I have been taught will now come to its fruitage. (8) Says Bahiṇī, "I have told you my secrets. What happens in the future you will see with your own eyes."

101 (1) To have my mind turned away from worldly things is in truth to me what it is to die during the

---

*See Bhagavadgītā 8-5 :—

अंतकाले च मामेव स्मरन्मुक्त्वा कलेवरम्

यः प्रयाति स मद्भावं याति नास्त्यत्र संशयः ॥

northward course of the sun. (2) I have no need of that northward course of the sun, as I have told you, my dear boy. (3) To have one's mind turned always towards worldly things, that is the southern course of the sun. (4) Says Bahiṇī, "This is the opinion of the *shāstras.* I have told you my belief out of my experience."

102 (1) I can remember some of my past births, but I feel in a hurry, because the time of my death is near. (2) There still remain to be told you other things of the past. It is true that the means I have employed are very powerful. (3) My body has shared all the fortunes that deeds in previous births have made necessary. My soul has passed through all these stages conscious of my true self. (4) In association with indifference to worldly things the stages of my births have been lived in truth, and this indifference to worldly things has been gained through obedience to my special duties. (5) The seventh stage was that of losing consciousness of body. This I gained through actual experience. (6) And now the fortunes of my body, as laid up in former births, have come to an end. I have a very clear witness of this in myself. (7) I have completed all the thirteen stages of my life, and the movements of my mind have ceased. (8) Says Bahiṇī, "Hold no doubts on this point. It has been through Right thinking that I have reached this condition of unconsciousness of body."

103 (1) My mind is ever indifferent to worldly things, because I have offered to God [Govinda] my senses [*indriya*]. (2) And this is the penance which I have taken internally, this absolute devotion expressed within

and without: (3) such as repeating and understanding the *mantra* (given me), and constantly thinking of Shri Rāma, and unceasingly worshipping my *sadguru.* (4) I will offer the ten kinds of gifts together with the four forms of speech including the *parā,* and I shall offer cows in the form of desires. (5) As for the penance of the *pancha-gavya* (five products of the cow), I consider it as worth but half a vowel. Instead I have drunk the holy "*soham*": I am Brahma. (6) I have bathed in the Ganges of Knowledge; shaving has been of my mind; and my consciousness has been that of being absorbed in Brahma. (7) This is always and for ever the only true penance, to have the mind fixed in its purpose. (8) Says Bahiṇī, "It is such a penance I have undergone. The *shāstras* alone know the *shāstras'* meaning."

104 (1) Desire is in truth the cause of births. This I know by experience. (2) And knowing this I have put aside desire, and the non-dual Brahma has become the desire of my soul. (3) I collected all my senses and administered a penance to them, namely a bath in the great *tīrtha* of Knowledge, devotion to God. (4) I had for a long while experienced the desires for sensual things, but to-day I have made them rootless. (5) Holding with singleness of devotion to the words of my *sadguru,* I have made pure all unholy desires. (6) Says Bahiṇī, "I have given penance to my mind, and now I am free through the enlightenment of my soul."

105 (1) It has taken three hundred and fifty-one years for my lives to be formed into these thirteen births. (2) When my mind found calm I passed my life as a

woman in the contemplation of Hari. (3) I tell you now with certainty that my heart has become unchangeable. (4) Says Bahiṇī, "I have now no further desires. My heart is in perfect peace in Brahma.".

106 (1) As long as you live in this body of yours you will acquire knowledge. (2) After this your births will be of a higher order, because in your various births you have been a *yogabhrashta* (one interrupted by death before completing his attainment of final deliverance). (3) In three of your births you will live in the sacred city of Benāres, with a mind indifferent to worldly things. (4) In one you will be born as a regular *sannyāsi.* In that life your heart will be at rest. (5) In your fifth birth, when you become eighteen years old, you will live a true and honoured life because of unconsciousness of body (i.e., consciousness of soul). (6) After that you will never have to be born again. I, therefore, tell you that you have no more worry after that. (7) Says Bahiṇī, "You will learn to know yourself; through the mercy and teachings of your *guru* you will gain knowledge."

107 (1) I have seen my death, and it is a good omen. (2) I have erected a banner on the top of my mind. I have met with the Universal Soul. (3) I have stopped my breathing. I have the certainty that "I am He" (*soham*). By this the physical flame has met the spiritual flame. (4) My store of merit or demerit is at an end. My physical life is completed and the store for my future birth is absorbed in Rāma. (5) Lust, anger, and illusion rise up day and night and with Yama Dharma cry, "Alas! Alas!" (6) I have enclosed my body with indifference to worldly things. I have kindled the fire of

knowledge, the knowledge of Brahma. (7) My bodily desires are now dead having seen their place in the grave. (8) The jar was carried round me and broken at my feet, and there came forth the loud cry of the great sentence, "I am Brahma." (9) I have dismissed with funeral rites my family, my name and my personality. I have offered my body to where it belongs (i.e., the earth). (10) Says Bahiṇī, "My body in its three forms has turned to ashes. Tukārām has indeed shown mercy."

108 (1) Turning into ashes the remaining part of my destined life, I have carried them to the sacred waters of joy of the non-dual. (2) By sprinkling the three-cornered altar of this body made up of three forms I have it in unconsciousness of bodily existence. (3) Wherever the eight feelings for the Qualitiless Brahma exist there the cow's urine has been sprinkled. (4) I have set up the banners of holy feelings. I have kept the *mantras* of devotion to Brahma in my memory. (5) Such rituals of sprinkling I have performed. Then follows the ritual which leads to *moksha*. (6) Says Bahiṇī, "In performing my funeral rites, I became in truth my very self."

109 (1) At the beginning of the first day the funeral ritual began and I offered my body to Brahma. (2) On the second day I lost my thoughts of duality, and non-duality appeared in the supreme Brahma. (3) On the third day there came the peaceful harmony of the three *guṇas* and the offering of the *Piṇda* came to an end in this way. (4) On the fourth day I found myself outside of the four casual bodies and recognized my true purpose. (5) On the fifth day I made an offering of my body (*piṇda*),

and saw my five vital airs on their way. (6) On the sixth day the six waves of distress became quieted. My feeling became steadied in the Universal Soul. (7) On the seventh day there was an end of the seven constituents of my body and I had an eternal refuge in the Non-dual. (8) On the eighth day occurred the destruction of the eight feelings (*bhāva*) and I enjoyed happiness through the experience of the Non-dual. (9) On the ninth day the nine forms of *bhakti* passed into the consciousness of the Universal Soul. (10) On the tenth day I saw the ten sense organs on their way. (11) The *Ashmā*, the *Uttarī*, and the five senses were thrown into the Ganges of knowledge. (12) On the eleventh day the eleventh sense organ with the *mana* I offered to the supreme Brahma. (13) The bull in the form of Indifference to worldly things was let loose, and was driven to lodge in the wilderness. (14) I made a sacrifice of all the rest that Fate had destined for me, with the purpose that hereafter there should be no pollution from my dead body. (15) On the twelfth day the ceremony of offering to my *manes* (ancestors) will bring my desires to an end. (16) In order to check the power of desire on the twelfth day the desires were thrown into the non-dual lake of the supreme Brahma. (17) I have set fire to the impression caused by illusion (*māyā*) on my heart, and my heart is now united to the term, "That thou art" and unity with Brahma has been attained. (18) As *satchidānanda* I have forgotten the idea of things to be seen, the seer and the act of looking; I have also forgotten the thing contemplated, the one contemplating, and the act of contemplation. (19) This destruction of the group of threes belongs to the twelfth day, by which my soul has attained its Brahmahood. (20) Both substance and shadow have disappeared (i.e., the idea of Universal Soul and its reflection in the individual soul) and this is the real meaning of the twelfth day. (21) I have seen the swan of "I am It" on its way. This then is truly the twelfth day. (22) Just as the sun in twelve months crosses the twelve zodiacal signs, so I have gone through the twelve days of my funeral and in this way the *shrāddha* ceremony of twelve months has been observed. (23) The moon's phases have sixteen as their limit, so I also have a limit of less or more. (24) Knowledge is my Ganges, and the *guru* is my funeral guide, and the Brahma manifestation is my Gayā. (25) According to my *guru's* teachings we shall perform the auspicious *shrāddha,* and offer it to Brahma helped by the consciousness that we ourselves are Brahma. (26) In this way then my body has performed the funeral ceremonies with resolution based on Right thinking. (27) Says Bahiṇī, "Now let the consciousness of this my body be laid aside: this is my fixed determination."

110 (1) Call a Brāhman, and we will perform the *mantra-bath.* We will complete the rite of alms-giving at the time of my death. (2) I must take the penance according to the prescription of the Vedas. You, the twice-born, are our divinities. (3) I salaam after bestowing the ten gifts; now be very tender towards me. (4) Only twenty-one hours are left before my death. Let there be a *diṇḍi* procession accompanied by cymbals and *kathās.* (5) The reading of the book, the *Dnyāneshvari,* is completed, and the rains are over. Let the Brāhmans stand ready. (6) The sound of musical instruments is resounding in the air. Hark! they are filling the ten directions. (7) Taking the special seat and assuming the posture for contemplation,

I see everything clearly because of the instruction of my *guru*. (8) The conch-shell, the disk, the club, and the *tulsi* garlands adorn the necks of Brāhmans. (9) Give attention and shout the names of Dnyāneshvar and Viṭṭhal and repeat them determinedly. (10) Listen to all I shall tell you. The death of my body is very near. (11) Says Bahiṇi, "I am now experiencing the union of the five *yogas*."

111 (1) I shall sit in contemplation facing the north; in the *yoga* posture, anticipating my death. (2) When it is three *ghatikās* (of twenty-four minutes each) before sunrise, (3) then, oh my son, sit at my back, with an attentive and self-reliant mind. (4) If you should hear any sound from without, let your heart be attentive to it. (5) Repeat aloud the names of God. It is a great day for rejoicing. (6) At whichever place I touch my hand, know that there is my life. (7) Three and thirteen making sixteen *ghatikās*, I have to sit in the posture of contemplation. (8) Nine of these *ghatikās* I shall repeat without ceasing the names of God. I have already told you of my heart's resolve. (9) Of the seven *ghatikās* that remain they are to be divided as I will tell you; all my sense organs will flock to their place of rest. (10) For four *ghatikās* I shall remain absorbed in contemplation. Let your own mind be at rest. (11) When thirteen *ghatikās* have passed in this way, my tongue will sing in memory of my *sadguru*. (12) Tukārām's name will be in my mouth, and I shall think concerning Gaṅgādhar (her husband) and the saints in my *guru's* line. (13) After that I shall fix my eyes on the tip of my nose and turn the fists of my hands. (14) I shall put a rosary around my neck with my own

hands, and givng my heart its freedom I shall remain so. (15) All the vital airs of my body will cease to work, will rise in my throat, and pass quickly into my head. (16) I shall hold Nārāyaṇ in my meditation. My soul will then become one with Him and remain so; (17) He, the indivisible, the non-dual, the pervader of the heart. My thought of Him will be that of the Non-dual. (18) Says Bahiṇī, "Such will be the happenings at my death; I have told you with certainly what is to take place."

112 (1) Wave the lights, wave the lights before the *sadguru.* Let us brighten the flames of our hearts. (2) The *piṇda* is lost in *piṇda* (i.e., my body is absorbed in Brahma). The flame of my life is now pervading the whole universe. (3) I have now occupied the seat of joy and peace; I will do reverence to the knowledge of the Non-dual. (4) Intelligence is the inmost part of the *Satchidānanda. Satchidānanda* is its lustre. (5) That lustre shines in my eyes, and Bahiṇī has disappeared in the mass of Intelligence.

113 (1) After the jar is broken the space within remains as a part of space. (2) So when the body is gone there remains Intelligence as the part of Brahma. (3) When the water has dried up who talks of where the reflection in it has gone? (4) When *bajri* is put on burning camphor it takes the form of the fire that burns it. (5) Likewise the name of Bahiṇī has passed into *Māyā* in the contemplation of the Non-dual.

114 (1) Now, finally, I tell you people, keep holy and true feelings in your heart. (2) In this Kaliyuga there are

sants (saints) to be found from house to house, just as plentiful as the cheapest vegetables. (3) Says Bahiṇī, "Right feelings will save you all. This is all I wish to say."

115 (1) [TO HER SON] As soon as you heard my letter read, you hastened at once. You jumped to your duty, my dear son. (2) You performed the thirteenth day for Rukmiṇī. My voice trembles, my throat is choked with emotion. (3) You have fulfilled your duty to all. You have done so in mind, body, speech and all your feelings. (4) In seeing you my joy has increased. My throat is choked with the emotions of love. (5) My death is fixed for the month of Āshvin, the first day of the bright fortnight of the moon. Listen, I have plainly told you. (6) Do not ever be sorrowful in your heart over this my death. And do not overstep the limits I set for you. (7) Your sonship has to-day come to its fruitage. You have arrived for my death. (8) Says Bahiṇī, "Now child, ask whatever you have to ask. Let there be no ground for bad men to doubt."

A VERSE BY BAHIṆĀBĀĪ'S SON, VITHOBA

116 (1) *To fill their bellies they play the hypocrite and from house to house loudly proclaim their teachings.* (2) *They lack understanding themselves, but give knowledge to others, pretending contemplation like a herron.* (3) *Self-deceived, they seek to deceive others. Taking them by the hand they lead them to hell.* (4) *Says Viṭṭhal. "What am I to do with the fate written on their foreheads? They feel no disgust for sin."*

CHAPTER IV

MANAHPAR ABHANGS

THE CONTROL OF THE HEART

NEED OF A SADGURU

117 (1) With all my heart I will cling to the feet of the *sadguru.* Unceasingly I will contemplate him. (2) If I do so, then, Oh my heart, what will be left of you there? You will find yourself in the net of contemplation. (3) Yes, I will place my trust on the words of my *sadguru,* for whom I have a love that can never die. (4) I will always remain the slave of my *sadguru,* absolutely indifferent to worldly things. (5) I will offer at his feet my body, my power of speech and my heart. I will hold my *sadguru* in my heart. (6) Says Bahiṇī, "Oh my heart, rid yourself of the idea of self, and come as a suppliant to the feet of the *sadguru.*"

118 (1) As chief of all means of salvation stands that of the service of a *guru,* which changes one into Brahma Itself. (2) I will, therefore, approach his feet, and there dwell, and then, Oh heart, who will care for you? (3) There are *Shāstras* and the *Vedas* and many great systems of philosophy, but a *sadguru* is superior to them all. (4) Says Bahiṇī, "If I have the favour of my *svāmi sadguru,* he will show my heart the easy way (to salvation)."

119 (1) Who would think of putting poison in the poisonous *Bachnāg* plant? Or add bitterness to the bitter *vrindāvan?* (2) So, Oh my heart, the love of worldly things is a part of you. You enjoy them as one enjoys sugar. (3) Who would think of placing stench in filth? One of the habits of the crow is the eating of that filth. (4) Says Bahiṇī, "Oh heart, worldly things are the roots to your life, and there you remain as a slave for ever."

THE HEART'S NATURAL INCLINATIONS

120 (1) No person would put himself to the trouble of going to sow grass-seed in a forest. (2) So you, Oh heart, naturally seek enjoyment in worldly things. I tell myself this; I do not have to go to others to learn this. (3) Many kinds of trees grow on mountain sides, flourishing naturally in the soil. (4) Who prescribes their duties to animals and birds? Each one of them does what by nature belongs to them to do. (5) Says Bahiṇī, "Oh my heart, such is your natural instinct, your worldly desires have been millions of millions."

121 (1) Who thinks of giving bitterness to the *Nimb* tree? The sugarcane is sweet, but who makes it so? (2) As is the seed, so is the fruit. This is the explanation of sweetness. The meaning of this is very plain. (3) Who would think of placing poison in the root of the poisonous *Indrāvana.* Who would think of supplying nectar to the mango.? (4) Who would add poison to the *Bachnāg* plant? One does not have to supply sweet fragrance to flowers. (5) Who ever adds sharpness to the taste of the mustard

plant? Who has to create sweetness in the date? (6) Says Bahiṇī, "According to the seed comes the fruit, either good or disgusting to our taste."

122 (1) Who has to tell swine, dogs and asses to eat filth? (2) One acts as one is constituted by nature. Why then should people feel troubled thereby? (3) Who has to tell a serpent to bite? People have to suffer from the anger of the scorpion. (4) Who has to whisper into the ear of the tiger or wolf to remain in the forest and kill other animals? (5) The tick and the bedbug live on blood. Do people have to tell them to do so? (6) Says Bahiṇī, "According to the effects of our former births we also act, without being told what to do."

123 (1) Who has to place sap in the root of the banana, the palm or the beetlenut tree? (2) If the seed is of the sweet kind, so will be its fruit. The saint understands the reason for this. (3) The jack-fruit, the mango, the *sitāphal* and other fruits are sweet, because of the sweetness that lies in their roots. (4) Says Bahiṇī, "If the seed is sweet, then the fruit will be nothing but good and worthy of being eaten by all."

124 (1) Oh my heart, your nature of attachment to worldly things was formed in a former birth, therefore the power of worldly things is great in you. (2) I, therefore, pray you to listen to me. I have made my organs of sense willingly obedient to me. (3) But if you do not mind what I tell you, I shall not let anything remain of my body. (4) I shall fast, I shall stop my breathing. In the hottest season I shall sit in the midst of five fires (four at the sides,

and the sun above); (5) I shall torture my body by hanging head downward over a smoking fire; I shall wander to all the sacred bathing places of the earth; (6) in practising the *yoga* I shall sit in contemplation; I shall adopt extreme fasting; (7) I shall put my body to the saw. Then what will you gain by all this? (8) Says Bahiṇī, "Oh my heart, obey what I tell you. If you don't, you will have to go begging."

125 (1) I have found Right-thinking [*viveka*] and Indifference to worldly things [*vairāgya*] as the true way. So now, Oh heart, who is going to pay any respect to you! (2) I shall seize and compel you to contemplate. Then at once the (seductive) power of my bodily organs will decline. (3) I shall make you the judge of yourself. Oh heart, look to yourself. (4) Says Bahiṇī, "In gaining the credit of this you will be the gainer, and find yourself in peace."

RIGHT-THINKING THE TRUE WAY

126 (1) By the power of Right-thinking [*viveka*] I have acquired indifference to worldly things [*vairāgya*]. Now Oh heart, how are you going to exercise your authority? (2) Now consider, and look within. (3) Lust, anger, covetuosness, pride and envy are carrying on their enmity against you. (4) Says Bahiṇī, "I have acquired Right-thinking as the counsellor directing me to a fixed resolve."

127 (1) Oh heart, you will say, 'I deceived Indra, I destroyed the reputation of Brahmadeva. (2) What do

you amount to, you fool? The *Vedas* and *Shāstras* sing my praises. (3) I turned Nārad into a female. Don't question my power. (4) I sent Shiva wandering into the jungle. I made Vishṇu madly in love with Vrindā. (5) I deceived Vyāsa, I robbed *rishis*. Who can equal me in power?' (6) Says Bahiṇī, "Such was the response of the *mana*. I listened and remained silent."

128 (1) Indra at the time of Ahilyā's marriage made this determination, 'I, mighty one, will enjoy her.' (2) Such was his desire, but did he not know it? He did not know that one's desires create one's own bondage. (3) Nārad asked for the very same gift. And he also was prevented from his intention. (4) Brahmadeva had his intentions fixed on beautiful Bhavānī. (Shiva's) thumb cost him the loss (of a head). (5) Shiva has always sensuous desires, therefore, his *mana* holds him in bondage. (6) Even Vyāsa, was not without sensuous desires. He got into difficulty. Any wonder at that? (7) Says Bahiṇī, "Oh heart, it is true that wherever a man has (evil) intention, there you bring him into difficulty."

129 (1) As for myself I am without a desire. This I myself bear witness to. My mind seeks enjoyment not for a single moment. (2) So now, my heart, how are you going to exercise authority over me? The footsteps of Vithobā are without desire (for worldly things). (3) I have seen Him in my thought, I have sung His praises in understanding and contemplated Him, [Viṭṭhal] in my soul. (4) I have strained out of me evil passions, and put them away, and now in Viṭṭhal I have continued peace. (5) Pāṇḍuraṅg Himself has become lust, anger, covetousness, and

envy. (6) Says Bahiṇī, "Oh heart, having taken account of my purpose, I am looking forward to the eternal peace."

130 (1) For this some practise celibacy, and abandon worldly things. For this purpose they go into the forest to live. (2) Freedom from desires is achieved by restraining desires, and then the mind will regard with disgust all sensual desires. (3) For this reason also, some perform the *yoga* rites, sacrifices, austerities, prescribed duties, and they resort to the forest. (4) Says Bahiṇī, "If desire for sensual things leaves one, then, Oh heart, who is going to worry himself about you?"

131 (1) In subduing my organs of sense and action I have brought Right-thinking (*viveka*) to my aid. It will make known to me the joy of oneness with the (supreme) *Ātmā*. (2) Oh heart, what authority have you over me now? I advise you to keep quiet. (3) Right-thinking will change desires into non-desires. And in the presence of peace, anger will stay away. (4) Covetousness will assuredly die. The enemy of envy will burn it up in the furnace of Knowledge. (5) The pure *guṇa* of Goodness will drive away the three *ahaṅkārs* [*buddhi, chit* and *mana*]. Be sure of this, Oh heart. (6) It will subdue under itself the passions of desires, longings and cravings; (7) and the organs of sense will have to obey. For Right-thinking is the fortune of him who is absorbed in Brahma. (8) Says Bahiṇī, "Right-thinking [*viveka*] is the cream of all thinking. Ask anyone who understands the Soul."

132 (1) He who makes Right-thinking his companion, the support of his sin is broken. (2) Now I have made Right-thinking my helper. So, Oh heart, I am not

going to bother myself about you. (3) If Right-thinking is joined with indifference to worldly things, *bhakti* becomes the servant of Right-thinking. (4) Says Bahiṇī, "Oh heart, Right-thinking is a true friend. Who needs now pay attention to you?"

133 (1) Through Right-thinking I will give attention to the Vedānta philosophy. I will acquire the non-dualistic experience of oneness with Brahma. (2) Oh heart, I will lay this wager before you, therefore, give yourself to knowing the supreme *Ātmā*. (3) The right result of listening (to the scriptures) is meditation. And in this deep meditation there is rest (for the soul). (4) Says Bahiṇī, "Oh heart, become a good heart. Why should we quarrel from now on?"

134 (1) I shall entwine all my ten organs of sense and action around Hari's feet. Then you will be bewildered. (2) Therefore, Oh heart, join with my organs of sense in going as a suppliant to the feet of God, [Achyuta] [Vishṇu]. (3) With determination let the understanding, the will, the conscious self, the thoughts and purposes, belong to the *Ātmā*. (4) Says Bahiṇī, "Putting aside evil, sensuous desires, let there be the embracing of God's feet.

135 (1) "Oh *Mana*, Right-thinking [*viveka*] has seized, tied in a bundle and taken away, all your vehicles. (2) So now you sit down and meditate within putting aside the cause of desires. (3) The ten organs of sense and action have become your enemies and have become the friends of Right-thinking. (4) Says Bahiṇī, "Oh *Mana*, you have now no form nor name. Your power has been cut short."

136 (1) I have turned my eyes to the meditation of God [Keshava] and my ears to listening to the praises of God [Hari]. (2) Right-thinking has shown my organs of sense and action the way of happiness, and having connected them (with that happiness) they think of nothing else. (3) It has turned my power of speech into praising God's name, and the service of God [Keshava] with free hands. (4) It has turned my feet to visit sacred bathing places and places of pilgrimage, there to see God. My organs of action are to be judged by these uses. (5) Right-thinking has turned to use all my ten organs of sense and action. So, Oh *Mana,* because of this, you have lost your power. (6) Says Bahinī, "The senses which have been appointed by me to do the bidding of *Viveka* will not now come back to serve sensual desires."

137 (1) He whose soul is not pure within him, and who is ever engrossed in things of sense, (2) he can never acquire true knowledge. And how can there be final deliverance [*moksha*] without that knowledge.? (3) He who has no desire or love of the means (of deliverance), he is but a molten image of faults. (4) Says Bahiṇī. "Knowledge is at the side of a saint, provided his soul is ever at the feet of God."

138 (1) Oh my heart, my dear one, my gool one, hear my request. I plead with you. (2) Put away your thought of self, and your self-consciousness, and live happily in peace. (3) How long are you going to wander suffering uselessly, and in vain, unprofitable effort weary yourself? (4) Why are you after an illusory mirage? Why

are you willing to suffer the eighty-four lakhs [8,400,000] of births and deaths? (5) What will you gain by it? Be ashamed of yourself before good men. (6) Says Bahiṇī, "The path the saints have taken has led them safely to whole-hearted devotion to God "

139 (1) The path that Shuka, Vāmdeva, Vyāsa, Parāshara, and other great ones took, (2) the path by which they became happy and freed from fear, Oh my *mana,* follow that same course, *Bāpā!* (3) It is the path that Vashishṭha, Arundhati, Sanaka, and others took so quickly. (4) It is the path by which Bali, Bibhishaṇa, Pralhād and Vālmiki arrived at happiness. (5) And of how many more would you have me tell you, belonging to all the four castes, who have attained to happiness, even in this world of care? (6) Says Bahiṇī, Oh *Mana,* by this same path, I have clung to the feet of God with devotion."

140 (1) Oh heart, it is you who are responsible for actions in a former birth, and for those in this birth, because of which I have to experience joy and sorrow. (2) It is through you that there is such an experience as bondage of the soul and deliverance. Otherwise what connection would they have with me? (3) The mistaken thought of "I" and "mine," this duality, you have developed in me. You are at the root of both, goodness and sin. (4) If only you were unfickle in your actions, who would have to experience joy and sorrows? (5) Oh heart, it is through your reasoning that the illusion has grown, of the individual soul [*jīva*] and the Universal Soul [*Shiva*] by use of names. (6) Says Bahiṇī, "I plead, Oh *Mana,* for compassion. Deliver me, a lowly one, from the hands of Death [*Kāla*]"

141 (1) Eternity, Time, Hours, Minutes and Seconds, all these have you as their cause. (2) Where there is no Eternity, there is no Time. You, Oh heart, are the cause of these unreal appearances. (3) The size of an atom becomes the measure of the infinite smallness of Brahma through you. (4) The five elements, the sun and moon, the day and night, appear to exist through you. (5) All this reckoning of time, and all the phenomena of nature, but for you, would be non-existent. (6) Says Bahiṇī, Eternity moves along, but it is through your deception, *Bāpā*!"

142 (1) Oh heart, you are a pervader greater than the Pervader [Brahma], because you pervade the whole universe. (2) So how can I anywhere find happiness for myself? Therefore, I have to plead with you. (3) Oh heart, wherever your influence extends, there is no place for happiness. (4) Oh heart, wherever you spread yourself, there the very thought of joy ceases to be. (5) So, if you can have mercy, it will mean the gain of joy. And for this I hold you by the feet. (6) Says Bahiṇī, "You have deceived overmuch, and for that reason I am despondent."

143 (1) Although Brahmadeva was so great, a mine of austerities, yet you deceived him. (2) Such is the game you play, and contact with you means that you cause one to suffer distress. (3) After deceiving Vishṇu you deceived Nārad. (4) Says Bahiṇī, "Oh heart, with these many things to say of you, your pranks are beyond my ken."

144 (1) Because of you, Oh heart, many forms of *yoga* practices have been adopted. (2) Mines-of-austerities [*Yogïs*] make use of these means, but, Oh heart, you are not controlled. What else can I say? (3) Some by closing the apertures of the body send the vital airs [*prāṇa* and *apāna*] up through the orifice in the crown of the head. (4) Some unclothed, with bare heads, or with matted hair, and in rags, wander about as mutes. (5) Some have themselves buried in the earth alive. Others wander in the forests without food. (6) Says Bahiṇī, "On account of you, Oh *Mana,* men with various practices wander about in their indifference to worldly things."

145 (1) In order to bring you, Oh *Mana,* under control, there is but one essential condition, and that is that many good deeds must be contained in the bundle of deeds one carries. (2) In that case one's *mana* is conquered, and it becomes just as one wishes. (3) One who carries in his bundle of austerities a great heap of austerities finds his *mana* in his grasp. (4) Says Bahiṇī, "And then the *mana* is as straw. One needs the condition of possessing good deeds (in one's bundle of deeds)."

146 (1) If the *mana* is conquered what is there remaining to be conquered, the heart that has turned the universe upside down? (2) Do the necessary good deeds [*puṇya*]. Conciliate the heart, but first embrace the feet of the *sadguru.* (3) If by adopting these means the heart is subdued, then final union with Brahma is fully assured. (4) If the *mana* is not controlled, how can one

gain knowledge? And the means to be employed will be in vain. (5) If the *mana* is not in its right place, what is the good of craving after union with the supreme *Ātmā*? It is merely deceiving the ignorant. (6) Says Bahiṇī "In this case one acts for himself just as the characteristics of an eater are known by the one serving him."

147 (1) On account of you, Oh heart, I shall go from here and remain at the feet of my *sadguru*. (2) Then we shall see of how little account you are. If you should come there, you will get into trouble. (3) On account of you, I will carry a club. With devotion I shall cling to the feet of my *sadguru*. (4) Says Bahiṇī, "By the favour of my *guru* I shall destroy you with the whole universe."

148 (1) If it were not that you were addicted to worldly things, what connection, Oh heart, would I have with you? (2) My joy would naturally be yourself, and who would have to weary themselves over means (to final deliverance)? (3) If you turned away from this worldly life, and gave yourself to the spiritual life, then who would care to seek their enjoyment in the things of this world? (4) Says Bahiṇī, "Oh heart, it is your connection with worldly things that gives so much trouble to one's life."

149 (1) Through the favour of my *sadguru* I shall overmatch your cleverness. I shall punish weak desire, Oh heart. (2) Then you will give your face a very pitiful appearance. It will be you who will not know how to get happiness. (3) You will be like one without a protector.

I shall quickly make you one who is indifferent to worldly things. (4) Says Bahiṇī, "I will make you drop your pranks. I shall fasten on your feet the manacles of Right-thinking."

150 (1) A bitter nimb tree is full of fruit. It is a happy time for the crows. (2) Intoxicated by it, they cry Caw, Caw! But they lack the knowledge of good taste. (3) Oh *Mana,* do not become intoxicated by lustful desires. Do only that which is for good. (4) The swan feeds on pearls, and the crows laugh at them. (5) But they do not know the sweetness of those pearls in their thinking, their mouths being filled all the time with their babbling. (6) Wherever one gets his delight, there he finds his exhilaration, but he does not know the full taste of oneness with Brahma. (7) Says Bahiṇī, "How can filth and musk ever be alike? True knowledge is hard to get."

151 (1) He who has laid up in his possession a great bundle of good deeds, his mind turns with loathing from the enjoyment of worldly things. (2) He then becomes the companion of fortune, and our own friend, and saviour. (3) He who has given up everything for the happiness of his soul, and looked for help in his indifference to worldly things, (4) he in whose heart there has arisen a distaste for worldly things, he has become the master of his own happiness. (5) Such men, in what is left of their faṭe, pass their life in absorption into Brahma. (6) Says Bahiṇī, "Oh heart, leave me alone now. Let me enjoy final absorption into Brahma."

CHAPTER V.

BHAKTIPAR ABHANGS

VERSES IN PRAISE OF BHAKTI

BHAKTI DEFINED

152 (1) *Bhakti* is the very highest means of salvation. Through it heaven [*Vaikuṇṭha*] is at once in one's grasp. (2) So let your heart be steady. Let your love be unbroken, and you will arrive at Vishṇu's heaven. (3) Knowledge and indifference to worldly things [*vairāgya*] are servants to *bhakti*. Before *bhakti*, all other means disappear. (4) Says Bahiṇī, "*Bhakti* is at the root of indifference to worldly things. Let your heart become fixed in this thought."

153 (1) He whose trust is firm in the teachings of the saints, his *bhakti*, forsooth, will have a new form. (2) He who lets his heart listen to their instruction, will indeed arrive at final peace. (3) The teachings of the saints are on the authority of the scriptures. Give yourself immovably to the exercise of *bhakti*. (4) Says Bahiṇī, "He whose longing is for the feet of the saints is to be recognized as on the *bhakti* path."

154 (1) He who is ever singing the praises of God and repeating His names and attributes, is the one whom I would describe as a man of *bhakti*. (2) Not a moment passes with him without repeating God's names. And he

has always the craving for *bhakti;* (3) eyes contemplating God [Hari], praises on one's lips, ears ever listening to the *shāstras* that tell of deliverance; (4) hands used for service, and feet for walking around the image of God [*pradakshiṇā*]; this is the path for peace and rest of the soul. (5) And this all the hours of the day without rest in humble attitude at the home of saints. (6) Says Bahiṇī, "*Bhakti* is the true giver of salvation, but with it there is need of the service given to the saints."

155 (1) As a fish is in distress when out of water, as the *chātak* bird longs for the appearance of a cloud, (2) so one's heart should long for *bhakti*. *Bhakti* is true peace. (3) (As is the distress) when an only son is kidnapped by an enemy, or that of the deer in the grasp of the hunter, (so is the soul without *bhakti*). (4) As the faithful wife is all in a flutter when her husband is absent, as a bumble bee gives up its life when there are no more flowers, (5) as a thirsty man longs for water, as the *chakor* bird longs for the moonbeams, so, (6) says Bahiṇī, "When one has a craving for the *bhakti* of Hari, it is then that one should notice the emotions of the heart."

156 (1) Without *bhakti* what is the value of living? All is vain without it. Such an one loses at the very first sight all that life could mean to him. (2) No one should even look at him. Why did his mother give birth to such an one! (3) He neither serves nor reverences good men, nor does he listen with attention to the scriptures. (4) Says Bahiṇī, "He who is without devotion to God [Hari], how can he acquire a heart indifferent to worldly things?"

THROUGH BHAKTI COMES PURITY OF HEART

157 (1) Through *bhakti* there comes the purity of heart which regards the multitude of visible things as vanity. (2) He, in whose heart there moves indifference to worldly things, to him worldly things are as vomit. (3) Sensual things are to him like the untrue water of a mirage. He regards everything as if it were illusory. (4) Says Bahiṇī, "Until the heart becomes pure, it will not be freed from the allurement of this worldly life."

158 (1) When in one's heart there arises indifference to worldly things, then he does not care for association with what appeals merely to the senses. (2) What can such an one lack of joy? He it is rather who is ever joyous. (3) He cares not for association with wife, son, wealth, and loves not the play of his organs of sense and action. (4) He cares not to see, to speak or to hear. He cares not for dainty food, nor the enjoyment of worldly pleasures. (5) He cares not for wealth, nor for his family connections. Nor does he care for the "I" in his body. (6) Says Bahiṇī, "As soon as the mind can become indifferent to worldly things, immediately the longing for this worldly life is snapped asunder."

159 (1) When a husband has gone away to some distant town, all enjoyment seems like poison to the devoted wife. (2) So repentance acts in the body when in the heart there is the recognition of the *Ātmā*. (3) When the man sensually inclined fails to realize his full desires, his enjoyments are to him like poison. (4) When the money of an avaricious man is stolen, he has no longer a moment's joy. (5) When a fish is taken out of the water, everything

is poison to it. (6) Says Bahiṇī, "So is it when one has not acquired God [*Brahmaprāpti*]; each moment seems to him an age."

160 (1) He who does not care for the hereafter in heaven, nor for the wealth Indra might give, and to whom in this life all things seem to his thought as poison, (2) he is the one truly indifferent to worldly things, and the one who has the right to true knowledge; and he is the one who acquires the true realization of oneness with Brahma. (3) To the house of such an one come all the *Siddhis,* but because of his indifference to worldly things, his mind cares not for them. (4) He has love only for Hari, not for Rambhā, Tilottamā, Urvashi and Menakā. (5) To him the sandalwood paste, and other methods of enjoyment seem poisonous, if without love for God [Hari]. (6) Says Bahiṇī, "He who has complete indifference to worldly things in his heart, Knowledge is his servant."

161 (1) He who has learned that this worldly life is not the true life, such an one cares not for the objects of sense. (3) While in the discharge of his worldly affairs he acts like one indifferent to them, having left all desires for them. (3) Such a one becomes a witness of the *mana* with its characteristic of good and evil thoughts. (4) He witnesses also to the *buddhi* [reasoning faculty] with its will, the mind with its determination, and the self-consciousness with its purpose. (5) He recognizes all the relationships of this world as of *māyā* origin, his fixed principles being founded on the non-dual Brahma. (6) Says Bahiṇī, "*Māyā* is neither existent nor non-existent. Such is the truth taught by my honoured *guru.*

CHAPTER VI.

SADGURUCHI THORAVI

THE GREATNESS OF THE SADGURU

MĀYĀ DEFINED

162 (1) If we say that *Māyā* is non-existent, (we are wrong, because) it is seen. If we say it is existent, (we are wrong, because) it does not exist, from the standpoint of true knowledge. (2) Now a *sadguru* through the certainties of right-thinking, clears away all confusing doubts (on the above theme). (3) Brahmadeva, Vishṇu and Shiva are the three *guṇas* of *Māyā*. And one must not assert that *Māyā* is included in the idea of Brahma. (4) *Māyā* is imaginable; Brahma is unimaginable. In no way can the mystery of Brahma be known. (5) Whether *Māyā* is a substance with parts or without parts is a subject which there is no way of knowing. (6) "But," says Bahiṇī, "In order to know this mystery one must cling to the feet of a *sadguru.*"

163 (1) If one should say that *Māyā* has developed from Brahma, (how can this be true)? For it would identify Brahma with its *upādhi,* [i.e., with that which makes a thing look different from what it is]. (2) In order to settle such a point there is need of a *sadguru's* explanation, by which the idea of a difference between the two, due to wrong thinking, is cleared away. (3) For example, if we say that *Māyā* is not a part of Brahma, still we must not

say that *Māyā* is independent of Brahma. (4) Says Bahiṇī, "Such are the perplexing questions regarding *Māyā*. He who can truly clear away these perplexities is indeed a *guru*."

164 (1) Brahma is non-dual. This is on the authority of the *Vedas*. How then can one speak of *Māyā* as being a separate entity? (2) So whom can one ask about the place that *Māyā* holds, if it is not a *sadguru*? (3) The precious metal and gold are different only in name. One recognizes their unity by one's commonsense. (4) Water and wave, these differ in name only. To the eye of knowledge, in everything there is this same unity. (5) A piece of cloth and the threads with which it is woven are evidently one and the same thing, when seen with careful attention by the eye of knowledge. (6) Says Bahiṇī. "When thus viewed through Right-thinking one sees unity of *Māyā* in Brahma."

165 (1) If one says that *Māyā* is unreal, (one is in error, because) everything that is seen is directly due to *Māyā*. (2) To what then should one hold? or what should one give up? On whose experience can one rest? (3) In Brahmā, Vishnu, and Shiva; and their *avatārs,* the greatness of *Māyā* is seen. (4) Says Bahiṇī, "If one then should say that *Māyā* is unreal, (one is in error, because) one sees in *Māyā* the existence of the three *guṇas*."

166 (1) If one says that *Māyā* is real (one is in error, because) knowledge discloses its unreality. Through experience also non-duality remains (as true). (2) To say that *Māyā* is real (one is in error, because) it nowhere

really exists. Now what enlightenment can I give my mind (in this problem)? (3) Can darkness remain in the presence of the sun? So *Māyā* is not to be seen where Right-thinking [*Viveka*] exists. (4) Says Bahiṇī, "After a saint has become enlightened as to *Ātmā,* he should never say that *Māyā* is real."

167 (1) He who has received the full favour of his sadguru finds the idea of *Māyā's* reality removed from his mind. (2) All else is ignorance that lies in confusion of thought, and means the never-ending troubles of one's earthly life [*samsāra*]. (3) Those whose mistaken thinking has absolutely disappeared, they end by becoming Brahma. (4) Those whose passions have ceased to exist in their hearts, they with ease become the Unchangeable One. (5) Those who lose the desires that belong to the body, they are the only ones who become the Lord-of-the-universe. (6) Says Bahiṇī, "What and to whom shall I tell this, for the knower of *Māyā* is very rare?"

168 (1) He who dwells in the home of the sun, knows no darkness even in his dreams. (2) So he who no longer sees *Māyā* through personal experience he is in association with Brahma Itself, Joy-without-a-second. (3) Does the touchstone know either the gold or the iron? He who has no selfish desires, has no temptations. (4) Says Bahiṇī, "Water never gets thirsty. It is in perfection that the feelings find their purity."

169 (1) By association with the sun the mirage appears as water, but the sun does not recognize it. (2) So *Māyā* has the appearance of being in Brahma, but in reality

it does not even touch Brahma. (3) Nearness to a magnet makes the bit of iron move. Men act according to the movements of the sun. (4) Says Bahiṇī, "It is such an experience that is needed in order to live in happiness for ever."

170 (1) He who is at the same time seer, the thing seen, and the act of seeing, is Brahma, the Everlasting, the Eternal. (2) What shall I include (as being Brahma)? What shall I exclude? For even the pores of one's body contain many a universe. (3) Brahma is in Itself the object of contemplation, the contemplator, and the act of contemplation. So also is He the Object of Knowledge, the Knower and the act of knowing. Also He is Himself both Cause and Effect in one. (4) Says Bahiṇī, "There is no such thing as Duality, not even in a dream. My Rāma is light universal."

171 (1) Why look for *Māyā,* or the conception of ignorance or the sensual desires? (2) Brahma is in the form of the universe, undivided and the All. See that you realize this through experience. (3) Why think of Mind, Intellect, Self-consciousness (as entities)? God [Nārāyaṇ] is the All, within and without. (4) Says Bahiṇī, "All phenomena are the differences in qualities. But Brahma has no differences in Itself, It being self-existent."

THE THREE GUṆAS DEFINED

172 (1) The Universe is pervaded by the Three *Guṇas* [qualities]. From this God [Shri Raṅga] is entirely separate. (2) He alone is in the form of the Universe.

Realize it by experience. The importance of this doctrine a *sadguru* understands. (3) To see things contrary to their appearance is what is needed for the happiness of the mind. (4) Says Bahiṇī, "The *Guṇas* [the three qualities] are the sprouts from *Māyā.* But Brahma, because of non-duality, is the Supreme-of-all."

173 (1) Of the *Guṇas* [the three qualities], the *sattvaguṇa* [the quality of goodness] brings about the knowledge (of Brahma) which enables the mind to become fixed in the form of the *Ātmā* (Brahma). (2) Why should one go to seek *rajoguṇa* [quality of mixture of good and evil] and *tamoguṇa* [evil quality] in the world? By association with them you only increase the form of sin. (3) What is there that the quality of goodness does not possess? Just think of this in your own mind. (4) Through this quality of goodness you will attain heaven, also final deliverance (from births and deaths). Give thought to this in your own mind. (5) Through the quality of goodness [*sattvaguṇa*] and association with those who are good, the effects of *karma* will be destroyed. (6) Says Bahiṇī, "Goodness is the cause of final deliverance, and that pure knowledge (of Brahma) is what is needed."

174 (1) Perform with attention and self-devotion the morning and evening baths and prayers, the various repeating of God's names, and the regular daily rites. (2) In doing this drop all thought of selfish gain. Make the great sentence, "I am Brahma" a reality. In doing so salvation will be found ready at hand. (3) Perform the special duties of your caste, your sacrifices and your giving to the

needy. Do it all. (4) Says Bahiṇī, "Anyone who thus acts, it is because the guṇa of goodness [*sattvaguṇa*] has entered his heart."

175 (1) A cow is cared for, because of one's liking for milk. The mango tree is reared for its fruit. (2) If thus your acts are performed with the hope of fruit, recognize in it the *guṇa* of mixed good and evil [*rajoguṇa*] (3) What is the good of pouring jars of milk at the root of a grape vine (expecting to get milk), or giving invitations to dinner to rich persons? (4) Says Bahiṇī, "He, whose actions are of this kind, knowledge never comes to him."

176 (1) He, who does not accept the *Vedas* and *Shāstras* as authority, know him to be impure within and without. (2) Such a man should be recognized as one who is a true representative of the evil *guṇa* [*tamoguṇa*]. For him there are the horrors of hell for ten millions of *kalpas*. (3) The authority of the *Vedas* is to such no authority; and he shows no respect towards those of high repute. (4) Says Bahiṇī, "One should not even talk with one who by nature is so evil a man."

177 (1) He who is corrupt in his desires from birth to birth how can he acquire so supreme a thing as salvation [*moksha*]? (2) A crow that loves filth, how can it expect to be in the same rank as the royal swan? (3) One who loves evil deeds, one who is inclined towards unrighteousness, is one who is blind, and seeking, as he does, his protection in the evil *guṇa* [*tamoguṇa*]. (4) Says Bahiṇī, "One should not even look into the face of such. Know him to be simply hell itself."

THE SADGURU BRINGS DELIVERANCE

178 (1) The snare of the three *guṇas* is laid for the soul. O God [Keshirāj], when will it be removed? (2) When the soul feels such anxiety within it, it may count on deliverance. (3) Lust, anger, envy, these enemies (of the soul) are all around one. Do Thou, Infinite One, now show Thy mercy. (4) Says Bahiṇī, "In this worldly existence they are especially blessed on whom the *sadguru* shows his favour."

179 (1) One does not need the reading of the *Vedas* or *Shāstras*. The supreme spiritual riches are acquired by a different means. (2) Go as a suppliant to your *sadguru* with all your heart's feelings, and as a natural consequence you will acquire Godlikeness [*Brahmarup*]. (3) One does not need austerities, rites or ceremonies. The means for acquiring the spiritual life are very different from these. (4) One does not need idols, sacred bathing places, sacred cities, or pilgrimages. Hunt rather for the mystic verses of the *Vedas*. (5) There is no need for the practice of *yoga,* for sacrifices or breath-control. The secret of the means (for acquiring salvation) is very different. (6) One does not need (the adoption of the threefold division of domestic life), the unmarried but chaste period [*brahmacharya*], the period of householder [*grihastha*], or the period of abandoning all worldly things [*sanyāsa*]. All such ceremonials without limit are also valueless. (7) There is no need for the five-fire austerity, or for hanging over a fire, drawing in its smoke. There is no need for the life of a naked *yogi*. (8) Says Bahiṇī, "Deliverance is through a *sadguru* alone. It is not obtained through living in forests."

180 (1) Words and their meaning belong to this visible creation. They disappear in the invisible. (2) As to what this means the able *sadguru* will enlighten one, explaining the meaning of the *Vedas* and *Shāstras*. (3) The enlightener of the intellect, and the instigator of thought, disappear in the invisible. (4) All the expressions of the bodily organs belong to the form of the universe. They disappear in the *nirguṇa* Brahma. (5) Says Bahiṇī, "Where it concerns the Indescribable, there the motherly *sadguru* explains."

181 (1) Our human bodies are subject to the law of *prārabdha*. Our souls being of a different nature have a different law. (2) And one should not bring upon oneself the joys or the sorrows that belong to (our bodies). One should remain steadfast in Brahma, the Soul (of the universe). (3) Says Bahiṇī, "I will tell you the characteristics of this, which you are to seek for at the feet of the *sadguru*."

182 (1) Identify your body with the universe, but stand aloof from it as Witnesser. (2) Become yourself the All, and yet be apart from the All. Learn this from the mouth of the *sadguru*. (3) Consider the malodorous as equal to gold, and go to the non-dual state of Brahma. (4) Considering desire and longing, as *Māyā*, live happily among men. (5) Be yourself in everything, whether in men or in forests. (6) Says Bahiṇī, "The root itself is lost, but look at its form through the insight of Knowledge."

183 (1) Blackness and whiteness when washed may disappear, but can fire drop its burning nature? (2) So also Fate will never forsake one. Even a wise man's head receives a blow. (3) Can water give up its characteristic of coolness? Then how would one expect the mind to give up its fickleness? (4) Says Bahiṇī, "This question can be solved when one gazes on the feet of one's *sadguru.*"

184 (1) Everybody has become a *guru,* and proceeds to preach, but none of them know of the greatness of the favour of the *sadguru.* (2) They tell of many forms of knowledge and contemplation, of repetitions of God's names, of religious actions and austerities; but know ye that the characteristics of a *sadguru* are impossible for them to attain. (3) Claiming the authority of the *Vedas* and *Shāstras* how have these professors of mystic powers become the enemies of God? (4) They tell you *mantras,* forms of worship, and talismanic mysteries, but no one in that way reaches the feet of the *sadguru.* (5) Says Bahiṇī, "Why care in vain for one's body? Rather let us worship at the feet of the glorious *sadguru,* where all the attainable things are to be found."

185 (1) My line of *guru* ancestry is from the great Chaitanya. In remembering his greatness I am also great in heaven. (2) I make my *sāshtāṅg namaskār* to him. Let us wave our offerings before the Saint and royal Chaitanya. (3) Chaitanya is the all-pervading *sadguru.* He has manifested himself to me in the form of Tukārām the merciful. (4) I am always contemplating him in my heart. The subject of my heart's contemplation is [Tukārām] both in inner thought and outer action. (5) I know not religious

baths, givings, repetitions of divine names, methods of sitting and bodily postures, but I do know to contemplate for ever the feet of Chaitanya. (6) Says Bahiṇī, "I have obtained deliverance through the contemplation of my *sadguru*. With love, with the reverence of worship, let us wave our lives as offerings before him."

186 (1) .Chorus :—And now my *sadguru*, Lord and King, and my very life. I will place my head at his feet. He will make me to remember Him. I will contemplate Him with a steadfast mind. He will show Himself to my eyes. (2) At the sight of Him thoughts of duality will vanish. *Māyā* will not even touch me. He on whom the shower of nectar falls will rejoice in his happiness. (3) I have a great longing for Him. How can I tell you how much? Says Bahiṇī, "He then will tell me of the seed that produces deliverance [*mukti*], indeed He will."

CHAPTER VII.

ANUTAPAPAR ABHANGS
VERSES ON REPENTANCE

BAHIṆĪ, AS AN ANXIOUS SEEKER AFTER TRUTH

187 (1) The fire of remorse is kindled in my heart. Have mercy on me now, oh Lord of the world. (2) I am in great distress through the three forms of affliction. I do not want worldly things. I do not even want heaven. (3) My sense organs are kindled into a roaring flame.

Have mercy on me quickly, O God [Pāṇḍuraṅg]. (4) Says Bahiṇī, "Happiness itself has become sorrow. Such is the conclusion Right-thinking has brought to me."

188 (1) Looking again at facts, who am I here? One knows that one's body is perishable. (2) By what means do our sense organs act? Who is here as lord of the universe? (3) The earth, water, light, air, and this ether, where were all these created? (4) Says Bahiṇī, "One should investigate these things. With a lively interest one should inquire."

189 (1) If we think of all these things in our minds, or look for some place where we may ask, (2) wherever we ask we find our doubts are not solved. (3) If we enquire of the *Shāstras,* life is too short. One's *karma* is certainly entangled with *karma.* (4) Says Bahiṇī, "How then shall I, an anxious seeker (of truth), become free from the snare of this worldly life?"

UNSATISFACTORY RELIGIOUS TEACHERS

190 (1) Wherever I go to enquire there I find pride. They glorify their own knowledge. (2) No one who really understands the heart tells me. On whose words then shall I rely to give my mind rest? (3) They tell you very many rules, and methods, various forms of worship and various *mantras.* (4) Some prescribe repeating of *mantras* sitting in the five different postures, such being the importance ascribed to how one sits. (5) Others tell you of sacred waters, of austerities, and rites. Others again

tell you an infinite number of ceremonials in worship. (6) Says Bahiṇī, "My mind is not at rest. The battlefield of ignorance I see everywhere."

191 (1) I see them sold to lust, conquered by anger, marked with envy in all their feelings. (2) If I should seek advice of those who possess no Right-thinking, what happiness can they give me? (3) Those who give a gift with the hope of some return, they become the servants of selfishness and slaves of ignorance. (4) Says Bahiṇī, "Such people are devoured by *Māyā*. How can they deliver us?"

192 (1) He whose heart suffers over the sorrows of others, he indeed should be recognized as a saint. (2) If you go to such an one, he will remove that suffering of your heart. Indeed he will remove your sorrow at once. (3) One who makes benevolence his daily companion, that man has peace throughout his whole being. (4) Says Bahiṇī, "Such a man does not distinguish between his own interest and that of another, for he has the eye of knowledge and acts through Right-thinking."

193 (1) The whole of a sandalwood block may be worn down into a pulp, and in becoming so it gives pleasure to men. (2) So a good man in giving happiness to others through his thoughts, his speech and his acts, is not made unhappy thereby. (3) Water gives gratification to men, and favours grass and vegetables in just the same measure. (4) Says Bahiṇí, "So (God) has become *avatārs* in the saints, and in every way has helped mankind."

VALUE OF REPENTANCE

194 (1) Now through repentance the mind becomes indifferent to worldly things, and the attraction of objects of sense is broken. (2) When the heart will feel sick of rebirths then only the sense organs can be held under control, (3) and when lust and anger are deported, then only one will lose the longing for heaven and samsār (life in the world). (4) Says Bahiṇī, "When this change takes place in the heart, it is then and there that the blessing of the *sadguru* is realized."

195 (1) If you regard this life as the really true one, you will find yourself robbed in your own home. (2) Giving reality to your determination and Right-thinking, take that which is imperishable as the essential of life, you fool! (3) Looking at this present life you see it corrupted in a moment. So do not set your heart on the things of this life. (4) Says Bahiṇī, "This body of ours, and all worldly things, lack reality. What the realities of the heart are I have already told you."

196 (1) If you give up worldly things thinking them to be unreal that means you are being robbed, my dear sir. (2) Be it known that it is by sifting unreality that the Real can be attained, but for this one needs Right-thinking. (3) Although the body is of the Unreal, yet by its means one attains the eternal peace in the intense love of Brahma. (4) Borax, for example, though classed as insignificant, can combine with gold, and even tools of iron are useful in making ornaments. (5) The eating of bachnāg (gloriosa superba) is beneficial, as it prevents death from more deadly

poisons. (6) Says Bahiṇī, "The unreal can attain the real, if one acts according to the instructions of the *sadguru.*"

197 (1) You have, as it were, borrowed this quintuplet body, in order to attain the essentials of the way of deliverance. (2) Now if you adopt a lazy attitude (in its use) you will bring about the destruction of your well-being. (3) It is like bringing horses to your home on hire. You feel that the work for which they were hired must be done with speed. (4) Says Bahiṇī, "The owner will take away what belongs to him; but our cause will suffer, (if we do not make a speedy use of it.)"

THE QUINTUPLE CHARACTER OF OUR BODIES.

198 (1) Earth, water, light, air, and ether are the natural elements in this universe. (2) By taking portions of each He made substances with them of special names, in order to save men in this earthly life, for their good. (3) Bones, flesh, skin, veins and hair are the special quintuple from the element earth. (4) Saliva, urine, perspiration, semen and blood are the quintuple He composed from the element water. (5) Hunger, thirst, sleep, laziness, and sexual intercourse are the distinguishing characteristics of the quintuple borrowed from the element light. (6) Moving, turning, contracting, stopping and extending are, be it noted, from the element air. (7) Anger, hatred, fear, shame, and temptation are without doubt qualities inherent in these quintuples. (8) Thus the characteristics of the quintuples, making twenty-five in all, He brought together with great effort. (9) Establishing a law of one hundred

years of life, He connected them with the three *guṇas*. (10) The four Vedas were appointed as oarsmen and a sacrifice was given to God. (11) Says Bahiṇī, "He created the NAME as a ferry-boat to save all mankind as they cross the ocean of this worldly existence."

THE NAME OF GOD, THE SAVING FERRY-BOAT

199 (1) If our boat takes the path of *sattvaguṇa* (goodness), it is sure to arrive at heaven; (2) for as our thoughts are, so we go to the place we have thought of. It is necessary, therefore, to think beforehand what is for one's good. (3) If anyone takes the path of *rajoguṇa* (the *guṇa* of activity), they arrive again in this world. (4) If anyone takes the path of *tamoguṇa* (evil), their boat will take them to hell. (5) If the boat is pushed off from the landing place of pure-goodness (*sattvaguṇa*), they will arrive at eternal peace in the state of Brahma. (6) Says Bahiṇī, "This very boat (or Name) either saves or kills, according to one's desires."

WHO GOES TO HEAVEN?

200 (1) It is true, perfectly true, that the *Vedas* promote obedience to duty. A *tāpasi* (performer of austerities) is one who possesses heavenly riches. (2) He goes to heaven through the power of truth (*sattvaguṇa*), having cast aside every path of *karma* (salvation through deeds.) (3) He is one who shows mercy, forgiveness, compassion towards all creatures, unselfish, and of a pure heart. (4) He is one who has a strong determmation

and courage, is kindly and courteous in his speech, and without deceit. (5) He is one who is always content, who does not violate the teachings of the *Vedas*, and who is for ever happy in his heart. (6) He associates himself with saints, he serves his *guru*, and in him there is no idea of separateness from others. (7) He lives in indifference to worldly things, being only a witnesser of this worldly life, and he has only the mind to care for what happens to come to him. (8) Says Bahiṇī, "It is such a man who goes to heaven. And he who has the perfect knowledge of the Soul (*Ātmā*) goes to final deliverance (no return through rebirth)."

WHO COMES BACK TO THIS EARTH?

201 (1) He who in this bodily life performs his deeds with the wish to enjoy the fruit of those deeds, and who holds the delusion of duality, (2) he, be it known, will possess this earthly life again; such an one is to be recognized as a *rajoguṇī* [one possessed with the *rajoguṇa*]; (3) one who has pride, one who for ever retains anger, one who always seeks an opportunity to sleep; (4) one who ever wears a garland of allurement-of-sensual-objects around his neck, and who so looketh upon a woman as to lust after her. (5) Even should the wealth of Indra come to his home [a multimillionaire], he is not content even with that, (6) sinful, hard-hearted, with a mind fixed on earthly things, one who can never be trusted, (7) a miser, an insulter, a hater of mankind, and one whose mind is not free from doubts. (8) Says Bahiṇī, "He who possesses a mind working in that way will have to receive a rebirth into this mortal world."

WHO GOES TO HELL?

202 (1) He who violates the prescribed rules, who does not respect the *Vedas,* who acts disrespectfully towards the great, (2) such an one is born into the class destined for hell. He is to be considered a low wretch, a *tamoguṇī* [evil, through the evil *guṇa*]. (3) He destroys by first gaining the confidence of others, a murderer, a man without moral principles, and a dullard. (4) He eats what is forbidden, sucks what should not be sucked, and merrily drinks what should not be drunk. (5) He does not fear in his heart the primal cause of hell itself, and he acts naturally with sinful heart. (6) Says Bahiṇī, "Such an one is a *tamoguṇī.* He, foolish one, will fall into hell."

THE EFFECT OF THE THREE GUṆAS

203 (1) The body is a molten statue, composed of the three *guṇas.* In this body the activities are according to the *guṇas.* (2) Therefore, be a witnesser of the acts of these *guṇas.* If you do so, how can you be affected by the illusion of duality? (3) Even Brahmadeva and the other gods are in fear of the three *guṇas.* The three *guṇas* are snares that destroy. (4) The three *guṇas* are a chain fastened upon one's life, whereby great harm has been done. (5) He, whom the serpent of the three *guṇas* has bitten, may be considered as already dead. (6) Says Bahiṇī, "To ward off these *guṇas,* there is but one thing, and that the favour of a *sadguru.*"

204 (1) The one substance [Brahma] that alone exists is outside of these *guṇas.* The right-minded understand this idea. (2) It is in all things, and yet separate

from all things. It cannot be perceived by the senses, because of its indivisibility. (3) We may speak of It as a visible thing, and yet not visible to the eye, because, It is not distinctly perceptible. (4) Says Bahiṇī, "It has no name, form or quality, and yet is for ever in all things."

205 (1) The ending of one's sensual desires should be recognized as a festival. (2) Such is the understanding of good men, namely, those whose minds have witnessed the facts, (3) when they feel weary of the objects of sense they leave them behind and march onward. (4) The heart with a firm resolution turns its back on them. (5) Knowledge burns up the effects of former births, and desires become inactive. (6) Says Bahiṇī, "A steady mind, that is the eternal *samādhi* [state of meditation]."

206 (1) That which is beyond the three *guṇas*, has no form, yet is visible to the eye; its lustre gives light to the eye itself. (2) That form is unperceivable, still it can be grasped by the mind through proper understanding. (3) It is a substance with qualities, without qualities, and beyond perception; and where the sense organs become inactive. (4) Says Bahiṇī, "It is not to be found in sound, yet sound is in It, within It, and without It."

207 (1) The odour of earth, the liquidity of water, and the substance of light belong to the *Ātmā* [Universal *Soul*], (2) but it cannot be seen without the eye of knowledge. And for this one needs the sight-promoting pigment of the favour of a *sadguru*. (3) Form which exists in air, and light in ether, belong to the *Ātmā*. (4) Says Bahiṇī, "The All is beyond all, and this can be seen only by the eye of knowledge."

208 (1) If one tries to see It, sight itself vanishes. and even scientific knowledge disappears in It. (2) The form of It [*Brahma*] cannot be seen by the eye, even though one attempts it, although it is by Its portions that there is such a thing as great and small. (3) When one tries to investigate It, the power of investigating is lost in the attempt. The border line between It and the other is here. (4) Says Bahiṇī, "But all these attempts to know It cease at the moment one sees God [Devarāṇā]."

209 (1) From Knowledge as Nanda [father of Krishṇa] and Intellect as Yashodā [mother of Krishṇa] at Gokul, there was one born into the community of the cowherds. (2) His lovely complexion filled to its fulness every eye. (3) The nine months completed, as it were, the nine forms of worship, and then Krishṇa, the Eternal One, was born. (4) Says Bahiṇī, "In form He was dark complexioned and beautiful. He removed the burden of the troubling monsters."

210 (1) The sun in the heavens is reflected in the water; does that mean that the sun has sunk into the depths of the water? (2) So the *Atmā* is untouched by the body, although essentially one with the senses. (3) At the very sight of the magnet the bit of iron begins to move; just so does the *Ātmā* act in the body. (4) When the moon is at its full the ocean reaches its high tide; so the body acts through the influence of the *Ātmā*. (5) When the Spring comes there come with it flowers and fruit; so the body moves by the power of the *Ātmā*. (6) Says Bahiṇī, "The *Ātmā* is outside of everything, (hence cannot be experienced), but the whole material universe is known by experience."

THE PHILOSOPHY OF THE ĀTMĀ PUZZLES BAHIṆĪ

211 (1) Where is the *Ātmā*? Where is it not? This the mind is unable to make known. (2) Therefore, the *sadguru* when he speaks of the *Ātmā* with confidence, does so that the characteristics of the *Ātmā* may be known. (3) What is Its town, what is Its place? I myself do not know. What shall I accept (as true)? (4) What is Its classification, what Its relative position? This I have not the power to grasp. (5) Who was Its mother, and who Its father? Who knows the exact truth regarding It? (6) Says Bahinī, "Whom shall I ask for Its history? While puzzling over this, ages have passed."

212 (1) If *Māyā* is real, then it is vanquished by Knowledge. If called unreal, that can never be. (2) Experience, in the form of an eye of knowledge, understands. *Māyā's* innumerable forms are ever increasing. (3) Whatever form *Māyā* gives is a real form. But sound is certainly of *Māyā* form. (4) But Knowledge also is *Māyā*, so is contemplation but *Māyā*. Without *Māyā* how could sight increase? (5) So long as this duality lingers in the mind, so long the three worlds [universe] will consist of *Māyā*. (6) Says Bahiṇī, "But *Māyā* does not let one call her a deceiver, read the *Vedas* and other *Shāstras* and see."

213 (1) When a jar is broken the space in it is still in space. (2) Just so when the body has disappeared, the individual soul [*jiva*] and the universal soul [*Shiva*] enter the sphere of the illusory. (3) After the water has evaporated, how can the reflection in it remain? (4) Says

Bahiṇī, "There seem to be two, but know that this is because of *upādhi* [that which makes a thing look differently from what it is]; as a rose behind a glass makes the glass appear red."

PUZZLED BAHIṆĪ REJOICES IN THE WORSHIP OF GOD

214 (1) As my footsteps turn toward Paṇḍharī, I feel the reality of Brahma-joy. (2) In the procession are musical instruments, and innumerable banners, drums and the solemn sound of voices. (3) The dances of Hamāmā, and Humbari give delight, as all openly show themselves the followers of Vishṇu. (4) Says Bahiṇī, "Such is the joy of the road to Paṇḍharī. Where it is can only be seen by the eye of one blessed by good fortune."

CHAPTER VIII.

SANTAVARNANAPAR ABHANGS
VERSES DESCRIBING SAINTS AND SAINTHOOD

215 (1) He who has not the least pride will in every point show a holy sainthood. (2) It is such a *sādhu* who can save men, who can remove confused ideas and give true knowledge; (3) a knowledge that is as pure as the sun, both within and without, and that in its outer forms mainfests itself in actions. (4) Like a jewel or like camphor, pure within and without, it tells men of the hidden

things of the mind. (5) He whose slave is mercy lives ever absorbed in joy. (6) Says Bahiṇī, "He who is filled with a kindly spirit towards all creatures is recognised as possessing the characteristics of a saint."

216 (1) All the sacred bathing places long for the coming of the saints. And who can count their good deeds? (2) While essentially Brahma in form, they have become *avatārs* to save mankind. (3) Brahmadeva and the others desire to meet them. Their deeds resemble a shower of life-giving nectar. (4) Says Bahiṇī, "Such men in their natural talk deliver the seeds of Vedāntic thought."

217 (1) The course of the Ganges is as far as the ocean alone. In the same way the *Vedas* have a flow of language until they reveal Brahma. (2) So also the human mind moves upward to the same great end [Brahma] and then as certainly after reaching the summit it dissolves. (3) A devoted wife's faithful longing increases only in the case of her husband. The sun manifests his glory in the heavens. (4) Says Bahiṇī, "Such is the teaching of the saints, the experimental knowledge of which comes to one's life through the mind."

218. (1) Nectar possesses a sweetness that is characteristic of its nature; so a flower (possesses a natural abundance of fragrance). (2) So those who perform deeds naturally, they are the *Vedas* manifest in a bodily form. (3) A saint has truly in him the qualities of a touchstone, just as the sun is to the precious stone, the quartz, and the diamond. (4) Says Bahiṇī, "So the saints by their very nature possess peace of mind. The riches of the saints consist of all their deeds."

219 (1) Saints and sinners are alike in body, but you recognize the difference between them by their deeds. (2) I may express it thus, also that the fruits of their deeds are different. Knowing ones recognize this through the eye of knowledge. (3) The touch stone [*paris*] and the quartz crystal have similar forms. To the sight, oil and melted butter look alike. (4) A bit of glass and a precious stone at first glance seem alike, but their inner nature is quite different. (5) A true and a false coin look the same. Buttermilk and milk look alike, but they are different in character. (6) Says Bahiṇī, "First determine whether one is a hypocrite or a true saint, and then thereafter (reject or) accept him according to his true character."

VALUE OF ASSOCIATION WITH SAINTS

220 (1) Association with saints leads to the purification of the heart. That association with the saints produces advancement in things good. (2) Therefore one should make oneself their slave. By doing so one will come to know the substance of one's self. (3) Association with saints brings about the destruction of all faults. All pride will disappear through association with them. (4) By this association one will learn one's true self, and knowledge that is hidden will be made plain. (5) By this association with the saints one's true eternal nature will be revealed to one's sight. By this association eternal deliverance can be obtained in the shortest of time. (6) Says Bahiṇī, "One should seek association with one who is without attachment to worldly things. Such an one will know the various ways of attaining the supreme spiritual riches."

221 (1) Association with saints leads the heart to indifference to worldly things. It also gives one peace of mind. (2) A saint is the noblest jewel of all men. What one therefore needs is the determination of full devotion to him. (3) Through this association one can become impressed with knowledge and experience. Through association with saints one may have happiness in this bodily life. (4) Says Bahiṇī, "What association with saints implies, those devoted to God fully understand."

222 (1) A saint is a great physician able to cure the diseases of this worldly life. Listen while I tell you of his process. (2) He gives to a life a very small portion of medicine,and drives all diseases far away. (3) As a congenial diet he prescribes the rejection of sensual appeals, and causes him to be served with emotions of the heart that are founded on the Truth. (4) Says Bahiṇī, "Thus understanding one's heart they devise the method of cure."

223 (1) A tree that comes in contact with a sandal-wood tree becomes exactly like it. (2) So if one comes in contact with a saint, one naturally becomes a saint. (3) The little rill that flows through a village, when it finally mingles with the Ganges river, takes on the form of the Ganges through association with it. (4) When iron comes in contact with a touchstone [*parīs*] it takes a different form and becomes gold. (5) When a wick comes in contact with a flame it is then able to give out a continuous light. (6) Says Bahiṇī, "He who associates, therefore, with good men, he find himself as one truly blessed in this worldly life."

224 (1) Association with evil men makes one evil. You can easily see the reason of this. (2) When camphor comes in contact with what is malodorous its true nature is lost. (3) Sweet milk is spoiled by contact with sour milk. The narcotic *bhāṅg* makes a man a fool in but a moment. (4) Says Bahiṇī, "Association overpowers one, so determine with whom it is to be by consulting with good men."

225 (1) Recognizing (who are good and who bad), make your association accordingly. In so doing you will gain happiness in your heart. (2) Be assured that this is the method (that comes) from Right thinking. And one should not hold in one's mind any attachment (to evil). (3) Recognizing the path of goodness you will attain from every side happiness through your association with good men. (4) Says Bahiṇī, "The scriptures have been composed for the very purpose of informing mankind of the right and the wrong way."

226 (1) The importance of association with saints is very great. By it the wise become possessed with goodness. (2) For this reason one should serve the feet of the saints. In a moment one's heart becomes steadied. (3) The moment the speech of a saint is heard, all assume the divine form (*Brahmarupa*). (4) Says Bahiṇī, "The very sight of a saint is deliverance itself. I ask you to learn this through actual experience."

227 (1) What good fruit is there in wandering to sacred waters so long as the heart is not pure? (2) The heart becomes pure through the reverential beholding of a saint [*darshan*]. (3) What can idols of stone say to you? Are they able to give joy to one's heart? (4) Says

Bahiṇī, "He in whose teaching there is no uncertainty, he will bring about directly spiritual consciousness [*videha*]."

228 (1) A saint performs all his duties while in the world, yet not of the world. (2) Therefore, one should serve the feet of saints. They become the cause to one of final deliverance [*moksha*]. (3) The buttermilk and the butter will never become one again, for the coming of the butter in the buttermilk is due to a different cause. (4) The lotus leaves will never mingle as one with the water (from which they have sprung), even if they remain there (in the water) all their life long. (5) Says Bahiṇī, "So one may remain in this worldly existence [*prapanch*] and yet not be affected thereby, because found at the feet of saints."

229 (1) The saints have shown their merciful favour. The building has arrived at its completion. (2) Dnyānadeva laid the foundation, and erected the temple. (3) His servant, Nāmdeva, built the wall surrounding it. (4) Eknāth, the disciple of Janārdan, erected its pillar in the form of his (commentary on the) *Bhāgavata Purāṇa*. (5) Tukārām became its pinnacle. Now then worship in this temple at your leisure. (6) Says Bahiṇī, "The flag above it flutters in the wind. I have clearly described this temple."

230 (1) In this ocean of worldly existence the saints are the true vessels (for crossing). They understand how to carry passengers across. (2) By the power of devotion the saints make their followers cling to their waist, and thus these merciful ones carry one to the other side; (3) or forming a raft in the form of God's Name show you the

shore of final absorption. (4) Says Bahiṇī, "In days past many have been taken over by the saints; the saints are true rafts."

231 (1) Or the saints may be thought of from another point of view, namely, that of physicians. They seem also like the adepts in magical words. (2) These have saved lives (by their *mantras*) from the evil eye of serpents. Their ability seems extraordinary. (3) (They have saved even) when the poison of the five-headed serpent was causing intense pain, and many waves of agony were dashing upon them. (4) Says Bahiṇī, "When the saint looks toward one who is poisoned, his poison loses its power. A wonder indeed!"

232 (1) With saints also there is knowledge in all its power, by which ignorance is driven away. (2) Therefore one should go to the saints and fall at their feet, and with heartfelt emotion seek refuge there. (3) Through the mercy of saints comes the destruction of sensual desires, and the finding of the Eternal Supreme Brahma. (4) Says Bahiṇī, "A saint is very God in visible form. Why should one then not take to heart his witness?"

233 (1) By association with saints comes concentration of mind. By association with saints comes the use of sacrifice. By association with saints mental habits are formed. (2) For these reasons one should love the saints. They form the direct road to final deliverance. (3) For association with saints is in itself a sacred bathing place. By association with saints one visits sacred places. By

association with saints there is added to one the accomplishment of using *mantras.* (4) Says Bahiṇī, "By association with saints one obtains knowledge. By association with saints one's mind gains the characteristic of steadiness."

BAHIṆĪ'S LOVE FOR SAINT TUKĀRĀM.

234 (1) As my sight fell upon a certain saint, [Tukārām] my emotions were completely overturned. Everything seemed changed. I was driven to silence. (2) The illusions as to visible things were lost. The idea of duality decamped. The very heavens became overfilled with the joy of Brahma. (3) My mind became concentrated; my sight became fixed, as I saw with my eyes the one Indivisible Reality, (4) where words fail to describe, where final absorption takes place, and where the good heart is freed from its passionate desires. (5) When Bahiṇī came into contact with that saint [Tukārām] her heart was filled with love for him, and all other bonds being broken she ended in oneness with the Indivisible one.

235 (1) Oh Mother dear! To-day my life has come to its fruition. I have seen the feet of saints and good men. Through the dust on their feet all physical burdens have disappeared, and an unending joy is mine. (2) To-day my happy fortune has come to its fruitage. I have seen the feet of *sādhus* and saints, and I am filled to overflowing with love. This joy has naturally filled me with happiness. (3) I existed as the One, then became the many-formed. Seeing the form of the Universe, I filled it all. According to the maxim of the banyan tree and its seed, how it grew, so I myself grew and became everything. (4)

Thoughts came and went, illusions disappeared. Until to-day *Prakriti* had created this law. Now according to the maxim of the rope and the serpent my illusions have proved false. I danced (with joy) as I saw the dust of the feet (of the saints). (5) Says Bahiṇī, "By it my pride and the burden of the sorrows of this worldly life have been removed. I have met Tukārām. Blessed is my life. I have easily become one whose purpose is accomplished."

CHAPTER IX.

BODHAPAR ABHANGS

THOUGHTS ON THE MORAL LIFE

(Partially translated).

(236 to 238 not translated)

THE IMMORAL ARE AFRAID OF DEATH

239 (1) Oh, let not Death come, says the man. Oh let not Death come. Even one who knows from experience what (true) joy is, yet he takes pleasure in sensual things. (2) He to whom wife, son, wealth, and daughter are dear, he hovers around them as a bumble bee hovers (around a flower). So also the man who takes delight in being honoured and publicly praised, whose pleasure is in such things; (3) one whose heart is in pleasures such as are

enjoyed by kings, full of desires, and cravings, lustful and addicted to evil habits, a drunkard, a libertine, one who is evil by nature; (4) one who is priest in order that he may attain the desired heaven of Indra and its delights with beautiful damsels. Says Bahiṇī, "A man of this character is indeed afraid of the terrors of death."

240. (1) But the wise man is not afraid of death. He is not afraid of death. It is like the bubble on the ocean. It disappears by the very force of the wind that brings it (to the shore). (2) All material things are of *māyic* origin, hence illusory. How can there be destruction for such? Just as a dream is seen to be illusory, so is the body of that same nature. (3) Just as when solid ghee is melted, it turns again into solid *ghee*. When the golden ornament is melted it is still gold. What fear can it have of being melted? (4) Says Bahiṇī, "To him who knows himself by direct experience, the idea of duality cannot come there. Whether his body falls or does not fall, he who has this direct experience of himself, finds his death to be but absorption into Brahma."

241. (1) Casting aside ideas of one's greatness, go quickly as a suppliant to the saints. (2) He will drive away from you all the anxieties of your heart, and your heart will then rest in peace. (3) But when you go as suppliant to the feet of the saint go with perfect confidence in him, throwing aside all pride of knowledge. (4) Says Bahiṇī, "The saints are, in truth, a mine of compassion. Serve them with the fixed determination of your heart, my good sirs."

FALSE SAINTS

248 (1) Outside they have the guise of a saint but within there is a riot of sensual desires. (2) Such have become the saints of this *Kali Yuga.* They do not follow the teachings which they teach. (3) When they see an assembly before them, they are dumb; elsewhere they bark like dogs. (4) To one's face they talk well, but behind people's backs there is a flow of shamelessness. (5) Says Bahiṇī, "These actors! I wonder where a wench gave them birth."

CHAPTER X.

NAMAMAHATMYAPAR AHBANGS

VERSES IN GLORIFICATION OF GOD'S NAME

THE LONGING FOR GOD

393 (1) He whose nature glows with love unbroken, will sing aloud God's names ever and ever. (2) That alone can be truly called *bhakti;* this the wise understand by experience. (3) Let not one moment of time pass unfilled by God's names. Oh my soul, let your affection rest on Pāṇḍuraṅg. (4) Says Bahiṇī, "Life must all pass away, therefore, let no time pass unfilled by (the repeating of) God's names."

394 (1) Just as a fish is filled with fear when deprived of water, so is he in whose heart is the love of the divine names (he dreads the failure of using them). (2) That love the wise call *bhakti*. Those other than wise vainly babble about it. (3) Just as a thirsty person loves a drink of water, so it is with one who feels a longing to sing aloud God's names. (4) Says Bahiṇī, "A barren woman longs for a child. So a *bhakta* (longs for and) loves the joy of God's names."

395 (1) You cannot buy *bhakti* in the market-place. You cannot find it by wandering in the forest. (2) In exchange for *bhakti* you have to give your heart as its value: any other consideration is without meaning. (3) Look you, *bhakti* is not to be found in the home of the learned. It is not to be found in the palaces of the rich. (4) *Bhakti* is not to be sought in the dwellings of kings or their officials. (5) Says Bahinī, "In order to acquire *bhakti*, one must possess the perfect and Right thinking."

PEACE OF HEART WHERE BHAKTI IS

396 (1) Where the heart's trust is, there *bhakti* is found. Where there is *bhakti* there is knowledge; and by that knowledge the heart has peace, (2) for you naturally acquire the power of contemplation when the heart humbles itself in the presence of the divine names. (3) One who lives in the company of saints and listens to their counsel is always on the alert for faith, devotion, knowledge and peace. (4) Says Bahiṇī, "One needs *bhakti* as a cause, and this results in the acquiring of the state of eternal peace."

397 (1) If the heart's devotion is pure, then the final deliverance will be perfect also. The *Vedas* bear witness to this, as you can see. (2) But if the heart's devotion is imperfect it makes for utter destruction, for in it pride will be found. (3) *Bhakti* is final deliverance. *Bhakti* is deliverance. *Bhakti* is true indifference to worldly things. (4) Says Bahiṇī, "One needs a *bhakti* that is firm. Then nothing is mystic to him."

398 (1) The *Guru-mantra,* God, and medicine, when used with trust all become fruitful. (2) Worship, therefore, this trust with confidence. And now I have told you the secrets of the heart. (3) If you worship a stone-image with trust, you will receive the desired thing. (4) Says Bahiṇī, "He whose trust is pure, heaven is in his very hand."

399 (1) Trust came to fruitage in the case of Vālmiki. By that trust the seven *rishis* became the *Pliades* [seven *rishis*]. (2) Therefore, the Seeker after final deliverance should possess the same trust [*bhāvārtha*]. It turns the pauper into a prince. (3) Trust came indeed to its fruitage in the case of Kaushika. To possess the spirit of trust is a necessity. (4) Says Bahiṇī, "Trust is the yielder of fruit in the form of what one desires. (With it) you may attain to the state of final deliverance in eternal peace."

400 (1) Through the might of *bhakti,* God provides us with what we desire. Such was the experience that came to Puṇḍalīka. (2) Therefore, *bhakti* must be at the

root. Wherever there is this trust there God is. (3) Entering into a dry Tulsi leaf, Krishṇa could not be weighed. (4) God Himself became the garment of Draupadi. For a handful of parched rice God gave a golden city. (5) With the one vegetable leaf (Krishṇa) satisfied the *rishis.* By trust Ganikā acquired heaven. (6) Says Bahiṇī, "To me trust is God. Of this I have not the least doubt."

401 (1) Around God's neck is the leading rope of Trust. Who is able to free Him of it? (2) If you will think deeply, you will see that God undergoes life in the womb for his *bhaktas,* and Bali (the Demon King) has made him (Vishṇu) his doorkeeper. (3) God is fastened to the peg of Trust. What mighty king is there who can untie Him. (4) Says Bahiṇī, "Who can free Him from the cord of Trust? God knows the value of Trust."

402 (1) This group of my five senses has combined and deprived me (of the happiness) of the hereafter. (2) Therefore, the association with saints is the good remedy for it. I myself have done so for my salvation. (3) The deer, drawn by the seduction of sound, loses its life in a moment of time. (4) The elephant is caught, because of its fondness for the female. It leads to his being subdued. (5) A moth is enticed by the brilliancy of the flame of a lamp and loses his life in pain. (6) The fish drawn by its greed of taste loses its life in a short time. (7) The bumble-bee through its passion for fragrance gets caught in the lotus-flower and loses its life. (8) Says Bahiṇī, "These five are lured by five objects of sense and they cannot escape loss of life."

BAHIṆĪ REJOICES IN GOD'S NAMES

403 (1) Let therefore not a moment pass without repeating God's names. Let your heart ever love to do so. (2) That is the real worship of God, which is offered by body, speech and mind. (3) Let there be the longing to listen in the company of saints, and in your heart let there be unbroken love. (4) Says Bahiṇī, "The heart knows no longer the pleasures of the senses, but gets its constant joy from the repeating of God's names."

CHAPTER XI.

BRAHMAKARMAPAR ABHANGS

THE DUTY OF BRAHMANS

THE SUPREMACY OF THE BRĀHMAN

404 (1) The powerful effects of austerities are very great. Take note of those superior beings of the past. (2) Vishvāmitra created another universe. This he did through the repetition of the Gāyatri *mantra.* (3) Vashisṭha placed the earth on the point of a blade of grass, due to the abundance of his austerities. (4) Who can fully describe the austerities of him to whom the light of the sun came to bear witness? (5) Agasti sipped up the whole ocean. He did this through the extreme rigour of his austerities. (6) Says Bahinī, "He who practises austerities, what difficulties are there for him?"

405 (1) Among all the castes the Brāhman is indeed the highest. So said the great ones in the past. (2) Therefore, Brāhmans should be worshipped with reverence. They are the door to final deliverance for all mankind. (3) The *Vedas* ever dwell in the mouth of Brāhmans. They know all their differences and meanings. (4) Says Bahiṇī, "He, whose kick made a mark on the breast of God [Vishṇu], his greatness is well known."

406 (1) God becomes satisfied through the mouths of Brāhmans. Look to actual experience for this. (2) Therefore, a Brāhman should be worshipped with bowed head; so all the scriptures say. (3) Through the *mantra* used by a Brāhman, God is installed in a stone-image, and through one's devotion God manifests Himself. (4) Says Bahiṇī, "In this *Kali Yuga* it is he who is God: such indeed is the witness of the *Vedas*." '

407 (1) He, who succeeds in acquiring the water in which a Brāhman's feet are washed, he acquires the opportunity of visiting the sacred bathing places of the earth. (2) Therefore, a Brāhman is superior to all. At his door all accomplishments stand ready to serve. (3) He who obtains the favour of a Brāhman is blessed through tens of millions of *kalpas*. (4) Says Bahiṇī, "A Brāhman is one through whom sin is naturally burnt up by the mere sight of him."

408 (1) If one serves a Brāhman even for a moment, one's heart's desires will be fulfilled. (2) Therefore, one should worship them, bow down to them and in reverence prostrate oneself on the ground before them.

(3) If any one spends his life in the cause of a Brāhman, he will finally dwell in the heaven of Indra. (4) Says Bahiṇī, "Such is the greatness of the Brāhman. Final deliverance is a mere servant in his home."

409 (1) The command of a Brāhman, God honours with bowed head, for salvation is an obedient slave at his home. (2) Therefore, a Brāhman is a saviour in this *Kali Yuga,* and blessed is he who in this world serves him. (3) In a Brāhman's body God dwells, and in his mouth are the *Vedas.* (4) *Says* Bahiṇī, "How am I fully to describe him? His body is Right thinking in substantial form."

410 (1) Among all the four castes the Brāhman stands superior. He enjoys the *samīpatā* form of salvation. (2) The *Vedas* say that a Brāhman is Brahma itself. His spoken word is honoured in the three worlds [heaven earth, and hell]. (3) No Brāhman has ever gone to hell. All the gods worship him. (4) Says Bahiṇī, "Look you, his body is the very abode of the Gāyatri *mantra.*"

BUT WHO IS A BRĀHMAN?

411 (1) But who in reality is to be called a Brāhman? This question belonging to Right thinking needs to be looked into. (2) Only after doing so should one adore and worship him with love. He is a giver of salvation of a surety, so say the *Vedas.* (3) But his life, body, caste, colour, actions, duties, all these qualifications must be searched. (4) Says Bahiṇī, "Knowledge and learning should belong to the Brāhman. Through Right thinking of the mind, look at this question."

BIRTH DOES NOT DETERMINE BRĀHMANHOOD

412 (1) If one says he is a Brāhman, because he possesses life, that conveys no meaning. (2) Life is the same principle in all living beings, in beasts, birds and the out-caste. (3) There will be many living beings hereafter, there have been many in the past, but that in itself does not bring Brāhmanhood. (4) Says Bahiṇī, "In all living creatures the principle of life is the same. One should not claim Brahmanhood because of it."

BODILY FORM DOES NOT DETERMINE BRĀHMANHOOD

413 (1) If one says, he is a Brāhman because of his bodily form, it cannot be maintained, as seen by Right thinking. (2) First enquire what makes a Brāhman, and then you may worship him and live in joy. (3) The body is essentially one in all living creatures. In all are to be found the five elements [earth, air, fire, water and ether] by their very nature. (4) Everybody experiences childhood, youth and old age. Such is known to be the states of the body. (5) Where there is a body, there is life; where life is, there is a body. That does not determine a Brāhman. (6) Says Bahiṇī, "In all creatures the essentials of the body are the same. This, Sir, is a well-determined fact."

414 (1) Old age, death and fear are alike for all. How can they distinguish the Brāhman? (2) Therefore, let your mind choose Right thinking, and recognize the true meaning of the word "Brāhman." (3) A man burns the

bodies of his mother and father. Why should he not be considered a slayer of a Brāhman, [if it is the body that makes the Brāhman]? (4) Says Bahiṇī "It is not the body that determines the Brāhman. This is clear to the understanding, through Right thinking."

COLOUR DOES NOT DETERMINE BRĀHMANHOOD

415 (1) Now if one should say he is a Brāhman because of his colour, that does not correspond with one's experience. (2) Careful thought will show that Brāhmans are beyond the thought of colour. (3) It is not true that a Brāhman is white, a Kshatriya red, and a Vaishya yellow. (4) There is no such distinction as that a Shudra is black. The structure of the human frame is one and the same. (5) Says Bahiṇī, "Colour does not make the Brāhman; let your mind be settled on the truth of this."

416 (1) Now to call a man a Brāhman, because of his caste, does not satisfy the mind. (2) Having curbed desire, consult the *Vedas* what the answer is; and what remains is easily settled. (3) The *Rishi* Shringi was born of a deer. Gautam was born at the point of the Kusha grass. (4) The *Rishi* Jambuka was born from the Jambul tree. Vālmiki came from an ant-hill. (5) Vyāsa was born from a fisherwoman. Vishvāmitra came from a Kshatriya woman. (6) Vashiṣṭha was born of Urvashi (the nymph), and Agasti from Kalasha (an earthen pot). (7) Everyone knows about Nārad that a house-servant gave birth to him. (8) Says Bahiṇī, "It is not caste-birth that makes one a Brāhman. The marks of a Brāhman are quite different."

MERE LEARNING DOES NOT DETERMINE A BRĀHMAN

417 (1) If we should say that because a man is a Pandit, he is a Brāhman, the mind does not tolerate that definition. (2) The knowing Right thinker chooses a better designation. A Brāhman must be one possessed with true knowledge. (3) Kshatriyas, Vaishyas, Shudras, Brāhmans and others, all display vast learning. (4) All castes are able to explain words and sentences and even poetry. All these castes understand the meaning of their poetry. (5) Even Muhammadans exhibit learning. But who regards these as truly Brāhmans? (6) Says Bahiṇī, "People should know in this way whom eventually to call a Brāhman."

MERE DUTIES DO NOT DETERMINE A BRĀHMAN

418 (1) If we say a Brāhman is one who performs certain duties, and actions, (that is not true), because actions are prescribed for all four castes. (2) Therefore, to say that a Brāhman is distingushed by having prescribed actions, is wrong, because his characteristics are different from that. (3) Each caste acts according to actions prescribed for them. They are not to be called Brāhmans because of that. (4) Says Bahiṇī, "If one is considering actions, Brāhmanhood does not consist in these being prescribed him."

419 (1) The authority for each one's actions is in the *Shāstras.* The special duties of each caste are there prescribed. (2) But how can one call them all Brāhmans because of that? One should let one's mind think of that. (3) The *Shāstras* do not prescribe actions to some special caste. The command of those in authority is to all castes. (4) Says Bahiṇī, "If all walk according to the *Vedas,* how could they all be called Brāmans?"

RELIGIOUS DUTIES DO NOT DETERMINE THE BRĀHMAN

420 (1) Now to say that religious duties define the Brāhman, seems to be without authority. (2) The Brāhman is different from a mere follower of *dharma;* the wise understand this. Men endowed with knowledge recognize him intuitively. (3) The Brāhman, Kshatriya, Vaishya and Shudra all have religious duties prescribed. (4) The giving of food, the giving of money and cows, all this alike are the duties of each. (5) Says Bahiṇī, "Religious duties do not make the Brāhman. The test of a Brāhman is quite different."

421 (1) The religious duties whereby one gains heaven does not make the good Brāhman. (2) One is called a Brāhman who knows Brahma. Others are called Brāhmans, merely because born of Brāhman parents. (3) The many sacrifices, gifts, religious ceremonies, and austerities do not specify the Brāhman. (4) Says Bahiṇī, "How often shall I tell my mind this? How then is a Brāhman to be recognized?"

WHAT MAKES A TRUE BRÀHMAN?

422 (1) I will tell you in short now who a Brāhman is. One who has stored up (in his mind) the teachings of the *Vedas*. (2) One who has made himself an authority on the *Vedas*, a superior, noble *guru* for all. (3) There is no one so great as a Brāhman through whom is obtained absorption into Brahma. (4) By his word one attains the authority to possess final deliverance. By his look alone the effects of past births are burnt up. (5) There is not the least difference between Brahma and a Brāhman. Learn this non-duality from him. (6) Says Bahiṇī, "Who is it who knows his characteristics? The wise recognize him through their Right thinking."

423 (1) Though in the environment of the *guṇas*, he is not overcome by them, nor in the very least is he overpowered by actions. (2) Yet he alone is to be recognized as a Brāhman among men, who even in his dreams does not come in contact with duality. (3) He is one free from the six waves [grief, illusion, hunger, thirst, decay, and death]. He does not so much as touch the six mental affections. He is not found in connection with faults. (4) Says Bahiṇī, "He never deviates from the truth. Such an one alone is a Brāhman."

424 (1) He is one who in his contemplation sees no differences [only the One Substance]; in whose heart is the priceless Supreme Brahma. (2) He alone is a true Brāhman according to the teachings of the *Vedas;* all others are heretics. (3) He is one who has seen one Soul [*Ātmā*] in all creatures. He is a molten image of peace. (4) Says Bahiṇī, "As the ether is everywhere, so he in this world is one in them all."

425 (1) In his inner (thought) and outer (action) the Brāhman represents the One, Indivisible, Non-dual Brahma in his direct actual experience. (2) He alone should be called a Brāhman whose eternal peace is in the supreme Brahma. (3) Indifference to worldly things is his slave and experimental knowledge is in the very palm of his hands. (4) Says Bahiṇī, "He is one from whom lust and anger have all gone, and what remains is his Brāhmanhood.'

426 (1) He is one who has attained the nine virtues, peace of mind, restraint of mind and the others; and is always rich in his possession of contentment. (2) A Brāhman is one who stands highest, the supremest of the supreme, through whom degraded mankind attain to final deliverence [*moksha*]. (3) All his evil longings, his infatuation for sensual enjoyment, his hypocrisy, his pride, have all gone; and in his actions his mind preserves its unchanging mood. (4) Says Bahiṇī, "He whose evil longings have disappeared, know him to be a Brāhman, devoted to Brahma."

427 (1) One who always has Brahma in him, he alone is a Brāhman. (2) The *Vedas* and scriptures bear witness to what I have said. I have not in this reserved a secret. (3) He whose organs of sense ever find their objects in Brahma is a Brāhman in accordance with this meaning. (4) Says Bahiṇī, "He who lives his life in Brahma is a Brāhman. It is not a question here of caste."

428 (1) One, who goes around singing the praise of Hari, is called a Haridās. He, who has a saint's characteristics, is called a *sant*. (2) We make the name fit a man's actions. One does not have to proclaim it to all the people.

(3) One who works in gold is called a goldsmith. A physician is named from his profession as a physician. (4) Says Bahiṇī, "Likewise whoever lives his life in Brahma, he is declared by the *Vedas* to be a Brāhman."

429 (1) One who knows Brahma is called a Brāhman. The *Vedas* are a witness to this. (2) Look to your own case for an experience of this fact, after having taken the witness of the scriptures. (3) Because the sun has twelve phases and gives light, one does not hesitate to call it the sun. (4) One who carries in his body the marks of a king, only he is a king. That which turns iron into gold, that alone is a touchstone [*parīs*]. (5) That which brings every wish to realization is the wish-cow [*kāmadhenu*]. That which can keep death away is *amrit*. (6) Says Bahiṇī, "So, he alone who knows Brahma, is a Brāhman."

430 (1) One who is bent on acquiring knowledge, a keen observer, one whose heart is indifferent to the enjoyment of sense objects, (2) he alone is truly a Brāhman among men. In your mind, notice the wonderful character of that man. (3) There is no wish in his heart to enjoy the fruits of his actions. He merely acts naturally according to the duties prescribed for him. (4) Says Bahiṇī, "He who is free from the idea of any distinctions, he alone is to be recognized as a Brāhman."

431 (1) He who has loving devotion, knowledge, and indifference to worldly things in his heart, he may be said to have acquired the *Vedas*. (2) Consider him alone as a Brāhman, as a knower of Brahma, and truly a Brāhman of excellence. (3) He who truly holds indifference to

worldly things as his wife, becomes a fire-keeper on account of his fire-of-knowledge. (4) He founds all his daily and occasional duties on the teaching of his *guru*. The Right thinking of his mind is continual. (5) He is Brāhman to whom peace, compassion, forgiveness, kindly feeling, and an enlightened mind are recognized children. (6) Says Bahiṇī, "It is after seeing such characteristic in one that the *Vedas* call him a Brāhman."

432 (1) The words of a *guru* may be likened to fire, and the burning faggots to sensual desires. (2) Therefore, one who possesses this fire is called a Brāhman. He kills all sensual desires, and enjoys the desires that remain. (3) The real householder is one who is possessed with desire and anger towards the effects of ignorance as taught in the *Shāstras*. (4) Says Bahiṇī, "It is such that are true Brāhmans. According to the teachings of the *Vedas* it is such that are Brāhmans."

433 (1) He, in whose heart the fire of knowledge blazes because of his *guru's* teaching, and in whose heart that fire remains, (2) he alone in this world should be called a Brāhman. This I have already described from self-experience. (3) One who makes a burnt-sacrifice of his sensual desires in the fire of knowledge, makes a true and complete burnt offering of the heart. (4) Says Bahiṇī, "It is one who is marked with such characteristics; he alone in fact is a Brāhman."

434 (1) One is an astronomer, one a reader of the Purāṇs, one an *agnihotri* [Priest of the sacred fire], one a wandering ascetic at sacred bathing-places. (2) But the

real Brāhman is the one who knows Brahma. Thereby he becomes in actuality God Himself. (3) Some are Pandits, some are students of the *Vedas,* some are Brāhmans enthusiastic in repeating the Gāyatri *mantra.* (4) Says Bahiṇī, "There are Brāhmans, so called, because born of Brāhman parents; this I have already declared."

435 (1) One who has effected the unity of the universe with his own being, and who has experienced the great sentence, "I am Brahma", (2) he truly is called a Brāhman; he has experienced Brahma in actual manifestation. (3) Such an one has lost the powerful force of the idea of "I" and "Thou." By knowledge he has made one the individual and the Universal Soul. (4) Such an one, with his four causal bodies purified, goes to the fourth state of absorption in Brahma. (5) Where there is the unending repetition of the great *mantra,* "I am the Supreme Soul [*Soham Hansa*]" there absorption is truly eternal. (6) Says Bahiṇī, "Those who know Brahma, they are Brāhmans, and their very sight brings final deliverance."

TRUE AND FALSE TEACHERS

436 (1) One is certain that *mukti* [final deliverance from births and deaths] lies in the teachings of the *guru.* One devotes himself to the contemplation of the Qualitiless One [Brahma]. (2) But know that *moksha* [final deliverance from births and deaths] is something quite different. It is the wise who attain the eternal peace. (3) In the opinion of some, *moksha* lies in the worship of God as possessing qualities. Others think that *moksha* is to be found in God as without form. (4) Some conceive of

moksha as follows :— *Moksha* refers to those means of salvation, namely, *bhakti,* knowledge, and indifference to worldly things. (5) Some say that *moksha* means accomplishments through the *yoga* practices, or they call the scriptures the way of *moksha.* (6) Some exalt *moksha* as the result of their actions, while others claim that *moksha* lies in the discarding of the fruits of one's actions. (7) Some imagine *moksha* to be victory over one's mind; others say that *moksha* is one of the side-results of contemplation. (8) Some by argument seek to prove the existence of the one great Substance (*mahāttatva*). Others drink intoxicating liquors, and eat meat as a method of attaining *moksha.* (9) Some give free rein to their organs of sense, and think that is the clear way to *moksha.* (10) Some consider the reading of the *Vedas* as *moksha,* others call moksha the worldly life itself. (11) Some cruelly torture their bodies, thinking that that is the way to *moksha.* (12) Some drink in the smoke of the five fires in the forest, and contend with others that that is the way to *moksha.* (13) Some are ascetics, wearing long matted hair, and performing austerities, and maintain that *moksha* is in that manner of life. (14) Some are always thinking of the combination of the five elements, contending that this is at the root of the state of *moksha.* (15) Some take the vow of silence, some repeat *mantras,* some practice austerities, some perform religious ceremonies, and consider that they gain *moksha* thereby. (16) Some assume the five attitudes in worship, and say it is by this that *moksha* is gained. (17) Some adore divinities in a variety of forms, while others regard *moksha* as the state of the heart. (18) Says Bahiṇī, "*Moksha* is quite different from all this, and it is the wise who understand its true nature."

437 (1) Men thus regard *moksha* in a variety of ways, but no one has the actual experience of it. (2) You will, however, find *moksha* in the destruction of desires, and then will come the welfare of the soul in the great sentence, "Thou art That". (3) In the word, "Art" is to be found the root of the unity of the "Thou" and the "That." (4) Says Bahiṇī, "When the mind [*vritti*] becomes immovable, then the curtain of this worldly life is torn down."

438 (1) The ear, the skin, the eye, the tongue, and the nose are the five organs of sense. (2) The *ātmā* is absolutely distinct from these. This you can realize by the experience of your mind. (3) The mouth, the hands, the feet, the phallus and the anus are the five organs of action. (4) The functioning mental organs of emotion, thought, cognition, feeling and consciousness are five in number. (5) Sound, touch, form, taste, and smell are the powerful appeals to the sense. (6) Says Bahiṇī, "Thus we have found twenty-five organs, but now, O mind, acquaint yourself with the nature of the 'That' [Brahma]."

439 (1) The five sheaves surrounding the *ātmā,* the three classes of afflictions, and the well known human passions, when these are destroyed, (2) it is such an one who can be truly called a Brāhman. I have considered the question well, and have told you the truth. (3) The Brāhman is one who has considered the truth of things and has cast aside the six waves [sorrow, desire, hunger, thirst, birth, and death], and the six passions. (4) Says Bahiṇī, "Where desire has been destroyed, there the Brāhman is, the real knower of Brahma."

440 (1) He who has uttered the *mantra* hundreds of thousands of times and has understanding, finds with joy the word *sat* [existent, i.e., Brahma]. (2) He who is devoted to Brahma can be called a Brāhman. And naturally he has an experimental knowledge of it, though in flesh. (3) Unchangeable, perfect knowledge has found entrance in him. He becomes lost in unconscious contemplation. (4) Says Bahiṇī, "Such are the marks of a Brāhman according to the strict definition of the *Shāstras.*"

441 (1) (The Brāhman is one) who offers to that word *Sat* [existent i.e., Brahma] the fruits of his peculiar duties, and becomes an unchangeable devotee of Brahma. (2) Such an one I call a pure Brāhman, to meet whom means salvation. (3) He is one who cannot endure self-pride, and in his actions there is no selfishness. (4) Says Bahiṇī, "When one meets such a Brāhman, it is as if absorption into Brahma had come to one's home."

THE STATE OF A SINNER

442 (1) God is far from him. Religious practices have ceased, and kindness towards living beings has left him. (2) What can one do? Evil deeds have been laid up in a former birth, and sensual pleasures in this life seem attractive. (3) The names of God do not come to his lips; he has no love for worship; and the idea of indifference to worldly things gives him pain. (4) Says Bahiṇī, "Where one does not like saints, and great souled *sādhus,* that is the place of sinners."

443 (1) The heart is ever inclined to sensual pleasures. To his understanding of Brahma there is added no devotion to the *Ātmā.* (2) Where one's deeds laid up in a former birth are not pure, his body is as it were a molten statue of sin. (3) He is one in whom there is pride, lust anger, and envy, and who loves unholy deeds. (4) Says Bahiṇī, "He who pays no respect to the authority of those who are superior, they are to be regarded as morally low."

444 (1) Just as the rising sun is useless to the blind, and the moon useless to the fox, (2) so is the man who is without knowledge. Although the *Ātmā* is directly before him, yet the proof of it does not enter his mind, because of his foolishness. (3) What value is the moonlight to the crow? What use can a monkey make of clothes? (4) What is song, tune and measure to a deaf man? It is like laying down principles to a dog. (5) What a beautiful woman of the highest type is to an impotent man, acts of enjoyment are to the lifeless man. (6) "So," Says Bahiṇī, "is the way of righteousness to a fool. Although instructed regarding it, there is no effort to live such a life."

445 (1) He who has no purpose, no love, no goodness of heart, and who knows not the life of one indifferent to worldly things, (2) such an one can never acquire knowledge, and how much less *Moksha.* (3) Is there any doubt about the meaning of this? For action, one is in need of strength. (4) Says Bahiṇī, "According as a *bhakta* purposes in his heart, so he attains final deliverance through his heart's devotion."

446 (1) When ghee comes in contact with fire it melts; salt dissolves when thrown into water. (2) The

characteristics of association are felt by them. The natural power is intensified. (3) Iron in contact with the touch stone [*parīs*] becomes pure gold; and in the month of Māgha, trees and creepers blossom. (4) Says Bahiṇī, "When the moon drops its soft light at full moon it naturally gives the tidal motion to the sea."

447 (1) By association with the worst of ill odours camphor is spoiled. Salt ruins milk. (2) Therefore, association with anything should take place only so far as it administers to the happiness of man. (3) If saffron comes into contact with lamp-black, it will show the effects of that association. (4) Says Bahiṇī, "One should seek only such association as will naturally lead to final deliverance [*moksha*]."

448 (1) If the nimb tree comes into contact with the sandalwood tree, the characteristics of the sandalwood tree are impressed upon it. (2) Such must be recognized as the effect of association with the good, and the mind must do its Right thinking along this line. (3) Through association with the flower, a common cotton thread receives honour. By association with the Tulsi plant the earth (in which it grows) also is honoured. (4) Says Bahiṇī, "Therefore, create a wholesome association, and having formed it, rest your soul's devotion upon it."

REPETITION OF THE GĀYATRI A BRĀHMAN'S DUTY

449 (1) The mark of a Brāhman is his repetition of the Gāyatri mantra, which is the primal *mantra* of the *Vedas*. (2) Anyone who says that any other *mantra* is

superior, should be thought of as dull of mind and low in morals. (3) The primal *māyā* is said to be the equalization of the three *Guṇas.* The Gāyatri *mantra* is to it the essential Brahma. (4) The knowledge of this seed of *Oṅkar* is the knowledge of divine essence. (5) Through it has come the knower of the *Vedas.* The Gāyatri is well known as the Mother-of-the-*Vedas.* (6) Says Bahiṇī, "He whose repetitions are those of the Gāyatri *mantra,* he is one who partakes exactly of the essential nature of Brahma."

450 (1) The duties belonging to caste, and those of the *āshrams* [the student, the householder, the forest life of retirement, and the ascetic life], should be carried out perfectly, and God should be held in one's heart with singleness of devotion. (2) The Brāhman who does not in this way perform the duties of a Brāhman should be considered as degraded and sinful. (3) Without entertaining any sinful idea, the first duty in the morning should be the bath, the prayers and the repeating of the *Gāyatri,* made faultless by being repeated one hundred and eight times. (4) Then should follow ablutions (*tarpaṇ*), which duty applies especially to gods, *rishis,* and ancestors. (5) Then should be repeated with reverence portions of the *Bhagavadgītā* and the names of God. This should be thoughtfully done and with feelings of love. (6) This should be followed by the worship of God according to the prescribed rituals, with incense and lights accompanied with the repeating of *mantras.* (7) After food is served to the gods offerings should be made to the Fire, and a well cooked morsel should be set aside. (8) After making these offerings to the gods, finally an offering of cooked rice should

be made to the crows. (9) Any guest who may come at that time should be regarded as a divine being, God in form. (10) He should be served first, and then the others, and then dinner should be partaken sitting in a line. (11) With every mouthful, God should be remembered. One should not eat without His being a witness to it. (12) Says Bahiṇī, "He who is thus scrupulous regarding his every action, and his relation to God, the attaining of heaven is in his very mind."

451 (1) The *Veda* is the individual soul. The *Veda* is the Supreme Soul. Through it there is the glorification of the Divine joy. (2) When the *Veda* did not exist, how could the universe have existed? And how could there have been the experiences of joy or sorrow to the soul? (3) The syllable, "Om" is an atom of Brahma. From that there arose the Veda. Then through the three *guṇas* there developed differences in the form of the universe. (4) The *Veda* was born with upward root, downward branch, and on it grew branches covered all over with leaves and flowers. (5) And as Chhand, Pada, Jatā, Krama, Araṇyaka and Brahmaṇs the *Veda* spread itself in Brahma form. (6) *Karma* is itself Brahma. Brahma itself is *Karma*. *Karma* and Brahma are not different from one another; thus say the *Vedas*. (7) The substance of the *Vedas* concerns itself with the One Substance and that is the essential meaning of the Vedānta, by which the differences is our worldly life are done away with, through our knowledge of the fact of non-duality. (8) The teaching is that there is one substance alone; there is no other. That alone can know Itself; the all of all, and the all in all every where. (9) Thou alone pervadest all

creatures. By experience know the joy of connection with the Non-different. (10) Says Bahiṇī, "One gets pure knowledge through relationship with the *Vedas*. Other knowledge is impure, belonging to darkness."

452 (1) Brahma exists at the beginning, middle and end of one's actions; such is the experience of the wise. (2) The Brāhmans who have these characteristics are alone true Brāhmans. All others should be recognized as low sinners. (3) With respect utter "*Om*" and offer with "*Tat*," and with "*Sat*" bring about the unity in Brahma. (4) Says Bahiṇī, "These also are without doubt Brahma themselves; realize the truth of this and be humble."

CHAPTER XII.

PANDHARIMAHATMYA.

THE GLORIFICATION OF PANDHARPUR

453 (1) The whole universe has truly today become Paṇḍharī (Paṇḍharpur) as I take on my lips the name Hari, Hari. (2) Joy has redoubled. To whom can I recount it, Oh Mother? Wherever I look, there my Hari fills all. (3) Illusion has passed away. The idea that the body is the "I" is lost. The great, great sentence, "That art Thou," no longer remains anywhere. (4) The consciousness of "I" is gone, *Bhāv* [presence] and *Abhāv* [absence] have disappeared. Says Bahiṇī, "I have seen the king of Paṇḍharī."

454 (1) My Protector-of-the-lowly, my Brother-of-the-lowly, my Hari, dwells at Paṇḍharī on the bank of the Bhimā. (2) He stands upright on a brick, and with parallel placed feet is beautiful to look at; with his lovely feet he stands a charming figure. (3) Around his neck sparkles the garland of jewels [*vaijayanti*], at his waist the yellow silken robe, (4) on his brow the upward mark of sandal paste, lovely earrings in his ears, all his body is anointed with paste. (5) On his head a jewelled crown gives him beauty, sparkling with jewels, and carrying strings of pearls. (6) His two rows of teeth flash with the light of diamonds. Says Bahiṇī, "Such an one I contemplate in my heart."

455 (1) Born into this worldly life, yet I have attained the union with Brahma; and that union I have found on the bank of the Chandrabhāgā. (2) His image of the colour of a dark cloud, with full open eyes, stands motionless on a brick. (3) Though outside of name and form, a spirit eternal, the essential *ātmā*, he has become manifest to the sight. (4) Look at Him, Indescribable, [Paṇḍharināth] who is unscrutinized by the *Vedas*, nay even higher than they, and qualitiless and unchangeable. (5) Indivisible, a mass of intelligence, He is seen to be the universal omniscience. Bahiṇī sees Him in her heart.

456 (1) My heart is entranced by Him. I see nothing but Him. I have seen the pure supreme Brahma. (2) I have become one with Him. My eyelids even do not move, as I long for absorption in Him. (3) My mind has forgotten itself. The idea of "I" and "Thou" has

fallen to nothingness. (4) I cannot recollect myself. I have forgotten myself. My sense organs have ceased to act. (5) They have ceased to be for use. My mentality has lost its vitality, while my thoughts have attained the *ātmā* condition. (6)My thoughts are fastened on Him. My mental wanderings are stopped. Bahiṇi is enjoying the *Ātmā* joy.

457 (1) As one's footsteps take the path to Paṇḍharī, the joy of Brahma comes directly to him. (2) You may look around, but there is no joy like that in the three worlds. You should see this with your own eyes at Paṇḍharī. (3) As you sing the name of Hari, as you clap your hands you find your joy in the waves of love. (4) The *diṇḍis* resound notes of Victory! Victory! The *mrudang* (drum) sends forth its sweet music. (5) They dance the *hamāmā, tipari* and *humbadi,* as they openly claim to be slaves of Vishṇu. (6) Says Bahiṇī, "Such is the joy along the way (to Paṇḍharī) which, one who is fortunate, sees with his eyes."

458 (1) Come! Let us hurry up and finish the journey, for Paṇḍharī, the original seat of our God, is yet far away. (2) Stop your idle tales and finish the journey. Pāṇḍuraṅg is waiting for us. (3) He who has a care for his own good, let him at every moment make full use of his time. (4) If the day sets, darkness will fall, and to the humble there is no better refuge than Paṇḍharī. (5) Whether the body shall die or live, stick to your determination of reaching Pāṇḍuraṅg. Let us not give up our devotion to Him. (6) Says Bahiṇī, "Let us reach there at the proper time, for then only shall we be in good time for the festal occasion."

459 (1) The glory of the Bhīmā river, pervading our whole being, is such that even Brahmadeva is speechless when attempting to describe it. (2) Blessed are the fortunate people of Paṇḍharī, who enjoy the happiness that the love of Viṭhobā brings! (3) It is here that the Bhīmā and Chandrabhāgā unite. How can one sufficiently praise their glory? (4) Besides this the God of Paṇḍharī is there. How can I describe my feelings at the glory of the sacred place? (5) Where these three meet, how can one sufficiently describe its glory? (6) Should one listen to the description of its glory, there would be no such thing as sin even in one's dreams. (7) Where bathing, gifts, and the vision of God take place, what can births and deaths do? (8) There is no measurement of time as day and night; there is always light there. There the Sudarshana (Vishṇu's disc) is for ever going round. (9) Even the gods come together here to bathe, riding here at midday in their *vimāns* [chariots-of-light]. (10) Who can describe the limits of the glory of this sacred place? But a sinful man, residing there, does not know it. (11) Blessed is Puṇḍalīk! Blessed his devotion! Through him the sacred place experienced its greatness. (12) Says Bahiṇī, "One must have a stock of *puṇya* to meet Viṭhobā.'

THE JOY OF PAṆḌHARĪ

460. (1) Blest of Fortune indeed are the pilgrims to Paṇḍharpur. They have on them the mark of Viṭhobā in all their rebirths. (2) In meeting with such there are great benefits, and a million waves of joy. (3) Who is able to describe the holy lives of the people of Paṇḍharī? They constantly look upon the glorious face (of God). (4) They bathe in the Chandrabhāgā. They (go to the

temple to see (and worship) God. They listen to the constant singing of God's praise, at the Great door of the temple. (5) They shout Victory, Victory! Crowds, in singing groups, move in lively procession. The very sky resounds to the loud acclaim of God's names, like peals of thunder. (6) The life of business and the spiritual life both go on happily together. And even in dreams no one sees Kali and Kāla (Sin and Death). (7) Here are to be seen the Tulsi altars; the drawings of the lotus flower with coloured powders, and the threshholds sprinkled with saffron water. (8) The hum and bustle of the city have the very form of Viṭṭhal. Indeed the people of Paṇḍhari are Viṭhobā Himself. (9) Even if one searched for it, as for some medicinal plant, one would not find (in Paṇḍhari) a single sinful act. Paṇḍhari thinks only of the final-absorption into Brahma. (10) In the city of Paṇḍhari are to be found those who have attained Final Deliverance even while living, [Jivanmukta] and Brahma Itself stands in the public squares in the form of Viṭṭhal. (11) Living creatures come and go through and over Paṇḍhari, so that even animals and birds have the opportunity of Final-Deliverance. (12) Says Bahini, "Blest and happy are we, as the name of Paṇḍhari comes to our lips."

461 (1) How can I sufficiently describe the joys of Paṇḍharī, joys that the four forms of speech fail to express, (2) where Puṇḍalīk made his home? Blessed is his family line, his father, his mother! (3) Who can draw the limit to the glory of Paṇḍharī, a place even Brahmadeva finds indescribable? (4) Says Bahiṇī, "No sacred city, the equal of Paṇḍharī, is to be seen anywhere on this round earth."

462 (1) Much have I heard, much have I sung, much have I seen of the glory of Paṇḍharī. (2) There is no sacred place the equal of Paṇḍharī anywhere, even if heaven is pointed out as one. (3) Where can you find such a Chandrabhāgā, such a bank as the Bhīmā, or such a god standing on a brick? (4) Such a sandbed, or such praises of Hari? And here and there you meet with crowds in groups of singers. (5) Tell me, pray, where is there such Haridās, such joyous love, such loud repeating of God's names? (6) Says Bahiṇī, "For the sake of us helpless ones, God created Paṇḍharī."

463 (1) The twenty-four idols have their seats, their postures and looks, but Paṇḍuraṅg is in the form of the *Nīrguṇa*. (2) At His feet both gods and sacred waters have their birth. And the idol is in truth that of Viṭhobā. (3) The origin of the *Vedas* and *ṣhāstras* is the letter "A", but Paṇḍuraṅg is the origin of everything. (4) The brick on which He stands is the symbol of the fifth state, that is the absolute absorption in Brahma. (5) Both his hands on his hips are an indication of many in one. (6) Says Bahiṇī, "He has stolen my heart. Blessed is he who has learned that sign."

464 (1) Among all sacred waters, that of Paṇḍharī is the chief of all. Looking all over the earth there is none equal. (2) Blessed are those fortunate ones who enjoy its love and happiness, and on whose lips are the constant loud repeating of God's names. (3) At the junction of the Bhīmā and Chandrabhāgā the dark complexioned Paṇḍuraṅg dwells. (4) On the banks of the holy *Pushpāvati* there is *Veṇunāda*. Here with feelings of love Govinda sported. (5) The three gods come here on

their *vimān,* choosing for their time the middle of the day. (6) The sacred city of Paṇḍharī is of the nature of Brahma, therefore, it is many times greater than all others. (7) Benares is *karmabrahma* (Brahma in the form of *karma*); Paṇḍharī is Brahma in the form of name. The Brahmagiri mountain is Brahma all in all. (8) In Paṇḍharī there dwells the three Brahmas, therefore Paṇḍharī is great. (9) Says Bahiṇī "Paṇḍharī is the greatest of all, such is the plain statement of the *Vedas.*"

465 (1) Blessed, blessed is Paṇḍharī where Hari lives! (2) Blessed, blessed is the Chandrabhāgā where Pāṇḍuraṅg dwells! (3) Blessed, blessed the *Padmāl* where Gopāl remained. (4) Blessed, blessed is Veṇunāda where Govinda danced. (5) Blessed, blessed is that sand-bed where He stands upright on a brick! (6) Blessed, blessed is Puṇḍalīk who obtained the presence of Hari! (7) Blessed, blessed is the Pushpāvati where Vrindā and Shripati stay! (8) Says Bahiṇī, "Blessed, blessed are those whose undivided love is on Pāṇḍuraṅg!"

CHAPTER XIII.

PUNDALIKMAHATMYA

THE GLORIFICATION OF PUNDALIK

PUNDALĪK THE UNDUTIFUL SON

466 (1) Listen to the glorification of a *bhakta* of Hari's. He, Puṇḍalīk, extended it to extreme limits. He made it encircle the very heavens. He drew to himself the good God in human form. (2) In all the three worlds

[earth, heaven, and hell] there was no one so sinful, so unholy as Puṇḍalīk. He paid no respect to his parents. His offerings to them were vile curses. (3) He would not listen to anything they asked him to do. Instead, he showered upon them foul abuse, thus heaping up sin. (4) Those parents through whom the happiness of this worldly life could have been made exceedingly happy, he made fun of them. Such a son he turned out to be.

PUṆḌALĪK IS CONVERTED

(5) Such actions on his part continued for some time. Then came a pilgrimage to Benares. The son carried along with him all the results of his evil deeds, as he trudged along the way. (6) But now suddenly the time for the dawn of good fortune came. His mass of sin began to crumble. The sufferings of both son and parents ceased. Righteousness now had its dawn. (7) Just as when a cow is attacked by a tiger, God rushes to its rescue, so God suddenly ran to the rescue of both the son and his parents. (8) Just as if a spring should burst from a solid rock, just as if a barren women should give birth to a son, just as if hair should grow on the palms of one's hands, so was it to have *love* come into the heart of Puṇḍalīk, but it did. (9) Understanding now the holy way of living, Puṇḍalīk felt deeply troubled and cried, 'I am an awful sinner, deep in sin. I have omitted the worship I owe to my parents. (10) What a sin I have carried on my plate! What anguish I have caused my parents!' So saying he was filled with sorrow at heart.

and embraced their feet. (11) And now he said, "What need have I now of Benares? My mother and father are my Benares." So turning back, he came to Māndesh, and sought for a forest called Atak. (12) Hunting for a hundred miles around he finally found a forest called Daṇḍakāraṇya, so dense, that while the singing of birds could be heard, none could be seen. (13) The trees stood extremely close to one another. Their tops could be seen swaying in the heavens, where the rays of the sun could find no opportunity for entrance. (14) It was in such a fearful forest that Puṇḍalīk began to live. Seeing here a a pool of water he gave it the name of Chandrabhāgā. (15) Here he began his parental service. He was moved with devotion. He regarded his mother and father as very God. At their feet he poured out the tender affections of his heart.

NĀRAD REPORTS PUṆḌALĪK'S DEVOTION

(16) Thus it continued for some time, until it happened that the *rishi* Nārad in his wanderings observed it, and said to himself, 'Some great and noble *bhakta* has come to light here.' (17) Seeing Puṇḍalīk's devotion to his parents, and that he was immovable as wood and considered all visible things with indifference, as if, who knows he may have met Him who dwells in the heart. (18) As the *Bharat Muni* Nārad watched him, he was filled with an uncontrolled joy in his heart. He was struck with extreme wonder, and tears flowed from his eyes. (19) After watching Puṇḍalik's devotion to his parents, Nārad hastened to heaven [*Vaikuṇṭha*] and said, "Oh God, I have seen

a strange sight. I am unable to contain my joy." (20) As he spoke his throat was choked with the emotion of love; his lips trembled; tears streamed from his eyes, and God said to him, "What is the matter with you?" (21) God embraced Nārad to his heart, and said to him, "Tell me quickly what is the strange thing that was happened. Let me know the secret of it." (22) Nārad then replied, "Oh Nārāyaṇ, I was wandering about, and I saw a strange thing. I ask you to listen to my story. (23) In the world of mortals there is a forest called Daṇḍakāraṇya, and I saw there also a country called Māndesh. (24) As I wandered about I came to that place, when suddenly I saw a strange sight. The sight gave my heart joy, which your own heart can understand. (25) In that forest there was a twice-born [Brāhman], rendering service there to his parents. Although I saw his remarkable devotion how can I sufficiently praise its nobleness? (26) The current of the wind may be turned backward; this round earth, may be turned upside down and one may even enter fire. All this is possible, but it is *impossible* for me to describe such devotion to parents. (27) It is possible to take a mouthful of poison. It is possible to dry up the six oceans. But how is it possible for me to describe the novelty of the limitless devotion to his parents, such as he was showing? (28) Of what value are other means compared with this and who thinks of wondering at them? I certainly am unable to describe adequately any means of greater value. (29) In seeing his devotion, Oh God, I don't know whether to say that one can obtain absorption in Brahma through it, or that Absorption into Brahma has actually come into this world of conflict."

GOD [KRISHṆA] AND NĀRAD COME TO SEE PUṆḌALĪK'S DEVOTION

(30) Hearing the unusual character of this devotion, God's heart was stirred with emotion. He took Nārad by the hand, and secretly departed with him. (31) Rukmiṇī [his wife] was in bed. Without letting her know, and leaving behind the Eagle [his conveyance], Krishṇa and Nārad started on their way (to the land of the mortals). (32) Behold this god, the chief jewel of *bhaktas*, walking on foot for the sake of his *bhakta*! He leaped down from heaven [*Vaikuṇṭha*] and in a moment arrived in Māndesh. (33) As he went along with Nārad in that country, Nārad pointed out to the lord of gods the great and the little forests. Suddenly he saw the chief of the *bhaktas* (Puṇḍalīk). (34) At the sight of him God was greatly astonished. Puṇḍalīk did not see Him. In fact he had no particular desire to see God. (35) Nārad, therefore, made God's presence known. "Oh Puṇḍalīk, God has come. See, He has come running here, for whom you suffer much severe pain." (36) Puṇḍalīk had become absorbed, however, in the one thing he was doing. Washing his parents' feet, he did not even turn his head to look at God, but tossed a brick towards Him, and God stood upon it. (37) The Lord of Vaikuṇṭha (who was Brahma Itself) placed his hands on his sides, and stood motionless on that brick. He fastened his sight on the tips of his nails, and thus gazed on the whole Brahma universe. (38) I know not whether his posture was that called Khechari, but His body was perfectly motionless. And as he looked upon Puṇḍalīk, the latter became altogether Shri Viṭṭhal. (39) He, into whose heart God enters, his heart is cleansed of all worldly things. Through His pervading power God

Himself lives in him whom He sees possessing the pure emotions of devotion. (40) God [Hari] had seen the *bhakti* of Puṇḍalīk, and so the Lord of Heaven had hastened down and entered into the heart of Puṇḍalīk. (41) And seeing the feelings of Puṇḍalīk He continued to remain in that place. He bore the glory of his fame, and founded the famous city of Paṇḍharī.

CONSTERNATION IN HEAVEN AT KRISHṆA'S DISAPPEARANCE

(42) Turning now to the events in heaven [*Vaikuṇṭha*]; when Rukmiṇī (Krishṇa's wife) awoke and looked about and she did not see Krishṇa anywhere. She fell into deepest concern. (43) When she looked for the Eagle [Krishṇa's conveyance], he was still there standing at the door. 'Mother' he cried, 'alas! alas! what has happened to Him, I do not know. (44) Whither has he gone! I know not for whom he has hastened. What can have been the distress that called Him? Shripati [Krishṇa] has stolen silently away.' (45) Rukmiṇī replied to the Eagle, 'I feel in my heart today that there is something wrong. Chakrapāṇi [Krishṇa] has gone away without telling me. What jewel of a *bhakta* could He have met?' (46) Just then there was a great ado (in heaven). The gods assembled together at once, remarking that a strange event had taken place. 'We know not where Gopāl [Krishṇa] has gone.' (47) The constant vision of Him was no more. The heavenly land was in depression of spirits. It was just like a widow bedecked with ornaments, for who was

there to appreciate her (the widow's) beauty? (48) All the gods began to weep. Rukmiṇī moaned aloud. A great sorrow overwhelmed them. They could find no trace of God.

NĀRAD EXPLAINS KRISHṆA'S DISAPPEARANCE

(49) Just then Rukmiṇī suddenly spied the Muni Nārad. The Mother of the world in humble tone asked him about Krishṇa. (50) Nārad noticed the ado all the gods of heaven were making, and he gave them the facts, telling them not to be troubled. (51) 'In the land of the mortals,' he said, 'there is a holy country. Here, one named Puṇḍalīk, a twice-born by birth, is carrying on strenuous religious rites. (52) He is living in a dense forest of great trees. Their tops sway in the heavens. The sun looking down with his eyes sees there eternal darkness. (53) In such a forest by the Chandrabhāgā pool the Brāhman Puṇḍalīk carries on his parental service. (54) The Lord of Heaven has gone to see that devotion. And seeing Puṇḍalīk's spirit of *bhakti* the God of gods has chosen to remain there. (55) Seeing Puṇḍalīk's whole-hearted devotion, the limits of which I do not know, the Lord of Heaven has chosen to remain there in preference to being in heaven".

THE GODS RUSH DOWN FROM HEAVEN

(56) Hearing Nārad's story, the gods rushed down to that spot (on earth). Seeing God standing there on a brick, they were struck dumb. (57) Though the groups

of God Brahma and others began to recite aloud the *Vedas* and *Shāstras* in praise of Nārāyaṇ, Nārāyaṇ [Krishṇa] Himself would not speak a word. (58) Then they cried, 'Alas! alas! Who has ever seen such devotion as that of Puṇḍalīk? It has made the Lord of Heaven stand on a brick. The wonderful nature of *bhakti* is extraordinary. (59) There are many severe means of attaining the presence of God. Some make use of breathings, and the soul is forced into the skull, and yet they have not attained God, Oh Nārāyaṇ. (60) There are many who in various painful ways attempt to find God, but fail. How has He been so easily pleased here?' (61) While the gods were thus thinking, and in their wisdom choosing the true reasons from the false, suddenly they came upon the clearing in the woods, where *bhakti* dwelt, in the form of the noblest parental service. (62) Then they exclaimed, 'This chief of *bhaktas* evidently knows the method of attaining Brahma. He has, therefore, obtained the actual presence of the Lord of *Vaikuṇṭha*, sealing his mouth and standing him on the brick. (63) 'Observe,' they said, 'this to begin with is the forest Daṇḍakāraṇya, and besides, it is the forest Brahmāraṇya. It is on the bank of the Chandrabhāgā river. The scene makes one's heart rejoice. (64) And in addition to all this, this chief of *bhaktas* seems like a rising sun. God has recognised the marks of Puṇḍalīk's devotion, and has taken pleasure in remaining here.' (65) Thus noticing the hearty desire (of Puṇḍalīk), God yielded to it, founded the town of Puṇḍalīk, and called it Paṇḍharpur. (66) With Rukmiṇi came all the host of *rishis*. They made the place a second heaven, and gave it the name of heaven on earth.

(67) Such is the river Chandrabhāgā; such the banks of the Bhīmā; such the sands of the river-bed; such was Puṇḍalīk chief among *bhaktas;* such the gods, such the city, such the acclaims of Victory, Victory at the great door of the temple. (68) Such are the banners, the flags and the conchshells, and the brass drums roll out their deep sounds. The big drums, the little drums and the horns, the cymbals and the hand drums make their musical sounds. (69) In every house *tulsi*-plants were seen in pots, the yards were sprinkled with water mixed with saffron and decorated with drawings of lotus flowers with powder made of crystals, and worship was conducted three times a day. (70) Blessed, twice blessed are the people of that place! Blessed are the city and its citizens! Blessed have become the butterflies, the bees, the beasts, the birds and the noble trees, (71) they who come and go over this sacred place, be they man, beast, bird or other creatures. And those who are found in this region of *Panchakrosh* never go to hell. (72) The very listening to this glorification of Paṇḍharpur is able to destroy the sin of killing ten million Brāhmans. And he who lives in Paṇḍharpur, what troubles can he possibly have? (73) He who listens to this story (of Puṇḍalīk and the description of Paṇḍharpur, brings about the salvation of forty-two families, and frees them from all future births and deaths. (74) Such is the greatness of Puṇḍalīk. It has increased the love of the spirit of *bhakti.* He has greatly extended the limits of *bhakti* and brought the good God to man. (75) Bahiṇī's devotion rests on Paṇḍharī. Her heart has become fixed on Pāṇḍuraṅg [Krishṇa] and her place is at His feet.

CHAPTER XIV.

PATIVRATADHARMAPAR ABHANGS

VERSES ON WIFELY DUTIES

BLESSEDNESS OF FIDELITY

467 (1) Listen, my dear ones, to the law regarding the duties of a wife. Blessed is the home-keeper of noble deeds! (2) By merely listening to this, one's soul will gain the final release. Without a husband one does not keep God in mind. (3) Blessed is she who knows herself as a dutiful wife. (4) She carries along at the same time her household duties, and her religious duties. Such an one bears the heavens in her hands, (5) she who understands that duties performed (*karma*) are Brahma, and that Brahma is the performer of duties. (6) And she whose mind constantly contemplates God, she is recognized in the three worlds as the dutiful wife. (7) She who holds no anger or hatred in her heart, she who has no pride of learning she who does not associate herself with evil, (8) she, who obedient to law, puts aside all sensual appetites, and in whom is not seen the selfish spirit, (9) she who is ready to serve saints and *sādhus*, and fulfils her husband's commands, she indeed is a blessed dutiful wife. (10) She who keeps the peace, who is forgiving and kindly, and compassionate towards all creatures, keeping in mind her husband's character, (11) she to whom her husband's words are like nectar, blessed is her birth, blessed her mother and father! (12) Says Bahiṇī, "Such an one has gained victory over this worldly life, and she has made a place for herself in heaven."

468 (1) How can I adequately relate the joy of God? It drives away all the sorrows of this worldly existence. (2) Therefore, one should associate himself with Him, the Giver of all happiness. (3) To see even the feet of God the heart is filled with joy and fully satisfied. (4) To see God in His actual nature is to dim the light of ten million suns. (5) If one does obtain the joy of God, one should remove one's head and hold it in one's hand. (6) Says Bahiṇī, "I do not know what good deed I did; I have obtained the joy of God."

HOW TO MAKE DOMESTIC LIFE HAPPY

469 (1) She who in everything accepts her husband's wishes in a noble spirit, and though it might mean even death will not violate his command, (2) blessed is she in this present world, blessed is her caste, her *gotra* (family line) and her family. For her comes the summons to heaven. (3) In body, speech and mind she submits herself to her husband, and the knowledge of Brahma plays at her door. (4) Without enquiring the right or the wrong of it, she is willing to give her very life to fulfil his wish. (5) She serves her husband as prescribed by religious rites, and is ever at his side like a slave. (6) Says Bahiṇī, "Such an one has saved both family lines by the power of her observance of her duty to her husband."

470 (1) Listen, my dear, if any one tells you of what is to your good, keep it in your mind, *Bāī.* (2) Do what is helpful to your domestic life. Therefore, hold in your attention what I tell you. (3) If you do as many good deeds as may be possible, and scores of noble actions, you

vill find yourself loving God. (4) Who can adequately describe that woman who is deeply devoted to God and overflows with self-delight? (5) One who is in love with her own happiness, bathing in public, and departing from recognized good conduct, (6) begins to act in a way to destroy obedience to duty, and get excommunicated by her relatives. (7) Such an one knows not her caste, her family line, her name or form. (8) "One should break the water jar over her name. She no longer belongs to this worldly life," so says Bahiṇī.

471 (1) Who is so extravagant of her own life, that while getting enjoyment out of it, (2) she would set fire to her own house, and then get happiness through enjoying its warmth? (3) Inspite of illimitable public criticisms, she does not give up His (God's or paramour's company). (4) Says Bahiṇī, "In body, speech and heart one's life should be in love with God."

472 (1) I have put away shame, and public custom, and fixed my actions on God. (2) Now what can men desire of me, and what need I fear, Bāī? (3) I have drawn the curtain of public shame and doubt, and will bestow my heart's love on God. (4) I have nothing to do with honour or dishonor from others. I shall enjoy the delight of being alone with God. (5) Says Bahiṇī, "I do not have to show my face to the public. God has made me so. What can I do?"

473 (1) Blessed in the three worlds, and to be praised, is the dutiful wife. She works out her own good. (2) And if one meets such an one, one's sins are quickly destroyed. (3) She who recognizes her husband's image in her heart, blessed is she in this world, and in the three

worlds. (4) In her listening it is only of his voice. In her contemplation she sees him only, and in that contemplation finds her happiness. (5) Her thoughts differ not in the least from his. Her comfort lies always in the happiness of her lord. (6) She puts lightly aside both light and darkness and stands upright at her husband's bedside ready for service. (7) The wish of her husband she learns from signs. And in silence she performs the actions he asks for. (8) When he speaks, her silence is neither that of a mere "yes," nor a total silence. She uses neither what has qualities, nor what is without qualities. (9) She enjoys the pure joy that is different from non-duality and separate from this universe. (10) She gets her very life without associating herself with this world. In her case the three [*triputi* doer, doing and effect] act in a special way. (11) The three [the thing to be known, the knower, and the knowledge] are finished in her case, and only a mass of joy remains for her. (12) Her thoughts have ceased, and all disappears. What remains for me to say here? (13) If such is the state of a woman, or a man, blessed is that dutifulness of wife or husband. (14) Says Bahiṇī, "Blessed is her birth, and her praise is spread through the three worlds."

GLOSSARY OF MARATHI WORDS USED IN THE TRANSLATIONS AND OF WORDS WHOSE TRANSLATION PRESENTS DIFFICULTIES.

It might have been possible to have used fewer Marāthi words in these translations but where there is no English word that exactly expresses the Marāthi word, or where it requires a whole English phrase to express the meaning of a simple Marāthi word, it has seemed to me better to keep the Mārāthi word, so familiar to India, and let the English reader learn its meaning by its context, or by the following glossary. English literature is already enriched by many Marāthi words. I see no reason why it should not still further enrich itself.

There are certain words, that are untranslatable except by a long explanation; others, where even the English word conveys only a part of the Marāthi meaning. I have translated these words and expressions as best I could, but it seems worth while to include some of these words, in a glossary in order that the reader, familiar with both languages, may understand why I have used the special English word or words, sometimes in opposition to Dictionary authorities, even Molesworth. Usage has to be considered, as well as etymological meaning. The glossary will furnish the examples that have suggested the above remarks. I have used Molesworth's definitions freely, as carrying authority.

RULES FOR PRONUNCIATION.

a as u in utter, butter, hut.
ā as a in father, far.
i as i in in
ī as ee in thee.
u as ou in you.
ū as oo in food.
e as a in ape, age.
ai as i in island, decline.
o as o in open, over.
au as ou in proud, plough.
g always hard, as g in gate, get.
ch as ch in church.

Other letters are pronounced very nearly as in English words.

A

Abhang. "A particular metrical composition in praise of the Deity." It is the popular meter of the poet-saints in their hymns of praise; the *abhangs* of Eknāth, the *abhangs* of Tukārām etc.

Abheda-bhakta. A *bhakta* who has the conception of no-difference (*abheda*) between the *paramātmā* and the individual *ātmā.* Abheda-bhakti is the worship of God in harmony with the conception of the identity of the *paramātmā* and the soul (*ātmā*) of the worshipper

Āchārya. Head of a religious order or sect.

Adhelā. A copper coin worth half a pice.

Agnihotri. The priest who maintains the Sacrificial fire.

Amrita. Nectar. The drink that prevents death.

Anugraha. Favor, grace, kindness, instructing in mystical verses of incantations.

Anushṭhāna. Performance of certain ceremonies and works in propitiation of a god.

Ārati. 1 The ceremony of (waving around an idol, guru etc.,) a platter containing a burning lamp. 2 The platter and lamp waved. 3 The piece of poetry chanted on the occasion of the ceremony of waving expressing praise or worship.

Āśrama. 1. The abode of saints and rishis. 2. The word is also applied to four conditions of living, the *Brahmacharya,* or the period of chaste youth, and study; the *Grihastha,* the householder in his married and secular life; The *Vānaprastha,* who as age comes on passes his worldly cares over to others, and goes into the forest for meditation, and the fourth the *Sannyāsi,* who entirely abandons all worldly cares, delights and passions, and is wholly absorbed in contemplation or the worship of God. These four *āśramas* are considered the ideal life for a Brāhmaṇ.

Ātmā. The soul, the soul of the universe, the human soul, the vivifying principle, the self, the ego. For clearness the soul of the universe is spoken of as *parama* (supreme) *ātmā,* to distinguish it from the individual *ātmā,* the two, however, in Vedāntic philosophy being identical. *Brahma,* or the *Parama-ātmā,* partially defined as *satchidānanda* (Existence, intelligence, joy) is the sole existing substance. The universe, as it appears in animate and inanimate forms, with their special names, is but the form in which the *ātmā,* the *paramātmā,* or *Brahma* manifests itself. The human soul, or *ātmā,* is, therefore, only a form in which the *paramātmā* appears. The great sentence, *aham-bramhāsmi,* I am Brahma, is the conscious acceptance of the philosophic postulate of the oneness of the soul of the universe with the individual soul.

Avatār. Etymologically it means, "one who has descended." A divine *avatāra* is the coming down to earth of such a divine being, as for example, Vishṇu in the form of Krishṇa, or Rāma. In Indian mythology, as well as in all popular conceptions, these *avatārs* are for the sake of combating some evil condition or conditions in this world, or, to save the world from its sin and misery.

Human *avatārs* are also recognized (*mānava avatāra*), that is, a good man who has died, reappears later in some other good man, to carry on, or to complete, the work of the former. Eknāth is spoken of as an *avatār* of Dnyānadeva, and Tukārām as an avatāra of Nāmadeva. Or Eknāth, for example, is spoken of as an *avatār* of God, making him, therefore, both divine and human.

B

Bachnāg. Poisonous root of the Gloriosa Superba.

Bhajan. 1 Adoration or worship. 2 Repeating the names of God as an act of worship. 3 A hymn, or verses sung in the worship of God.

Bhakta. 1 A worshipper, votary, or follower of; one devoted or attached to. While the above definition is etymologically correct, in usage, by the poet-saints, there is connected with it a moral idea. A *bhakta* implies a really pious man. A hypocrite is not a *bhakta,* though technically and outwardly he might appear to be one. 2. A special religious class devoted to the religious life.

As the different manifestations of God, and the various *avatars* appeal differently to different minds, there is a personal choice as well as the traditional, or family choice of the special manifestation of God. There is, therefore, a *Vishṇubhakta*, a *Śivabhakta*, a *Haribhakta*, a *Rāmbhakta*, a *Viṭṭhalbhakta*, and so forth.

Bhakti. Literally, worship or adoration. It is the attitude of the *bhakta* towards God. It always implies a moral idea of sincerity and purity of worship, accompanied with love. Again and again the poet-saints affirm that there can be no *bhakti* without sincerity and love. *Bhakti* is, therefore, more than mere worship, which can be so easily a mere outward form. *Bhakti* must be the true feeling of the heart, of reverence, and love of God, whether expressed in outer forms of worship, or in the mental worship (*Mānaspujā*)

Bhaktimārga. Bhakti-mārga, the way of *Bhakti.* Three ways are recognized for the deliverance of man from the succession of births and deaths, with their sins and sorrows, and with their good deeds and joys, as well. The *Dnyānamārga* (The Way of Knowledge) holds the highest place in the minds of philosophers, because, when by true Knowledge Ignorance disappears, all causes of sin and sorrow disappear. The *Karmamārga* or Way of Works is recognized by the poet-saints as a way, but a very hard way, and a very dangerous way. In the case of both of the above vays the danger is pride, and with pride comes a fall. The safe way, the sure way, the easy way, for all hgh or low, is the *bhakti-mārga,* in which a man throws himself on the mercy of God, *bhakti* on man's part, and mercy, forgiveness, and salvation, on God's part. With *bhakti* sincere, and the consequent gift from God of *moksha* (salvation, deliverance), a return to this earth is avoided, and there is eternal life in the presence of God. Because it is a sure and easy way for all, the poet-saints give the *Bhakti-mārga* the highest preference. Although, the word etymologically does not imply it, the usage of the poet-saints in strongest terms emphasizes the moral side of *Bhakti*, not only sincerity in *Bhakti*, but a pure ethical life is essential to the very idea of *Bhakti*. Eknāth's writings are especially emphatic on this importance of internal and external moral purity.

Brahma. The One substance of which all existing things consist. *Brahma* is the substance of which all things exist. Existing things have forms and names (*nāma* and *rupa*). That they exist and have *forms* and *names* is as real as is the real substance *Brahma*. To consider these forms, however, as different from *Brahma*, making a duality, is due to *ignorance*, that Ignorance personified being called *māyā*. (which see.)

Brahmachāri. A Brāhmaṇa who observes the strictest chastity for a time or for life from a religious motive.

C

Chakōr. A bird that is said to subsist on moonbeams. This idea is very frequently used in poetic figures and illustrations.

Charitra. Actions, deeds, proceedings, exploits, history.

Chātaka. A bird said to drink only from the clouds, hence always eager for the rain. The idea is very frequently used in poetic figures and illustrations.

Chiplā. A musical instrument; consisting of two sticks rattled together.

Chūl. A fireplace. In its simplicity it may be three stones so arranged as to have the fire between them, and the pot or pan resting on them, or a semicircular erection of earth to contain the fire in its cavity, and support the cooking vessel on its rim.

D

Dakshiṇā. Money or presents given to Brahmans and others on special occasions.

Darśana. Literally, sight, seeing, looking. In the religious usage of the word there is, however, much more than the physical sight, seeing or looking. There is an implication of respect, reverence and worship. There is no English word corresponding with this use of *darśana.*

Lasarā. A festival commemorating the period of the year when the Marāthā Kings started out on their campaigns.

Dhotar. The garment worn by men, consisting of a long piece of cloth wound around the body, tucked in front at the waist and also behind, taking the place of the European trousers.

Divāli. The annual festival of lights.

Dnyāna. 1 Knowledge in general. 2 Knowledge of a specific and religious kind, that which is derived from meditation and the study of philosophy; which teaches man the divine origin and nature of his immaterial portion, and the unreality of corporal enjoyments, sufferings and experiences, and the illusoriness of the external and objective universe; and which sanctifying him during life from earthly attachments and fleshly affections, accomplishes for him after death emancipation from individual existence and reunion with the universal spirit. In some parts of India the word is pronounced *gyāna.*

Dnyānamārga. The Way of Knowledge. (See *Dnyāna*).

G

Gāyatri. A sacred verse from the Vedas, repeated by Brāhmaṇs at their morning and evening devotions.

Ghatikā. A period of twenty-four minutes.

Ghāt. 1 A mountainous range dividing countries. 2 A pass or difficult passage over a hill. 3 Quay, wharf, stairs, landing place (on banks of rivers or tanks). Hence applied by washermen, tanners, dyers, Brāhmaṇs, etc., to their respective places of resort.

Ghi. Clarified butter, also known as *tūp.* The butter is melted, thus removing the water that may be in it, and then preserved in jars.

Guṇa. 1 A quality, attribute, affection, or property whether of matter or mind; a power, faculty, excellence, virtue; a property inherent or an affection supervenient in the most comprehensive sense. 2 The constitution of created things, as comprised in three *guṇas; sattva* (existence, truth, goodness, brightness etc.); *raja* (energy, passion, action etc.); *tama* (evil, darkness, ignorance etc.). All created things are a mixture of the three, *sattvaguṇa*, *rajoguṇa,* and *tamoguṇa,* and therefore, are spoken of as *saguṇa* (possessing these *gunas*), and Brahma, the *paramātmā* is *nirguṇa* (unpossessed by these qualities). In God, in good men, in good things the *sattva* predominates. In evil men or spirits or demons the *tama* predominates. The *rajoguṇa* is in all as the activity of either the good or the evil, or both. In God all is *sattva,* because it is the *sattva* that is in activity (*rajoguṇa*). In man there is a mixture of the *sattva* and *tama,* and the activity (*rajoguṇa*) makes man a mixture of good and evil, sometimes the good predominating, sometimes the evil.

Guru. A religious teacher; one who instructs in the *Śāstras.*

H

Harbarā. A vetch, gram. Cicer arientinum.

Haridās. Servants of Hari [Vishṇu]. Worshippers of Hari. Wandering singers who praise the deeds of Hari.

J

Japa. The repeating of *mantras* or the names of God. A rosary may be used so as to know the number of times the *mantra* or names have been used. As this outer form requires an inner reality, *japa* stands also for meditation, for worship, for prayer, indeed for the true spiritual life of a man. The correlative of *japa* is *tapa* (which see). *Tapa,* literally, religious austerity, is also extended in meaning to comprise the outer religious life of a man. *Japa,* his inner religious life and *tapa* his outer religious life.

Jiva, Śiva. When Jiva and Śiva are thus used together Jiva stands for the Individual ātmā, and Śiva for the Universal ātmā.

Jondhaḷā. A cereal plant or its grain. Hulcus sorghum.

K

Kaḍabā. The stalks with their leaves of the *jondhaḷā*, or *jvāri*, Hulcus sorghum, used for fodder.

Kailās. The Heaven of Shiva.

Kākiṇi. A weight of shells equal to 20 cowries.

Kaliyuga. The present, fourth age of the world, the evil age. Its duration is considered to be 432,000 years, after which the world is to be destroyed. The present year A.D. 1926 corresponds with the *Kaliyuga* 5027. The initial year is 3101 B.C. The four *yugas* are the *Kritayuga, Tretāyuga, Dvāparayuga* and the *Kaliyuga*. The four *yugas* together make a *Mahāyuga* (Great *yuga*) 4,320,000 years. It is this evil *kaliyuga* that has necessitated the frequent *avatārs* to check evil and to save mankind from its effects.

Kalpa. A day of Brahma, 432 million years of mortals.

Karma. 1 An act or a deed. 2 Religious action, as sacrifice, ablution, etc., 3 Destiny; destiny being only the allotment, to be enjoyed or suffered in the present life of the fruit of good and evil actions, performed in former lives. 4. Deed or action. As all actions through the laws of cause and effect determine the actions in the next life. Karma is equivalent also to fate.

Karmamārga. The law of works; the road to heaven through observance of rites and ceremonies and performance of virtuous deeds. (See Dnyānamārga, Way of Knowledge, and Bhaktimārga, Way of Devotion). The way of deeds. One of the three ways of Deliverance: Dnyānamārga, Karmamārga, and Bhaktimārga.

Kathā. A story, fable, exploits of Gods or heroes related with music and singing.

Kāvaḍ. A bamboo lath provided with slings at each end in order to contain baskets, jars etc. and carried on the shoulder. Used for carrying water, vegetables etc.

Kavaḍi. A cowrie. A shell used in making small change.

Kirtan. Celebrating the praises of a god with music and singing. Reciting the names of the deity. In practice, however, it is a religious service of song. The leader has a topic which he delivers in song. He is accompanied with a chorus leader, and musical instruments. Following their leader the audience may break out in ecstatic repetitions of the names of God, or of the lines of a chorus.

Kshetra. A sacred spot, a sacred city, a place of pilgrimage; also the human form.

Kulkarni. A village officer who keeps public records and keeps the accounts of cultivators in their relation to Government.

M

Mahant. 1. The chief or head of an order of Gosavis, Bairagis etc., a religious superior. 2. Applied to the head or leading man among paṇḍits, devotees, etc.,

Mahābhārata. The great epic relating to wars of the Pandavas and Kauravas, ascribed to Vyās as author.

Mahārāshtra. The great nation. The old name of the country occupied by the Marātha people, now included in the Bombay Presidency.

Mana. Mind. According to Western psychology the mind is the soul itself viewed as thinking or imagining. Mana, however, is regarded as an organ (indriya) of thinking and imagining and not a part of the pure Ātmā (Soul).

Maṇḍap. An open temporary structure, made with bamboo or other poles, with cloth roof and sides erected for festal occasions, for marriages, *kirtans* etc.

Mantra. A text, prayer, hymn or verse, which possesses mystical or supernatural power.

Māyā. This word is usually translated "Illusion," but this is not a satisfactory translation. Vedantic philosophy postulates that there is but one substance, called *Brahma*, or *paramātmā*, or *ātmā*. This substance appears in the form of the universe, and to the various *forms* there are *names* (nāma-rupa). These forms are temporary and changeable, and with the change of form the name disappears. It is due to Ignorance that these forms are supposed to be distinct from the One Substance. The reality of these forms is not denied, but that they are distinct from the One substance is denied. That they are distinct *i.e.*, that there is a duality, is the particular form of illusion which is indicated by the word *Māyā*. In usage Māyā becomes personified as the cause of the Ignorance (*adnyāna*) which sees duality where is unity. One of the stock illustrations is that of gold in the form of various ornaments, each with its own name. That the gold appears in the form of various ornaments is not denied, but that ornamental forms are permanent and distinct from the gold is denied. The ornaments can be melted; they disappear as ornaments, but the gold remains unchanged. To think the ornaments were distinct from the gold would be through Ignorance (*adnyāna*), and the cause of the ignorance, by a sort of personification is *māyā*.

Moḍi. Is the cursive writing of the Marāthi. The old Aśoka alphabet of the inscriptions, 250 B.C., gradually developed in time into the *Devanāgari*, used in transcribing Sanskrit literature, as also Marāthi literature. In business writing, however, haste being important, and the pen being lifted from the paper as little as possible, it led to a change in the form of the *Devanāgari* letters, which to the casual observer seem a different character, but which can be most easily traced back to the *Devanāgari origin.* The tradition that Moḍi was brought from the south, or that it was the invention of Hemachandra in the 13th century, may be due to the character of the southern cursive writing, and it could well be that Hemachandra adopted it as the form for official documents. There is no doubt, however, that the Modi has developed from the *Devanāgari* simply by rapid writing, with the lifting of the pen from the paper as little as possible.

Moksha. Deliverance of the soul from the body, its exemption from further transmigration, with all its joys and sorrows, sins and good deeds, and its absorption into the divine essence.

Mukti. Exemption of the spirit from further migration and the reabsorption of it into its source, the divine monad, Brahma, the substratum and substance of universal being. This deliverance from births and deaths, must be understood to include in the idea the deliverance from the sins and sorrows, even from the good deeds and joys of life, for each life is made up of these. The four forms of *mukti* are *sāyujyatā*, *salokatā*, *samipatā* and *sarupatā*, (see *sāyujyatā*).

N

Namaskār. Worship, obeisance, reverential or respectful address or salutation. It is performed by joining the palms, inclining the head and pronouncing the word *namaskār*. A *sāshtāṅga namaskār* is the prostration on the ground, so that eight parts (*ashta*) of the body touch the ground, and is the most profound method of showing reverence to God or man.

Nirguṇa. *Nir-guṇa.* Literally without a quality. *Brahma*, or *ātmā*, *paramātmā* the one substance which appears to us as the universe, cannot be described in human words. It is indescribable (*avāchya*). While the one substance cannot be described the forms in which it appears can be described, and their qualities determined. The forms with their names are, therefore, *saguṇa*, (Sa-guṇa) with quality. God, as a personal being, creator of the special form, in which the universe appears, is recognized as one of the forms in which the One eternal substance appears. God, therefore, is *saguṇa*, that is, he has qualities which can be described in human understandable words. *Brahma* is *nirguṇa*; God (*iśvara*) is saguṇa. The gods, all *avatārs*, idols, and the visions of God, are all *saguṇa* manifestations of the *Nirguṇ Brahma*, or *nirguṇa ātmā*. The *saguṇa iśvara*, being but the one of the many forms in which the *nirguṇa iśvara* appears, are, of course, to be identified as the golden bracelet is identified with the gold of which it consists. The poet-saints, therefore, in their hymns of praise, their invocations, their worship, and their prayers, make no distinction. They are addressed as well to the *nirguṇa* God as to the *saguṇa* God. This identity of the *saguṇa* and the *nirguṇa* is often asserted very definitely.

Nivṛitti. Cessation from worldly concerns and engagements; also Absorption into Brahma.

O

Ovi. A stanza of a particular metre of Marāthi verse.

P

Pada. A variety of metrical compositions, used in hymns or anthems. Very many of the poet-saints have written in this metre. (See the *Padasangraha* in the *Kāvya-sangraha* Series for examples).

Pādukā. An impression of a foot on stone, worshipped as the trace of some god or guru.

Pānsupāri. A roll of the Piper-betel leaf with Areca nut, cloves, lime etc. (See *Vidā*).

Pāp. Sin in the abstract, or an evil deed. It is the exact negative correlative of the word *puṇya,* goodness or holiness in the abstract, or a good or holy deed. That *pāp* and *puṇya,* evil and good deeds must receive a future reward of suffering or happiness is a part of Hindu philosophy, but this idea does not belong to the words themselves. Molesworth's Marāthi English Dictionary of 1831, founded on the Marāthi-Marāthi Dictionary of 1829, rightly defines these words. I differ absolutely from the Notes on these words in Molesworth's Second Edition of 1857, and from its definition of the word *puṇya* as "merit," a meaning it never has had in Sanskrit, or in the whole course of Marāthi literature, until influenced by Molesworth's second edition. See further discussion under *puṇya.*

Peth. A region or large division of a city. A manufacturing or a trading town. A market town. A ward of a city.

Pradakshiṇā. Circumambulation of an object, keeping the right side towards it. These objects may be idols, sacred trees, the *tulsi* plant, a temple, even a sacred city. Keeping the object to the left would imply irreverence.

Prahar. An eighth part of the day of 24 hours. A *prahar* is, therefore, a period of three hours. The *prahars* begin at sunrise, at six, hence *Donprahar* (two-praharas) is noon.

Prakriti. In philosophy *prakriti* and *purusha* are words that denote the material and the immaterial universe. *Prakriti* (Nature, matter, phenomenon) conceived as female, and *Purusha* (male, the soul, life, activity) by their union make the whole universe, an anthropomorphic expression of the idea expressed in English as "matter and mind."

Prākrit. In the usage of the Marātha poet-saints the *Prākrit* language means the Marāthi language. As distinguished from the Sanskrit (the polished language), it means the common vernacular of the people. As may be seen from the lives of the poet-saints and their works, they had to encounter a certain amount of opposition against their Marāthi, or *Prākrit* versions of the sacred Ṣanskrit texts. (See Eknāth's life, *Bhaktalilāmrita* Chapter 21).

Prārabdha. Deeds in former births determined the course of one's life in the birth previous to this. Deeds in the previous life have determined the course of one's present life. Deeds in the present life will determine the life in the next birth. This is the law of *prārabdha.*

Prasād. 1. Favor, graciousness, propitiousness. 2. Any thing (a fruit, flower, rice etc.) given by an idol, a guru, a saint, as a blessing or a mark of favor." 3. Food etc. presented to an idol or a holy person to be distributed, thus honored, among worshippers etc. 4. The sweetmeats and fruit distributed among the audience at the conclusion of a *kathā, kirtan,* or puraṇic reading.

Puṇya. Goodness or holiness in the abstract, or a good or holy deed. Its negative is *pap,* or sin in the abstract, or an evil deed. In the definition of this word as also in the definition of the word *pāp* I differ absolutely from Molesworth's Marāthi and English Dictionary, second edition of 1857. In a note it says, " The word bears not the feeblest implication of holiness, godliness or purity of spirit." On the contrary it implies all three. And by its using the definition of "merit" (not found in the edition of 1831) an idea foreign to the word has since then been attached to this noble word. "Merit," meaning a future reward of a good deed, is no part of the meaning of the word *Puṇya,* which is simply goodness or holiness in the abstract or a holy or good deed. The idea of merit belongs to Indian philosophy, but not to the word *puṇya.* Every *puṇya* will have its reward in the future, as will every *pāp,* but this idea is not in the word itself.

The first edition of Molesworth of 1831, founded on the Paṇḍits' Marāthi-Marāthi edition of 1829 has the correct definition. See also Monier-Williams Sanskrit dictionary under *puṇya* and *pāp*. The word *puṇya,* twice used in the Ṛigveda, many times used in the Upanishads, and Bhagavadgitā, and all through old Marāthi literature, is the exact negative of *pāp*. It, in no single instance, means "merit" as implying a future reward.

Puraṇpoli. A wheaten cake with stuffing of coarse sugar, pea flour etc.

Purāṇa. A particular class of Hindu sacred literature, generally regarded as eighteen in number. They deal with stories of the creation of the world, its destruction, its renewal, of gods, goddesses, and heroes. The eighteen are Brahma, Padma, Vishṇu, Śiva, Liṅga, Garuḍa, Nārada, Bhāgavata, Agni, Skanda, Bhavishya, Brahmavaivarta, Mārkaṇḍeya, Vāmana, Varāha, Matsya, Kūrma and Vāyu, but there are other lists of 18, slightly varying from this. Of the Purāṇs the Bhāgavata, giving the life and teachings of Krishṇa, has had the greatest influence on the thought and life of the Marāthā poet-saints.

Purāṇik. A Brāhman well read in the *Purāṇs.* A public expounder of them. On account of the vast extent of Sanskrit literature those who expound the sacred books have to specialize. There are those who make a speciality of expounding some Purāṇ and are known as Purāṇiks.

Purusha. See *Prakriti.*

R

Rāmayaṇa. The great epic relating the exploits of Rām, ascribed to Vālmiki as author.

S

Sadguru. Literally a true, or good guru (see Guru). While primarily the word applies to human teachers, or gurus, the poet-saints even applied it to god, for a *sadguru* is regarded as a manifestation of God. The Marāthā Poet-saints frequently refer to the high moral qualities, the sincerity, the unselfishness, to unhypocritical spirit, that marks a *sadguru,* as distinguished from a false guru.

Sādhana. The means employed to obtain deliverance from births and deaths and all that life implies in its sins and sorrows and even joys.

Saguṇa. See *Nirguṇa.*

Samsāra. 1 The world, mundane existence, human life, man's mortal state. 2. The affairs of life; worldly business; the vocations and engagements, the cares and troubles of secularity.

Sannyāsi. One who has cast off all worldly possessions, and carnal or natural affections, an ascetic. The poet-saints distinguish between the hypocritical, formal *Sannyāsi,* who outwardly appears only to have given up all, and the true and sincere *sannyāsi,* whose giving up of the world is genuine.

Santa. A saint, practically synonymous with *sādhu* (which see). He is one who has lost worldly desires and devotes himself to the worship of God. But whatever he may appear outwardly, no one is a *santa* without purity of heart and life. The appellation *Kavi-santa*, or poet-saints, designate those saints who were poets. The Marāthā poet-saints begin with Dnyāneśvara, about A.D. 1290, so far as their works are known, and continue to the present day.

Satchidānanda. Existence-intelligence-joy. Although *Brahma*, or the *paramātmā* cannot be described in human words (avāchya), yet because, it is believed to *exist*, to be that which takes the form of *intelligent beings*, and to express itself in beings feeling *joy*—*Brahma* being the substrate of these—this definition of Brahma is very frequently employed. It should be noted that these three words, *existence*, *intelligence* and *joy* are not adjectives, but nouns. They do not connote that *Brahma exists*, is *intelligent* and *happy*, but that the One substance, *Brahma* in taking form, appears in the form of existing things, in the form of intelligent beings, and those possessing joy and goodness.

Sādhu. A holy man; a saint or sage; one of subdued passions and of contemplative habits. The poet-saints give the word a moral emphasis, hence a *sādhu* is a man of pure character, one truly devoted to God, a spiritually minded man; a good man. A man can appear hypocritically a *sādhu*, and not be a *sādhu*, for a *sādhu* must be pure in heart and life. The wandering professional *sādhu*, called such, may or may not be sincere, but he is not considered a true *sādhu* without purity of heart and life.

Sāshtāṅga-namaskār. See *Namaskār*.

Sāyujya. The fourth of the four states in which *mukti* (final deliverance) is distinguished, *viz.*, absorption into the essence of Brahma. The four are *Sāyujya* (absorption into the essence of Brahma;) *Salokatā* (residence in the heaven of a particular deity); *Samipatā* (Nearness to the Deity); and *Sarupatā* (Bearing the likeness of God).

Sāvadhāna. Literally attention, heed. At the moment of marriage, the priests in solemn tone repeat the words, "*Sāvadhānam, sāvadhānam,*" and at that moment the curtain between the bride and bridegroom is removed, and the marriage is complete.

Siddhi. A supernatural power of faculty supposed to be acquirable through the performance of certain magical, mystical, or alchemical rites or processes. Eight are enumerated, *viz.*, *aṇima, mahimā, garimā, laghimā, prāpti, prakāmya, īshitva,* and *vashitva*. The powers or *siddhis* are personified as female beings, or *siddhis*, who come and serve those who by their austerities or otherwise gain those powers.

Shrāddha. A kind of funeral rite or ceremony in honor of the departed spirits of dead relatives, observed with great strictness at various fixed periods, especial honor being given to paternal and maternal ancestors.

Shudra. The fourth grand division of the Hindu body; also an individual of it. The four grand divisions are *Brāhmaṇa*, (the priestly caste); *Kshatriya*, (the warrior, military, governing class); *Vaiśya* (agricultural and mercantile class) and *Shudra* (the servile class, whose duty is to serve the upper three). The *atiśudra* also called *anāmik, antyaja,* are those still lower than the Shudra, and outside of the four grand divisions. Hence they are *aspriśya* (Untouchable) or *anāmika* (Unmentionable).

Shānti. Peace. Unruffled mind.

Shloka. A verse, a stanza, a quantity of four lines. A particular metre; praise. In the Marāthi commentaries the *Shloka* commented on is the Sanskrit text.

Shruti. The Vedas severally or collectively. The word is from the Sanskrit, meaning "hearing."

Skandha. A section of a book, a book, a chapter.

Stotra. 1. Praise, panegyric, eulogium. 2. A book or writing in celebration of the praises; also a hymn.

Svāmi. A master or lord, the master or lord of, also the proprietor or owner of. Applied to the Deity, a god, a king, or prince, a spiritual preceptor, a husband, a holy personage, a learned Brāhman, a *Gosavi, Sannyāsi* etc. It is used also as a title, Keshava-svāmi.

T

Tapa. Religious austerity, pious mortification of the body. It is especially connected with the *yoga* system, and the *yogis* carry it to its extreme limit. But it also has less austere usage, meaning the duties of life, the special duties of Brāhmans, Kshatriyas, Vaishyas and Shudras. It is, therefore, the correlative of *Japa, Japa* signifying the inner spiritual life, and *tapa* the outer religious life. (See *Japa*).

Tilak. The spot or line made with coloured earths or unguents upon the forehead. It is considered either as an ornament or as a sectarial distinction.

Tirtha. 1. A holy or sacred place, any place of pilgrimage, but especially particular spots along the course of sacred streams or in the vicinity of sacred springs. 2. A holy stream, or water brought from one. Water in which a Brāhman, sannyāsi etc., has dipped his foot, which has been poured over an idol; holy water.

Tulsi. A plant venerated by the Hindus, Holy Basil, Ocymum sanctum. It is usually grown in an earthen altar before the door of the house, or in the garden behind the house. Its leaf is used in offerings, in garlands, and its stalks also have sacred uses. Those worshipping the plant go around it, keeping it to the right (pradakshiṇā) with palm to palm, repeating a *mantra*, or prayer.

U

Upanishad. The oldest philosophical literature.

Upāsanā. Worship or religious service.

V

Vaikuṇtha. The Heaven of Vishṇu.

Vairāgi. An ascetic or devotee; one who has subdued his worldly desires and passions. The word is also applied to a class of religious mendicants. The word is also pronounced *bairāgi.* The poet-saints distinguish between the true and the hypocritical *vairāgi.*

Vairāgya. 1. Absence of worldly desire or passion. 2. Popularly, renunciation of all sensuous delight or gratification.

Vastu. The real as opposed to the unreal. Brahma. The Universal *Ātma. Substance.* The substance of which the Universe consists, namely Brahma.

Vedas. The oldest of the Indian Scripture. The four Vedas are; the Rigveda, the Yajurveda, the Sāmaveda, and the Atharvaveda.

Viḍā. A roll of the leaf of Piper-betel with Areca-nut, cloves, lime etc. It is usually chewed after a meal. It is distributed to an audience after a *kirtan,* or any public assembly, and is the final act. It is believed to be a digestive, and also as purifying the mouth. It is generally callel *pan-supāri* (leaf supāri nut). Many have the habit of chewing it constantly.

Videhi. Literally, one without a body (vi-deha). In usage, however, it implies a temporory or permanent absorption of the mind in a way to make one unconscious of the possession of a body, as when one is intensely listening to a *kirtan,* he is for the time being a *videhi.* Or when through a life of constant contemplation of the *ātmā,* or of God, the ascetic or devotee loses all thought of his body, or cold or heat, hunger or thirst, desires or passions, he is a *videhi.* A man is a *videhi* when the spiritual completely dominates the physical.

Viveka. Right-thinking. To the Vedantist right-thinking is the discrimination between reality and unreality.

W

Wāḍā. 1. A stately or large edifice, a mansion or palace. 2. A division of a town, a quarter, a ward, as Brahmanwādā, Mahārwādā. 3. An enclosed piece of meadow-field, or garden ground; an enclosure. 4. A cluster of huts of agriculturists, a hamlet.

Y

Yama. The god who rules over the spirits of the dead.

Yoga. Spiritual or abstract devotion; union with Brahma through abstract meditation, or contemplation; also the practice or exercise of this sort of worship.

Yogabhrashṭa. One who was interrupted in his preceding birth during the performance of *Yoga* (abstract meditation upon *Brahma*). As an example, a pious outcaste, devoted to Eknāth, is called a *Yogabhrashṭa.* In the Autobiography of Bahiṇābāi, a calf, because of its peculiar pious actions, is called a *yogabhrashṭa.* Indeed any pious person can be described as a *yogabhrashṭa,* as one whose pious life in a former birth was accidentally interrupted and has now a further opportunity.

Yogi. 1. A performer of the abstract meditation called *yoga.* 2. An ascetic or devotee in general. Popularly a *yogi* is supposed to be able to gain extraordinary powers through his practice of *yoga,* called *siddhis* (which see), and the ash-covered *yogi* is able to instil much fear in the minds of the ignorant. The poet-saints, of course, distinguish between the hypocritical *yogi* and the true *yogi* whose heart and life must be pure.

Yojana. A measure of distance equal to four *Kos,* roughly about eight miles.

संत बहिणाबाईचा गाथा

॥ श्रीविठ्ठल ॥

१ आदि परंपरा

अभंग १

आदिनार्थे उपदेश पार्वतीसी केला । मत्स्येंद्रें ऐकिला मच्छगर्भी ॥१॥
शिवहृदयींचा मंत्र पैं अगाध । जालासे प्रसिद्ध भक्तियोगें ॥२॥
तेणें त्या गोरक्षा केलें कृपादान । तेथोनि प्रकट जाण गहिनीप्रती ॥३॥
गहिनीनें दया केली निवृत्तिनाथा । बाळक असतां योगरूप ॥४॥
तेथोनी ज्ञानेश पावले प्रसाद । जाले ते प्रसिद्ध सिद्धासनीं ॥५॥
'सच्चिदानंद बाबा' भक्तीचा आगरू । त्यासी अभयवरू 'ज्ञानें' केला ॥६॥
पुढें विश्वंभर शिवरूप सुंदर । तेणें राघवीं विचार ठेविलासे ॥७॥
केशव चैतन्य बाबाजी चैतन्य । झालेसे प्रसन्न 'तुकोबासी' ॥८॥
एकनिष्ठ भाव तुकोबा-चरणीं । म्हणोनी 'बहिणी' लाधलीसे ॥९॥

२ आत्मनिवेदन

अभंग २

देवगांव माझें माहेर साजणी । वेरुळ तेथोनी पूर्व भागीं ॥ १ ॥
देवांचा समूह सर्व जया ठायीं । मिळालासे पाहीं 'देवगांव' ॥ २ ॥
हिमाचलाहुनी चालला अगस्ती । चतुर्मास वस्ती केली जेथें ॥ ३ ॥
तेथोनी पश्चिमीं शिवनदी वाहात । तीर्थ हें अद्भुत तीर्थांमाजीं ॥ ४ ॥
लक्ष तीर्थ जेथें मज्जनीं सर्वदा । लाक्षायणी सदा वास जेथें ॥ ५ ॥
स्थळ तें पवित्र देखोनी अगस्ती । अनुष्ठाना येती सूर्योदयीं ॥ ६ ॥
वर दिधलासे ऋषी अगस्तीनें । जाण लक्ष तीर्थें 'लाक्षा ग्रामा' ॥ ७ ॥
स्नान दान करीं जप अनुष्ठान । सिद्धि तेथें जाण होय नरा ॥ ८ ॥
अगस्ती राहोनी देवगांवीं जाण । शिवनदीस्नान करी सदा ॥ ९ ॥
बहिणी म्हणे ऐसें स्थळ देवग्राम । तेथें माझा जन्म झाला असे ॥ १० ॥

अभंग ३

'आऊजी कुलकर्णी लेखक ते स्थळीं । तयाचिये कुळीं जन्म माझा ॥ १ ॥
जननी 'जानकी' पिता 'आऊदेव' । देवगांव नांव स्थळ त्यांचें ॥ २ ॥
तयाचिये कुळीं नाहीं जी संतान । करिती संताना कांहीं बाही ॥ ३ ॥
लक्ष तीर्थीं नित्य करूनिया स्नान । शिव-अनुष्ठान आरंभीलें ॥ ४ ॥
किती येक दिवशीं झालें स्वप्न तया । माझीया पितया आऊजीसी ॥ ५ ॥
होईल संतान कन्या दोन पुत्र । ब्राह्मणें पवित्र सांगितलें ॥ ६ ॥
बहिणी म्हणे एका वरुषीं मी उत्पन्न । नवमास पूर्ण कन्या झालें ॥ ७ ॥

अभंग ४

करिती उत्साह बारशा ब्राह्मण । करूनी ब्राह्मण घरां गेले ॥ १ ॥
पिता आऊदेव गेला अरण्यांत । तंव अकस्मात लाभ झाला ॥ २ ॥
मोहर बांधिली पितांबरी गांठीं । सांपडली वाटीं वेरुळाच्या ॥ ३ ॥
घरां येउनीया आनंदें बोलती । कन्या आम्हांप्रती लाभाईत ॥ ४ ॥

विश्वेश्वर ब्राह्मण ज्योतिषी नेटका । तयानें पत्रिका संपादिली ॥ ५ ॥
होईल कल्याण इचेनी तुमचें । ऐसें पत्रिकेचें फळ वाची ॥ ६ ॥
बोलती देवलसी भाग्याची होईल । आयुष्याचें बळ फार आहे ॥ ७ ॥
बहिणी म्हणे ऐसें द्विजें सांगितलें । तयासी दीधलें वस्त्र गायी ॥ ८ ॥

अभंग ५

कन्यादान घडो हा अर्थ पाहोन । करावया लग्न द्विज आले ॥ १ ॥
तंव आकस्मात प्राक्तनासारिखा । 'शीऊराचा' सखा एक आला ॥ २ ॥
पूर्वील सोयरा लग्नाचा इच्छिक । विवेक पाठक रत्न नामी ॥ ३ ॥
लाउनी मागणें केलें वाक्प्रदान । नेमुनिया लग्न संपादिलें ॥ ४ ॥
तंव बंधू झाला माझे पाठीवरी । अनुष्ठाना करी पूर्वीचिया ॥ ५ ॥
म्हणती हें सभाग्य बंधू पाठीवरी । झाला हे निर्धारी गुण इचे ॥ ६ ॥
बहिणी म्हणे ऐसीं झालीं वर्षें तीन । त्यापुढें जें होणें तेंही बोले ॥ ७ ॥

अभंग ६

मौनस गोत्र माझ्या पित्याचें वरिष्ठ । भ्रतारही श्रेष्ठ गौतम तो ॥ १ ॥
शिवपूर नाम तेथील ज्योतिषी । मायबापें त्याशीं समर्पिलें ॥ २ ॥
द्वितीय संबंधीं वरुषा तिसाचा । नोवरा भाग्याचा ज्ञानवंत ॥ ३ ॥
बहिणी म्हणे त्याशीं कन्यादान केलें । आंदण दिधलें सर्व कांहीं ॥ ४ ॥

अभंग ७

लग्न संपादोनी जाले वरुष चारी । गोत्रजाचा वैरी पिता जाला ॥ १ ॥
वृत्तीच्या संबंधें कलह मांडला । माझा बोलाविला भ्रतार हा ॥ २ ॥
गोत्रजाची फेडा बाकीसाकी ऋण । मागती लेहून शेतमळा ॥ ३ ॥
आतां येथोनियां जावें परदेशीं । तरीच आम्हांसी सुख प्राप्त ॥ ४ ॥
तूं सखा सोईरा मित्र तूंचि जामात । आमुचा हा अंत पाहूं नको ॥ ५ ॥
घातलेसे बंदीं सोडवील कोण । सखा तूं होऊन सोडवावें ॥ ६ ॥
मग त्या भ्रतारें काढिले बाहेरी । निशिचिया भरीं मध्य रात्रीं ॥ ७ ॥

पिता माता बंधू मजही समवेत । गेले रातोरात गंगातीरा ॥ ८ ॥
प्रवरा-संगमीं केलें गंगास्नान । घेतलें दर्शन सिद्धनाथ ॥ ९ ॥
बहिणी म्हणे पुढें चालिलों तेथोनी । पाय वो संतुनी महादेवा ॥१०॥

अभंग ८

गंगा देखोनिया सिद्धेश्वर देव । तेथोनियां जीव निघो नेणें ॥ १ ॥
आवडीचा हेत पूर्वील संस्कार । श्रवणीं आदर कीर्तनाचा ॥ २ ॥
पुराण-श्रवण पूजा देवस्थान । ब्राह्मणपूजन प्रीति याची ॥ ३ ॥
संन्यासी सज्जन संत महानुभाव । यांचे पायीं जीव लागलासे ॥ ४ ॥
निघतां तेथून थोर वाटे दुःख । करंटें अदृष्ट काय कीजे ॥ ५ ॥
बहिणी म्हणे पुढें महादेवा जावें । भ्रतार गौरवें नेत आम्हां ॥ ६ ॥

अभंग ९

मागोनी भिक्षेसी क्रमीतसों वाट । सोसुनिया कष्ट नानापरी ॥ १ ॥
मायबाप बंधू भ्रतारेसीं जाण । महादेववन पहावया ॥ २ ॥
नरसिंहदर्शन घेउनी संपूर्ण । पांडुरंगस्थान देखियेलें ॥ ३ ॥
भीमाचंद्रभागा पुंडलीक भक्त । वेणूनादीं मुक्त प्राणीमात्र ॥ ४ ॥
पद्मालयीं स्थान देवाचें दर्शन । नामसंकीर्तन आयकियेलें ॥ ५ ॥
राही रुखुमाबाई सत्यभामा सर्व । देखियेले पूर्वद्वारयुक्त ॥ ६ ॥
महाद्वारांतुनी करितां प्रवेश । वाटलें मनास महासौख्य ॥ ७ ॥
पांडुरंग मूर्ती देखोनी पवित्र । संतोषले नेत्र इंद्रियेसीं ॥ ८ ॥
केली प्रदक्षिणा महा हर्षयुक्त । चित्त हें विरक्त करोनिया ॥ ९ ॥
वाटे मनामाजीं रहावें येथेंची । परी प्राक्तनाची दशा नाहीं ॥१०॥
जीव जावो परी पंढरीचें स्थळ । न संडावें जळ ऐसें वाटे ॥११॥
बहिणी म्हणे पंचरात्री पंढरीस । केला आम्हीं वास पुण्ययोगें ॥१२॥

अभंग १०

चैत्रपौर्णिमेस गेलों महादेवा । देव-यात्रा सर्वां पाहविलें ॥ १ ॥
जालें समाधान देखोनी शंकर । मार्गें अभयकर भक्तियोगें ॥ २ ॥
पंचरात्री तेथें क्रमोनिया जाण । सिंगणापुरस्थान तेथें आलों ॥ ३ ॥
कोरान्नीचे कण सहज मेळवूं । तेणें सुखी जीवू होय माझा ॥ ४ ॥
अमृताचे परी वाटे गोड अन्न । पाप जळे जाण भक्षिलिया ॥ ५ ॥
बहिणी म्हणे माझें वय वर्षें नव । जालें अंतर्भाव सांगितला ॥ ६ ॥

अभंग ११

भ्रतार विचारी सर्वांस विचार । रहावया थार एथें नाहीं ॥ १ ॥
ब्राह्मणाचे गांवीं जाउनी रहावें । ऐसें मनोभावें वाटतसें ॥ २ ॥
रहिमतपुरीं आहे ब्राह्मणसमुदाव । तेथें वस्ती ठाव सर्व करूं ॥ ३ ॥
बहिणी म्हणे पूर्व प्राक्तनाचे योग । न सोडी स्थळ त्याग केलीयाही ॥ ४ ॥

अभंग १२

रहिमतपुरीं सर्व जाउनी राहिलों । आवघींच लागलों भिक्षा करूं ॥ १ ॥
भ्रतार तो थोर स्नानसंध्या करी । देव तयावरी कृपावंत ॥ २ ॥
तेथील उपाध्या ग्रामींचा ग्रामस्थ । जावया उदित वाराणसी ॥ ३ ॥
ग्रामींचा व्यवहार चालावयालागीं । भ्रतार विभागी केला तेणें ॥ ४ ॥
देखोनी नेटका ज्ञानी विद्यावंत । सर्वही गृहस्थ तया पुसे ॥ ५ ॥
आपण काशीस जाऊनी तुम्हांसी । उपाध्या ज्योतिषी 'रत्नाकर' ॥ ६ ॥
तेंही केलें मान्य मग राहो तेथें । निर्वाह जाला येथें वरुषाचा ॥ ७ ॥
यावरी तो जाणा आलीया ग्रामासी । रक्षिलें आम्हांसी वर्ष एक ॥ ८ ॥
ऐसीं वर्षें अकरा जालीं मजलागीं । वाटे संतसंगीं असावेंसें ॥ ९ ॥
कथा आयकावी पुराण-श्रवणीं । ब्राह्मणपूजनीं चित्त रिझे ॥ १० ॥
तेथोनी प्राक्तनें वोढोनिया जाण । स्थळ तें त्यागून चालविलें ॥ ११ ॥
उदास अंतर नावडेचि कांहीं । प्राक्तनासीं नाहीं उपाय तो ॥ १२ ॥
बहिणी म्हणे पुढें कोल्हापुर क्षेत्र । जें अति पवित्र तेथें गेलों ॥ १३ ॥

अभंग १३

हिरंभट एक ब्राह्मण वेदांती । दोहीं शास्त्रीं गती यजुर्वेदी ॥ १ ॥
थोर भाग्यवंत पवित्र अग्निहोत्र । विद्यार्थी सर्वत्र पठण करिती ॥ २ ॥
तयाच्चिये गृहीं पाहोनिया स्थळ । राहोनी निश्चळ श्रवण होय ॥ ३ ॥
'जयराम गोसावी' त्यांची हरिकथा । नित्य भागवता श्रवण करूं ॥ ४ ॥
बहिणी म्हणे तेथें करोनिया वास । सदा निजध्यास आत्मचर्चा ॥ ५ ॥

अभंग १४

कोणे एके वेळीं आकराव्या वरुषांत । सोमवारीं वृत्त थोर झालें ॥ १ ॥
हिरंभटं यासीं गोदान दिधलें । द्विमुखी पाहिलें यजमान ॥ २ ॥
काळी ते कपिला काळें तिंचें वस्त्र । प्रदक्षणे पुच्छ निवेदिलें ॥ ३ ॥
सुवर्णाचीं शिंगें रुपियाचे खूर । वरी पितांबर पांघुरिला ॥ ४ ॥
सर्व उपचारें गोदान दिधलें । पहावया आले सर्वजण ॥ ५ ॥
उपजोनी वत्स गाय नेली घरां । वत्स पीत क्षीरा दोहाच्चिया ॥ ६ ॥
जाले दिवस दहा अकराव्या दिनीं । हिरंभटा स्वप्नीं द्विज बोले ॥ ७ ॥
ब्राह्मण हा तुझे आहे ओसरीस । कपिला तयांस निवेदीजे ॥ ८ ॥
स्वप्न परी साच केलें हिरंभटें । भ्रतारासी निष्ठें गाय दिल्ही ॥ ९ ॥
आनंदलें मन सर्वांचेंही जाण । गायी-शुश्रूषण घडे आम्हां ॥१०॥
नित्य मायबाप जाती तृणालागीं । पाळिती प्रयोगी जाण तोषें ॥११॥
गायीचें तें वत्स तेंही असें कपिला । माझे ठायीं तिला हेत बहु ॥१२॥
मीच सोडीं तरी वत्स रिघे दोहा । करितां दोहावा सर्वें माझी ॥१३॥
पाणी मीच पाजीं तृण घालीं मीच । मजविण काच मनीं वाहे ॥१४॥
मी जाय पाणीया ओरडे तें वत्स । गाय वाय पुच्छ सर्वें चाले ॥१५॥
करुनिया लोक नवलची राहाती । उगेच पहाती वत्स गायी ॥१६॥
मोकळेंचि वत्स असोनिया जाण । न वजे आपण गायीपाशीं ॥१७॥
तृण घालीं तरी भक्षिती आपण । पाजिल्या जीवन तेव्हां पीती ॥१८॥

रात्रीचे अवसरीं वत्स निजे सेजें । पुराणीं ते फुंजे श्रवणकाळीं ॥१९॥
कथेपाशीं जाय सवें तेंहि येत । उभेंची निवांत कथा परिसे ॥२०॥
गाय गोठा घरीं आपण कथेसी । जातां मी स्नानासी सवें चाले ॥२१॥
करिती अपूर्व हे तुझे संबंधीं । लोक नाना शब्दीं बोलताती ॥२२॥
कोणी म्हणे वत्स आहे योगभ्रष्ट । कोणी म्हणे नष्ट सवे इची ॥२३॥
कोणी म्हणती जन रिणाइत इचें । रीण फिटे तिचें तैंच तुटे ॥२४॥
ऐसें नानापरी वत्स तें न सोडी । मजही आवडी तयापाशीं ॥२५॥
न देखतां वत्स हेचि तळमळी । जलाविण मासोळी तैसें वाटे ॥२६॥
दळितां कांडितां वाहातांही पाणी । वत्साविण जनीं नावडे हो ॥२७॥
भ्रतार रागीट नावडेची तया । परी त्यासी माया उपजली ॥२८॥
म्हणे असो तुज नाहीं मुलबाळ । हाची तुझा खेळ जाण मनीं ॥२९॥
तुजही आवडी कथा-पुराणाची । संगती फुकाची तुज जाली ॥३०॥
तंव तये वेळीं जयराम गोसावी । तेथें तों स्वभावीं सहज आले ॥३१॥
कथा घरोघरीं ब्राह्मणाची पूजा । संतर्पणें द्वीजां आरंभिलीं ॥३२॥
रात्रीं कथा होती दिवसांही करिती । मायबापें प्रीतीं पाहाती तें ॥३३॥
तेथें तया संगें मीही जाय कथे । वत्सही तें तेथें सवें चाले ॥३४॥
जेथें बैसे माय तेथें मी आपण । वत्सही धांवोन सवें उभें ॥३५॥
हागेना मुतेना उभेंचि श्रवण । करित कीर्तन नामघोष ॥३६॥
आरती जालीया नमस्कार होती । आपणही क्षितीं ठेवी डोकें ॥३७॥
देखोनिया जन हांसती सकळ । परि ते प्रेमळ आल्हादचीं ॥३८॥
म्हणती योगभ्रष्ट पूर्वील हरिभक्त । गोवेषें विरक्त पहा कैसें ॥३९॥
तंव येके दिवशीं मोरोपंत कथा । करावया भक्तां पाचारिलें ॥४०॥
दिवस एकादशी प्रहरा दों कथा । मांडिली तत्त्वतां महानंदें ॥४१॥
जयराम गोसावी शिष्य समुहासीं । बैसले सभेसीं आसनीं ते ॥४२॥
टाळ मृदंगेसीं होतसें गायन । मिळालेसे जन सर्व तेथें ॥४३॥

तेथें आपणही मायबाप बंधू । कथा परमानंदू पहातसें ॥४४॥
समागमें वत्स मजपाशीं बैसलें । लोकीं त्याशीं नेलें दारवंटा ॥४५॥
म्हणती स्थळ नाहीं बैसावया जनां । पशू हे श्रवणा काय योग्य ॥४६॥
मी रडों लागलें वत्सालागीं तेथ । तंव जालें श्रुत गोसाविया ॥४७॥
ओरडतां वत्स मज ये रडतां । सांगती अवस्था स्वामीपासीं ॥४८॥
म्हणती एक मुली हिरंभटाघरीं । आली ते श्रीहरी-कीर्तनासी ॥४९॥
तिजसवें एक वत्स असे त्याशीं । सांगातें दिननिशीं हिंडवीते ॥५०॥
तें वत्स बाहेरी घातिलें अडचणीं । यालागीं ती रुसुनी रडतसे ॥५१॥
वत्स तें ओरडे बाहेरीं तिष्ठतें । रडत ही येथें गलबला ॥५२॥
साक्ष अंतरींचा तो स्वामी जयराम । वत्स-अंतर्याम ओळखीलें ॥५३॥
म्हणे आणा त्याशीं वत्साचें अंतरीं । काय नाहीं हरी आत्मवेत्ता ॥५४॥
कथेलागीं जीव होतो कासावीस । पशू कीं तयास म्हणों नये ॥५५॥
आणविलें वत्स बैसविलें आसनीं । पाहोनी नयनीं तोष वाटे ॥५६॥
मजही कृपावंत कृपेचिये शब्दें । बोलावी प्रारब्धें पूर्व पुण्यें ॥५७॥
कुर्वाळोनी दोघां पाहे पूर्ण दृष्टी । न मानेचि गोष्टी जनांलागीं ॥५८॥
कथा होत असे गजरें महा थोर । चित्त हें निर्भर वैष्णवाचें ॥५९॥
जयराम गोसावी याचें मनोगत । पुण्यशील सत्य उभय वर्ग ॥६०॥
कथेमाजीं वत्स उभेंचि तिष्ठत । रूपीं सर्व चित्त आणुनीया ॥६१॥
मुली हे लहान वय इचें थोडें । श्रवण हें आवडे नवल मोठें ॥६२॥
म्हणे इचे कोणी आहे ये कथेसी । मायबाप तिशीं सांगितला ॥६३॥
भ्रतार इयेचा आहे बहु योग्य । परि हिचें वैराग्य थोर दिसे ॥६४॥
मायबापासवें येतसे पुराणीं । वत्सही घेऊनी समागमें ॥६५॥
मग म्यां आपुलें आपण पाहिलें । चरणीं घातलें लोटांगण ॥६६॥
वत्सही तैसेंची पायावरी पडे । अपूर्वता घडे सर्व जनीं ॥६७॥
वाम सव्य दोनी होते दोघे जणे । वत्सा मज तेणें उठविलें ॥६८॥
कथा संपलिया लोक गेले सर्व । परि हें अपूर्व म्हणती जन ॥६९॥

हिरंभट आणि आणिकही जन । म्हणती हें चिन्ह कोणां कळे ॥७०॥
बहिणी ऐसें कोल्हापुरीं होय । पुढीलहि सोय तुम्हां सांगों ॥७१॥

अभंग १५

पिता-माता-बंधू-समवेत बिऱ्हाडीं । पावले ते घडी वत्सयुक्त ॥ १ ॥
दोन घडी रात्र होती ते समयीं । वत्स तयीं गायीं पाजीयेलें ॥ २ ॥
हिरंभटीं स्नान केलें अग्नीसेवें । कार्तिकाचे दिवे आकाशांत ॥ ३ ॥
सडे संमार्जन केलें स्नान तेथें । गायी[1] वत्स हातें कुर्वाळीलें ॥ ४ ॥
भ्रतारानें स्नान केलें आपुलिया । दक्षिणेची गया कोल्हापूर ॥ ५ ॥
तंव कोणी एक निराबाई होती । तिनें कथास्थिति सांगितली ॥ ६ ॥
भ्रताराचे कानीं कथेंतील सर्व । सांगाया अपूर्व म्हणोनिया ॥ ७ ॥
वत्साचें वृत्तांत माझेंही रुदन । भ्रताराचे कान वृत्त केले ॥ ८ ॥
जयराम गोसावी विदेही अवस्था । तेणें हात माथां ठेवियेला ॥ ९ ॥
थोर यांचें भाग्य तो यांशीं बोलिला । आशीर्वाद दिला योग्य तेणें ॥१०॥
जातीचा भिक्षुक अंतरीं बहु राग । धांवला सवेग गेहाप्रती ॥११॥
धरुनीया वेणी मारिलें यथेष्ट । हिरंभटा कष्ट फार झाले ॥१२॥
नावरे मारितां गायही ओरडे । वत्स तेंही रडे कासाविसीं ॥१३॥
अकरावें वरुष मज होतें तेव्हां । काय पतिसेवा अंतरलें ॥१४॥
मायबाप बंधू बोलती न कांहीं । भ्रतारें क्रोधही आंवरिला ॥१५॥
शांत झालीया पुसत तयांस । स्त्रियेवरी त्रास कासयाचा ॥१६॥
येरु म्हणे रात्रीं कथेंत प्रतिष्ठा । काय यांची निष्ठा देखियेली ॥१७॥
कैचें तें पुराण कैची हरिकथा । मारीन अन्यथा नव्हे येथ ॥१८॥
इतुकें बोलोनिया भ्रतार पुनरपी । क्रोध तो नाटोपो अग्नि-ऐसा ॥१९॥
बहिणी म्हणे तेव्हां देह संकल्पिलें । प्राक्तनाचें केलें कोण वारी ॥२०॥

---

१ पाठभेद—गौचीं शृंगें

अभंग १६

आलें मना तंव[1] मारिलें बळकट । बांधोनिया मोट टाकियेली ॥ १ ॥
हिरंभट म्हणे व्हा तुम्ही बाहेरी । हा दिसे हत्यारी चांडाळ कीं ॥ २ ॥
मग मातापिता हिरंभटालागीं । प्रार्थुनिया वेगीं स्थीर केलें ॥ ३ ॥
म्हणती कृपा करा आजि दिसभरी । प्रातःकाळीं दुरी ठाव पाहों ॥ ४ ॥
तयावरी वत्स गाय दोघे जण । न खाती तृण जळासही ॥ ५ ॥
देखोनी वत्सासी गायींचा वृत्तांत । मोट तो सोडीत तये वेळीं ॥ ६ ॥
आणिलें जवळीं गाय वत्सापाशीं । झुंबरली जैसी पुत्र माता ॥ ७ ॥
आपण देखीलें वत्स आणि गाय । म्हणे प्राण जाय तरी बरा ॥ ८ ॥
बहिणी म्हणे तया तृण-पाणी पाजी । न घेती ते माझी थोर माया ॥ ९ ॥

अभंग १७

न खाती तृण न घेती जीवन । आपणही अन्न टाकियेलें ॥ १ ॥
नुठती सर्वथा स्वस्थळापासून । येती सर्वजण पाहावया ॥ २ ॥
जयराम स्वामीस सांगितलें जनीं । पहावया निर्वाणीं तेही आले ॥ ३ ॥
भ्रतारें तयासी केला नमस्कार । आपुलें अंतर एकनिष्ठ ॥ ४ ॥
घातिलें आसन जयराम स्वामीस । हिरंभटीं त्यांस पूजियेलें ॥ ५ ॥
मिळोनिया लोक पाहाती लोचनीं । स्वामीही ते क्षणीं आनंदले ॥ ६ ॥
म्हणती ब्राह्मण तूं इचा भ्रतार । सांगतों निर्धार ऐक आतां ॥ ७ ॥
योगभ्रष्ट इचीं साधनें बळकट । तूं इसीं कष्ट करूं नको ॥ ८ ॥
स्वधर्मेंची तुझी करील ही सेवा । उद्धरील जीवा आपुलीया ॥ ९ ॥
तुझे पदरीं कांहीं पूर्वील सुकृत । तेणें ही सांगात प्राप्त जाली ॥ १० ॥
गायी आणि वत्स हें इचें सांगाती । अनुष्ठानीं होती ऐक्य भाव ॥ ११ ॥
हेंच इचा गुरु हें इचें साधन । तोंडील बंधन आपुलें हें ॥ १२ ॥
इचे समागमें करिती जे वास । तेही भक्तिरस घेती सुखें ॥ १३ ॥

---

१ पाठभेद—आतां

आयकसी तरी बरें होय तुझें । येथें काय माझें बळ आहे ॥१४॥
बहिणी म्हणे ऐसें बोलोनी जयराम । पाहे मनोरम सर्व चिन्हें ॥१५॥

अभंग १८

स्वस्थाना आपण चालीले जयराम । शिष्यांचा संभ्रम फार होता ॥ १ ॥
म्हणती जयराम अनुष्ठानीं तिघे । पूर्वींच्या प्रसंगें एकनिष्ठ ॥ २ ॥
अंतराय कांहीं अनुष्ठानीं राहिल्या । गायी या जन्मल्या पुण्यवेगें ॥ ३ ॥
हे मुली संपूर्ण आहे अनुष्ठान । चित्त शुद्धि जाण ईस आहे ॥ ४ ॥
ऐसें परस्परें बोलती उत्तरें । हे कानीं सादरें ऐकियेलीं ॥ ५ ॥
बहिणी म्हणे गेले स्वामी स्वस्थानासी । मागील वृत्तांसी जाण सांगों ॥ ६ ॥

अभंग १९

द्वादशी क्रमोनी त्रयोदशी आंत । वत्सासी देहांत-समय आला ॥ १ ॥
तेथ हिरंभट बोलियला श्लोक । सहज स्वाभाविक '*मूकं' करोति ॥ २ ॥
पूर्वार्ध श्लोकाचा सरताची जाण । बोलिलें आपण वत्स तेव्हां ॥ ३ ॥
यत्कृपा तमहं वंदे बोले शब्द । श्लोकउत्तरार्ध वत्स बोले ॥ ४ ॥
आयकिला सर्व लोकीं तो श्लोकार्ध । करिती संवाद परस्परें ॥ ५ ॥
तंव त्या वत्सें टाकियेला प्राण । आलें मी धांवोन तयापाशीं ॥ ६ ॥
प्राणासवें प्राण जाऊं पाहे माझा । प्राक्तनासी दुजा यत्न नाहीं ॥ ७ ॥
गाय हंबरडे दोहीवरी मान । टाकी परी जाण शब्द कैचा ॥ ८ ॥
बहिणी म्हणे देह प्राक्तनें राखिलें । पुढें काय झालें कोण जाणे ॥ ९ ॥

अभंग २०

जयराम स्वामीस कळला वृत्तांत । वत्सासी त्या अंतकाळ जाला ॥ १ ॥
श्लोकार्ध म्हणोनी प्राण वत्स त्यजी । योग लाजला जी तयापुढें ॥ २ ॥
मग सर्व श्रेष्ठ संत साधुजन । करीत कीर्तन वत्स नेलें ॥ ३ ॥

---

* गीताध्यान, श्लोक ८—मूकं करोति वाचालं पंगुं लंघयते गिरीन्
यत्कृपा तमहं वंदे परमानन्दमाधवम्

दिंडी पताकानें मिरविलें वत्स । गायसवें तुच्छ यानीं देहें ॥ ४ ॥
हुंबरे हाणोनी चाले मागें मागें । गाय अंतरंगें महा दुःखी ॥ ५ ॥
पुरुनिया वत्स आले सर्व जन । करुनिया स्नान गृहा गेले ॥ ६ ॥
गाय वत्सापाशीं जाऊनी हुंबरे । मागुती ते फिरे गृहासी ये ॥ ७ ॥
मज विलोकितां मी तों अचेतन । माझ्या देहीं प्राण आढळेना ॥ ८ ॥
ऐसें दिन चारी लोटलियावरी । प्रतिपदेमाझारीं मध्यरातीं ॥ ९ ॥
बोलिला ब्राह्मण येऊनी सन्मुख । सावध विवेक धरीं बाई ॥१०॥
सावध सावध सावध तूं मनीं । श्रवणीं ऐकोनी देह कांपे ॥११॥
तंव गाय नाहीं वत्स ना ते लोक । माय ते सन्मुख बैसलीसे ॥१२॥
बंधू पिता आणि भ्रतार बैसला । सोज्ज्वल लागला दीप असे ॥१३॥
तेथोनीयां मन करोनी सावध । स्मरणीं स्वतां सिद्ध चित्त केलें ॥१४॥
बहिणी म्हणे देह सर्वही विकळ । परि तें निश्चळ चित्त माझें ॥१५॥

अभंग २१

उघडोनी नेत्र पाहे जंव पुढें । तंव दृष्टी पडे पांडुरंग ॥ १ ॥
देखीली पंढरी ध्याना तेची येत । जयराम दिसत दृष्टीपुढें ॥ २ ॥
ब्राह्मण स्वप्नांत देखिला तो जाण । त्याची आठवण मनीं वाहे ॥ ३ ॥
न दिसे आणिक नेत्रांपुढें जाण । नामाचें स्मरण मनीं राहे ॥ ४ ॥
पूर्वील हरिकथा आयकिल्या होत्या । त्या मनीं मागुल्या आठवती ॥ ५ ॥
तुकोबाचीं पदें अद्वैत प्रसिद्ध । त्यांचा अनुवाद चित्त झुरवी ॥ ६ ॥
ऐसीं ज्याचीं पदें तो मज भेटतां । जीवास या होतां तोष बहू ॥ ७ ॥
तुकोबाचा छंद लागला मनासी । ऐकतां पदांसी कथेमाजीं ॥ ८ ॥
तुकोबाची भेटी होईल तो क्षण । वैकुंठासमान होय मज ॥ ९ ॥
तुकोबाची ऐकेन कानीं हरिकथा । होय तैसें चित्ता समाधान ॥१०॥
तुकोबाचें ध्यान करोनि अंतरीं । राहे त्याभीतरीं देहामाजीं ॥११॥
बहिणी म्हणे तुका सद्गुरु सहोदर । भेटतां अपार सुख होय ॥१२॥

अभंग २२

मच्छ जैसा जळावांचोनी तडफडी । तैसीच आवडी तुकोबाची ॥ १ ॥
अंतरींचा साक्षी असेल जो प्राणी । अनुभवें मनीं जाणेल तो ॥ २ ॥
तृषितांसी जैसें आवडे जीवन । तैसा पिंड प्राणावीण तया ॥ ३ ॥
बहिणी म्हणे हेत तुकोबांचे पायीं । ऐकोनिया देहीं पर्दे त्यांचीं ॥ ४ ॥

अभंग २३

संचितासी दग्ध करी ऐसा कोण? । सद्गुरूवांचोन जाण मना ॥ १ ॥
यालागीं सद्गुरु असावा उत्तम । जेणें निमे श्रम संसाराचा ॥ २ ॥
त्रिविध तापासी कोण करी शांत । सद्गुरु एकांत न जोडतां ॥ ३ ॥
जन्ममरणाची कथा कैं निवारे । सद्गुरु निर्धारें न भेटतां ॥ ४ ॥
वासना निःशेष निवारेल तेव्हां । भेटेल तुकोबा सद्गुरु तो ॥ ५ ॥
बहिणी म्हणे माझा जाऊं पाहे जीव । कां हो न ये कींव तुकोबा ॥ ६ ॥

अभंग २४

न बोलवे शब्द अंतरींचा धांवा । नायके तुकोबा काय कीजे ॥ १ ॥
अदृष्ट करंटें साह्य न हो देव । अंतरींची हांव काय करूं ॥ २ ॥
तेरा दिवस ज्यानें वह्या उदकांत । घालोनिया सत्य वांचविल्या ॥ ३ ॥
महाराष्ट्री शब्दांत वेदांताचा अर्थ । बोलिला लोकांत सर्वद्रष्टा ॥ ४ ॥
अंतर साक्ष आहे निरोपणीं हेत । जडे परी चित्त वोळखेना ॥ ५ ॥
बहिणी म्हणे मीच असेन अपराधी । अन्याय त्रिशुद्धी काय त्याचा ॥ ६ ॥

अभंग २५

बहुत अंतरीं शोक आरंभिला । कां मज विठ्ठला मोकलिलें ॥ १ ॥
त्रिविध तापानें तापलें मी बहू । जाइना कां जीऊ प्राण माझा ॥ २ ॥
तंव अकस्मात सातविया दिनीं । नामसंकीर्तनीं घोषयुक्त ॥ ३ ॥
तुकाराम रूपें येवोनी प्रत्यक्ष । म्हणे पूर्वपक्ष सांभाळिजे ॥ ४ ॥
नको करूं चिंता असें मी तुजपाशीं । घेईं अमृताशी हातींचिया ॥ ५ ॥

गाय केलें वत्स मुखीं निघे धार । अमृत हें सार सेवीं हेंची ॥ ६ ॥
ठेवोनिया कर मस्तकीं बोलिला । मंत्र सांगितला कर्णरंध्रीं ॥ ७ ॥
म्यांही पायांवरी ठेविलें मस्तक । दिधलें पुस्तक मंत्रगीता ॥ ८ ॥
कार्तिकांत वद्य पंचमी रविवार । स्वप्नींचा विचार गुरु-कृपा ॥ ९ ॥
आनंदलें मन चिद्रूपीं कोंदलें । उठोनी बैसलें चमत्कारें ॥१०॥
मंत्र आठवती तुकोबास्वरूपें । स्वप्नामाजीं कृपा पूर्ण केली ॥११॥
अमृत पाजिलें चवीं अनारसी । साक्ष ज्याची त्यासी मनामाजीं ॥१२॥
बहिणी म्हणे ऐसी कृपा सद्‌गुरूची । तुकारामें साची पूर्ण केली ॥१३॥

अभंग २६

जालें समाधान ब्राह्मणाच्या शब्दें । स्वप्नामाजीं पदें आठविती ॥ १ ॥
परी अंतरींच तुकोबाचें ध्यान । दर्शनावांचोन करितसें ॥ २ ॥
जयाचिया पदें होतसे विश्रांती । तेचि देहाकृति विठ्ठलाची ॥ ३ ॥
विठ्ठलासी तया नाहीं भेदभाव । ऐसें माझें मन साक्ष आहे ॥ ४ ॥
पांडुरंग तुका पांडुरंग तुका । वेगळीक देखा होय केंवी ॥ ५ ॥
कलियुगीं बौद्धरूप धरी हरी । तुकोबा शरीरीं प्रवेशला ॥ ६ ॥
तुकोबाची बुद्धि पांडुरंगरूप । मन तें स्वरूप तुकोबाचें ॥ ७ ॥
तुकोबाचें सर्व इंद्रिय-चालक । पांडुरंग देख सत्य आहे ॥ ८ ॥
तुकोबाचे नेत्र तेही पांडुरंग । श्रोतृ ते अभंगरूप त्याचे ॥ ९ ॥
तुकोबाचे हात लिहिताती जें जें । तेंचि तें सहजें पांडुरंग ॥१०॥
सर्वही व्यापार तुकोबाचे हरी । आपणचि करी अद्वयत्वें ॥११॥
बहिणी म्हणे रूपें व्यापक तुकोबा । ध्यान माझ्या जीवा हेंचि पाहे ॥१२॥

अभंग २७

भ्रतारें टाकिलें मोट बांधोनिया । न सोसी ते तया क्लेशावस्था ॥ १ ॥
चतुर्थ दिवशीं जीव टाकियेला । विठ्ठलें दाविला चमत्कारु ॥ २ ॥
ब्राह्मणाच्या रूपें येवोनी सांगत । सावधान चित्त करीं पुढें ॥ ३ ॥

अंतरीं सावध होउनी राहिलें । चित्त म्यां गोविलें तुकोबासी ॥ ४ ॥
वत्स गेलियासी दिवस सातवा । येवोनी तुकोबा स्वप्नामाजीं ॥ ५ ॥
केलें समाधान पाजिलें अमृत । वत्सासी करीत गाय भेटी ॥ ६ ॥
अमृता पाजोनी सांगितला मंत्र । जो कां हा सर्वत्र लोक जपती ॥ ७ ॥
मस्तकीं हस्तक ठेवोनिया कृपा । केली त्या स्वरूपा तोची जाणे ॥ ८ ॥
कृपेचा महिमा आहे तो अपार । वत्स बोले सार श्लोक-अर्ध ॥ ९ ॥
आठवे दिवशीं सावध इंद्रियें । अमृतें धालिये तुकोबाच्या ॥१०॥
तेधवां ती गाय देखिली सन्मुख । निमालीसे देख वत्स कळे ॥११॥
म्हणे या वत्सातें पाजिलें अमृतु । तयासी तो मृत्यु कदा नोहे ॥१२॥
अमर तें वत्स आहे मजपासीं । चित्त अमृतासी घेत गोडी ॥१३॥
बहिणी म्हणे इतुकें वर्तलियावरी । पुढेंही विस्तारीं सांगिजेल ॥१४॥

अभंग २८

जयराम समर्थ ज्ञानाचा सागर । साक्ष तें अंतर त्याचें तया ॥ १ ॥
बोलाविलें तेणें हिरंभटाप्रती । माझी तया स्थिति पुसियेली ॥ २ ॥
सांगितला तेणें वृत्तांत सर्वही । वर्तला जो कांहीं गृहीं त्याचें ॥ ३ ॥
स्वप्नागत गुरु तुकोबाचें रूपें । स्वप्नींचिये कृपें बोध केला ॥ ४ ॥
सावध होउनी ते मुली बैसली । गायीस गौरविली कुर्वाळूनी ॥ ५ ॥
दुग्ध दोहोनिया घेतलें तियेनें । पाणी आणि तृणें भक्षितसे ॥ ६ ॥
परी तें मुलीचें रूप पालटलें । पूर्ण तें दाटलें हृदय तिचें ॥ ७ ॥
तुकोबाचा छंद अंतरीं लागला । मायबापें तिला सांगताती ॥ ८ ॥
भ्रतार हा तिचा वेडावला राहे । उगाची तो पाहे तियेकडे ॥ ९ ॥
छांदिष्ट होउनी बैसली घरांत । तुकोबासी चित्त लावुनिया ॥१०॥
ऐसा हा वृत्तांत हिरंभट सांगे । जयराम निजांगें संतोषला ॥११॥
बहिणी म्हणे ऐसा निर्धार ऐकोनी । जयराम स्वामींनीं कृपा केली ॥१२॥

अभंग २९

कृपा उपजली जयराम स्वामीसी । आले पाहायासी भाव माझा ॥ १ ॥
देखोनी तयासी आनंद वाटला । कंठ कोंदाटला आनंदानें ॥ २ ॥
मनेंचि आरती केला नमस्कार । पूजिला साचार मनामाजीं ॥ ३ ॥
बहिणी म्हणे त्याचे मनांतील हेत । ओळखे निश्चित पांडुरंग ॥ ४ ॥

अभंग ३०

मजवरी दृष्टी कृपेची ओतिली । प्रेमाची गुंतली माय जैसी ॥ १ ॥
अंतरींची पूजा घेऊनी जयराम । गेला तो सप्रेम स्वस्थानासी ॥ २ ॥
उगाची बैसला आसनीं नेमस्त । करोनिया स्वस्थ चित्तवृत्ति ॥ ३ ॥
तंव कांहीं एक अपूर्व वर्तलें । तुकारामें दिलें दर्शनासी ॥ ४ ॥
केला नमस्कार भेटुनी आनंदें । अत्यंत आल्हादें स्वामी सखा ॥ ५ ॥
मजही दर्शन दिधलें अळुमाळ । घातला कवळ मुखामाजीं ॥ ६ ॥
मज म्हणे आलों जयराम-भेटीसी । तुजही मानसीं ओळखीलें ॥ ७ ॥
तुम्हीं आतां येथें नका राहूं कदा । आत्मज्ञानबोधा न संडावें ॥ ८ ॥
बहिणी म्हणे दिलें दर्शन दुसरें । मनाच्या व्यापारें तुकोबाचें ॥ ९ ॥

अभंग ३१

नवल जनांसी वाटलें म्हणोनी । येती ते धांवोनी पहावया ॥ १ ॥
भ्रतार हा माझा देखोनी तयांसी । माझिया देहासी पीडा करी ॥ २ ॥
न देखवे तया द्वेषी जनांप्रती । क्षणक्षणा चित्तीं द्वेष वाढे ॥ ३ ॥
म्हणे ही बाईल मरे तरी बरें । ईस कां पामरें भेटताती ॥ ४ ॥
काय आतां घुमारें येईल अंगासी । देव इचें पोषी पोट कैसें ॥ ५ ॥
बहिणी म्हणे ऐसी भ्रतारासी चिंता । जाणोनी अनंता कळों आलें ॥ ६ ॥

अभंग ३२

भ्रतार म्हणतसे आम्ही कीं ब्राह्मण । वेदाचें पठण सदा करूं ॥ १ ॥
कैचा शूद्र तुका स्वप्नींचे दर्शनीं । बिघडली पत्नी काय करूं ॥ २ ॥

कैचा जयराम कैचा पांडुरंग । माझा झाला भंग आश्रमाचा ॥ ३ ॥
आम्ही काय जाणों नाम हरिकथा । भक्ति हे तत्त्वतां नसे स्वप्नीं ॥ ४ ॥
कैचे संत साधू कैची भाव भक्ती । भिक्षुकाचे पंक्तीं वसों सदा ॥ ५ ॥
बहिणी म्हणे ऐसें चित्तांत भ्रतारें । चिंतोनी निर्धारें विचारिलें ॥ ६ ॥

अभंग ३३

विचारिलें मनीं भ्रतारें आपण । आतां हें त्यागोन वना जावें ॥ १ ॥
इसी नमस्कार करितील जन । आम्ही इसी तृण वाटों परी ॥ २ ॥
स्त्रियेशीं बोलती अनुवाद कथेचा । आम्हीं इसी नीचापरी वाटो ॥ ३ ॥
पुसतची येती इसी पहा जन । आम्हीं कीं ब्राह्मण मूर्ख जालों ॥ ४ ॥
इचें नांव घेती गोसाविण ऐसें । आम्हां कोण पुसे इजपुढें ॥ ५ ॥
बहिणी म्हणे ऐसें भ्रतार मानसीं । चिंतुनी चित्तासी बोध करी ॥ ६ ॥

अभंग ३४

म्हणे आतां मना स्त्रियेची हे दशा । आतां तूं सहसा राहों नको ॥ १ ॥
चाल वेगीं जाऊं तीर्थासी वैराग्य । आमचें हें भाग्य वोढवलें ॥ २ ॥
सासु-सासऱ्यांसीं केला नमस्कार । आहे स्त्री गरोदर मास तीन ॥ ३ ॥
आम्ही जातों तीर्थयात्रा करावया । देवलसी स्त्रीया यत्न कीजे ॥ ४ ॥
न पाहें मी मुख सर्वथा इयेचें । हीनत्व आमुचें कोण फेडी ॥ ५ ॥
भंडिमा सोसून कोण राहे येथें । ऐसिया स्त्रियेतें कोण पाळी ॥ ६ ॥
बहिणी म्हणे ऐसा बोलिला भ्रतार । मज पडे विचार मनामाजीं ॥ ७ ॥

अभंग ३५

काय म्यां अदृष्टा करावें आपण । आलें जें ठाकून सोसी जें तें ॥ १ ॥
नाहीं येत वारें अंगासी माझीया । घुमारीन काया नव्हे माझी ॥ २ ॥
स्वधर्म आपुला रक्षुनिया मनें । शास्त्राच्या श्रवणें देव साधू ॥ ३ ॥
भ्रताराची सेवा तोचि आम्हां देव । भ्रतार स्वयमेव परब्रह्म ॥ ४ ॥
तीर्थ भ्रताराचें सर्व तीर्थ जाणा । तया तीर्थाविणा निरर्थक ॥ ५ ॥

भ्रतारवचनासी उल्लंघीन जरी । पापें माझ्या शिरीं पृथिवीचीं ॥ ६ ॥
धर्म अर्थ काम मोक्षासी अधिकारी । भ्रतार साचारी वेद बोले ॥ ७ ॥
हा माझा निश्चय मनांतील हेत । भ्रतारेसी चित्त लावियेलें ॥ ८ ॥
भ्रतारसेवेनें सांग हा परमार्थ । भ्रतारेंच स्वार्थ सर्व आहे ॥ ९ ॥
भ्रतारावांचोनी अन्य देव जरी । येईल अंतरीं ब्रह्महत्या ॥१०॥
सद्गुरु भ्रतार साधन भ्रतार । सत्य हा निर्धार अंतरींचा ॥११॥
बहिणी म्हणे देवा भ्रतारांचें मनीं । तुवां प्रवेशोनी स्थिर केलें ॥१२॥

अभंग ३६

भ्रतार गेलीया वैराग्य घेऊनी । पांडुरंगा जनीं जिणें काय ॥ १ ॥
प्राणावीण देह काय पावे शोभा । रात्रीविण प्रभा चंद्राचिये ॥ २ ॥
भ्रतार तो जीव देह मी आपण । भ्रतार कल्याण सर्व माझें ॥ ३ ॥
भ्रतार जीवन मी मीन तयांत । कैसेनी वांचत जीव माझा ॥ ४ ॥
भ्रतार तो रवी मी प्रभा तयासी । वियोग हा त्यासी केवीं घडे ॥ ५ ॥
बहिणी म्हणे माझा जीवाचा निर्धार । बोलें पैं विचार हरी जाणे ॥ ६ ॥

अभंग ३७

भ्रतारें वैराग्य घेतलिया वरी । जीव हा निर्धारीं देईन मी ॥ १ ॥
वत्सासाठीं देह अचेतन पडे । हें तव रोकडें परब्रह्म ॥ २ ॥
भ्रताराचें तीर्थ न सांपडे जरी । अन्न खाय तरी मांस आम्हां ॥ ३ ॥
भ्रताराचें शेष न सांपडे तरी । पापें माझ्या शिरीं त्रैलोक्याचीं ॥ ४ ॥
चित्त हें भ्रतारावीण जरी जाये । तरी वास होय नरकीं आम्हां ॥ ५ ॥
भ्रतारदर्शनाविण जाय दीस । तरी तेचि रास पातकांची ॥ ६ ॥
बहिणी म्हणे मज आज्ञाची प्रमाण । ब्रह्म सनातन स्वामी माझा ॥ ७ ॥

अभंग ३८

पाषाण विठ्ठल स्वप्नांतील तुका । प्रत्यक्ष कां सुखा अंतरावें ॥ १ ॥
घेईन उदंड सेवासुख देहीं । साक्ष या विदेही आहे मज ॥ २ ॥

भ्रताराची सेवा पतिव्रता करी । तरी ती उद्धरी उभय कुळें ॥ ३ ॥
बहिणी म्हणे माझ्या जिवाची विश्रांती । भ्रतारें समाप्ती जन्ममृत्यू ॥ ४ ॥

अभंग ३९

भ्रतारें निश्चय केला मनामाजीं । जावें उद्यां आजि टाकोनिया ॥ १ ॥
तंव त्यासी व्यथा जाली शरिरास । झाला सात दिवस ज्वाळ देहीं ॥ २ ॥
ओळखीचे जन नायके उत्तर । आपण अहोरात्र तयापाशीं ॥ ३ ॥
दिधल्या औषध नेदी तया मान । जीव व्यथा फार पूर्ण सोसी ॥ ४ ॥
एक मासवरी अन्न विवर्जीत । व्यथा हे अद्भुत सोसीतसे ॥ ५ ॥
नाना देव कुळें देवतांची भाष । ठेविल्या विशेष बहु कांहीं ॥ ६ ॥
परी तया व्यथेलागीं न ये गुण । म्हणे तो मरण आलें मज ॥ ७ ॥
काय पांडुरंगा तुकोबासी निंदी । व्यथा तेचि संधीं आली मज ॥ ८ ॥
जरी तुकाराम निंदिला त्यागुणें । असेल दुखणें व्यथा मज ॥ ९ ॥
तरी चमत्कार दाखवावा सध्या । जीवीं विश्ववंद्या तुकारामा ॥१०॥
बहिणी म्हणे झाला अनुताप भ्रतारा । पांडुरंग पुरा अंतरसाक्ष ॥११॥

अभंग ४०

वृद्धसा ब्राह्मण येऊनी बोलतु । म्हणे कां रे मृत्यु इच्छितोसी ॥ १ ॥
वैराग्य कां तुज आलें असें मना । स्त्रीचा त्याग कोण्या गुणें केला ॥ २ ॥
आधीं इचा विचारीं अपराध अंतरीं । मग कोपा करीं प्रवर्तावें ॥ ३ ॥
वांचण्याची इच्छा असलिया मानसीं । तरी तूं इयेसी अंगिकारीं ॥ ४ ॥
स्वधर्माविरहित वर्तेल ही जरी । तरी तिचा करीं त्याग वेड्या ॥ ५ ॥
ही आहे विरक्त निश्चित हरिभक्त । तुवां पाहीं सत्य तैसें व्हावें ॥ ६ ॥
होईल कल्याण बोलत ब्राह्मण । भ्रतारें चरण वंदियेले ॥ ७ ॥
सांगितलें सर्व कारण आपण । देईं जीवदान आजी मज ॥ ८ ॥
ये व्यथेपासोनी वांचवीं स्वामीया । जीव तुझ्या पायां वाहीन मी ॥ ९ ॥
स्त्रियेसी सर्वथा न बोले आपण । हरीसी शरण जीवेंभावें ॥१०॥

केला नमस्कार प्रत्यक्ष उठोन । होईल कल्याण म्हणे द्विज ॥११॥
ऐकतें मीही दोघांचें बोलणें । घालीं लोटांगणें भ्रतारासी ॥१२॥
झाला तो अदृश्य ब्राह्मण तात्काळ । आरोग्य कुशल देह झाला ॥१३॥
बहिणी म्हणे देव कृपा करी तरी । सर्व सिद्धी द्वारीं तिष्ठतील ॥१४॥

अभंग ४१

आरोग्य तात्काळ व्यथेचा हारास । झाला दिसंदिस भ्रताराचा ॥ १ ॥
मग करी कृपा बोले समाधानें । द्वेषाचें हें ठाणें दूर केलें ॥ २ ॥
म्हणे आतां सर्व जावें येथुनियां । आपुलिया ठाया स्वस्थाना ॥ ३ ॥
देवें आपणासी ब्राह्मणाच्या वेषें । सांगितला शेष प्राक्तनाचा ॥ ४ ॥
तेचि आतां करूं हरिची वो भक्ति । मिरासीची खंती टाकियेली ॥ ५ ॥
माझी माय-बापें तयांसी सांगत । तुम्हीं जा निवांत देवगांवा ॥ ६ ॥
आपण अरण्यांत दोघे करूं वास । देवाच्या बोलास धरोनिया ॥ ७ ॥
होवो आतां कल्याण किंवा अकल्याण । आम्ही तो संपूर्ण भक्ती करूं ॥ ८ ॥
तुकोबाचे गांवीं जाऊनिया राहों । मनींचा दृढावो धरोनिया ॥ ९ ॥
ऐसी पालटली भ्रताराची बुद्धी । स्वामी कृपानिधि अंतरसाक्ष ॥१०॥
काय एक देव करील तें नव्हे । प्रत्यक्ष अनुभवें सर्वजनां ॥११॥
बहिणी म्हणे आवर्घी घेउनी चालिलों । तुकोबाच्या आलों दर्शनासी ॥१२॥

अभंग ४२

वत्साचिये माय कपिला सांगातें । धांवे एकचित्तें आम्हांपुढें ॥ १ ॥
माय बाप बंधु भ्रतारासहित । इंद्रायणी जेथ तेथें आलों ॥ २ ॥
करोनिया स्नान पांडुरंग-भेटी । आनंदली सृष्टी अंतरंगें ॥ ३ ॥
तुकोबा आरती करित होते तेथ । नमस्कारें स्वस्थ चित्त केलें ॥ ४ ॥
स्वप्नीं जो देखीला तेंच ध्यान तेथ । देखिलें नेमस्त पूर्ण दृष्टीं ॥ ५ ॥
बहिणी म्हणे तेथ भ्रतारें साष्टांग । केला अंतरंग भावयुक्त ॥ ६ ॥

अभंग ४३

माध्यान्ह जालीया पाहिजे तें अन्न । भ्रतार जाऊन ग्राम हिंडे ॥ १ ॥
तंव तेथ एक ब्राह्मण कोंडाजी । म्हणे तुम्ही याजी भोजनासी ॥ २ ॥
भ्रतार बोलिला आह्मीं पांचजण । इतुकीया अन्न कोण घाली ॥ ३ ॥
येरू म्हणे तुम्ही अवघींच भोजना । यावें नारायणा काय चिंता ॥ ४ ॥
जावें स्थळ तुम्ही पाहोनी राहिजे । माध्यान्हीं येईजे गृहाप्रती ॥ ५ ॥
बहिणी म्हणे आला भ्रतार अन्नासी । मेळविलें त्यासी सांगितलें ॥ ६ ॥

अभंग ४४

मंबाजी गोसावी त्या स्थळीं नांदता । गृह प्रवेशतां देखियेले ॥ १ ॥
जाऊनी तयासी मागितलें स्थळ । तो अति चंचळ क्रोध तया ॥ २ ॥
मारावया उठे घातलें बाहेरी । आनंदें वोवरी प्रार्थियेलें ॥ ३ ॥
तेथें राहोनीया भोजनासी गेलों । बहुत पावलों समाधान ॥ ४ ॥
वृत्तांत पुसिला कोठोनी आलांत । चालतसा पंथ कवण कार्या ॥ ५ ॥
कांहींबाही तया सांगितलें पूर्व । म्हणे रहा सर्व पर्वणीसी ॥ ६ ॥
सोमवारीं आहे अमावास्या पुढें । रहा भक्तिकोडें सुख घ्यावें ॥ ७ ॥
नित्य हरिकथा होतसे देऊळीं । तुकोबा माऊली वैष्णवाची ॥ ८ ॥
रहा येथें तुम्हां भक्षावया धान्य । देऊं हेंही पुण्य आम्हां घडे ॥ ९ ॥
बहिणी म्हणे मग राहिलों देहूस । धरुनी हव्यास तुकोबाचा ॥१०॥

अभंग ४५

देऊळांत कथा सर्व काळ होत । श्रवण करीत दिनरात्रीं ॥ १ ॥
तुकोबाची कथा वेदांतील अर्थ । पावे माझें चित्त समाधान ॥ २ ॥
तुकोबाचें ध्यान पूर्वीं कोल्हापुरीं । जें स्वप्नामाझारीं देखियेलें ॥ ३ ॥
तेंचि ध्यान डोळां प्रत्यक्ष देखोनी । आनंद लोचनीं हेलावत ॥ ४ ॥
रात्रंदिन निद्रा न ये तिळभरी । तुकोबा अंतरीं प्रवेशला ॥ ५ ॥
बहिणी म्हणे येती सुखाचे डोलावे । जाणती अनुभवें जाणते जे ॥ ६ ॥

अभंग ४६

मंबाजी गोसावी भ्रतारासी म्हणे । तुम्ही शिष्य होणें क्रियायुक्त ॥ १ ॥
माझा हेत आहे तुम्हीही हरिभक्त । दिसतां विरक्त उभय वर्गें ॥ २ ॥
ऐकोनी ते गोष्टी दोनचार वेळां । मग त्या प्रांजळ सांगितलें ॥ ३ ॥
आम्ही अनुग्रही आहों जी पूर्वीच । न वाटे त्या सत्य गोष्ट कांहीं ॥ ४ ॥
भ्रतारें त्याप्रती सांगितलें सर्व । कोल्हापुरीं पूर्व वर्तलें जें ॥ ५ ॥
ऐकोनीया द्वेष संचरला मनीं । म्हणे काय स्वप्नीं समाधान ॥ ६ ॥
नाहीं गुरुसेवा घडली जोंवरी । हस्तक हा शिरीं सद्गुरूचा ॥ ७ ॥
तोंवरी तो गुरू कासयाचा खरा । शुद्राचिया अंतरा ज्ञान कैचें ॥ ८ ॥
स्वप्नींचा अनुग्रह गुरू केला शुद्र । तोही बळिभद्र ज्ञानहीन ॥ ९ ॥
तुम्हांस वाळीस ब्राह्मणाचे पंक्ती । तुम्ही गुरुभक्ती नका सांगूं ॥१०॥
बहिणी म्हणे ऐसें मंबाजी बोलिला । द्वेषही मांडीला तेच क्षणीं ॥११॥

अभंग ४७

एके दिवशीं वाटे देखिलें आपण । मंबाजीसी पूर्ण हेतयुक्त ॥ १ ॥
नमस्कार करावया गेलें जंव । येरू हा न शिवे दुरी पळे ॥ २ ॥
म्हणे तुम्ही काय कोण याती नेणें । मी तो शुद्र म्हणे तुम्हांलागीं ॥ ३ ॥
सोनार कीं तुम्ही गोळक यातीचीं । तुम्हां ब्राह्मणाची क्रिया नाहीं ॥ ४ ॥
तुम्ही कोठें जाल भोजनासी जरी । दिवाणांत तरी घालीन मी ॥ ५ ॥
बहिणी म्हणे ऐसें ऐकोनी आपण । भ्रतारासी पूर्ण सांगितलें ॥ ६ ॥

अभंग ४८

महादाजी कुळकर्णी कोंडाजीपंतासी । सांगितली ऐसी गोष्टी तया ॥ १ ॥
मग त्यांहीं नेलें आपुल्या गृहासी । म्हणे कीं तयासी काम काय? ॥ २ ॥
परंतु तो द्वेष चालवी अत्यंत । मारूं पाहे घात चिंतोनिया ॥ ३ ॥
म्हणे हे ब्राह्मण तरी गुरू शुद्र । हेंचि तया छिद्र सांपडलें ॥ ४ ॥
द्वेष ही वाढला अत्यंत अद्भुत । सर्वही लोकांत कळों आलें ॥ ५ ॥
बहिणी म्हणे देव छळी नानापरी । निश्चय निर्धारीं पहातसे ॥ ६ ॥

अभंग ४९

आपाजी गोसावी पुण्यांत रहात । जो अति विख्यात राजयोगी ॥ १ ॥
तयाप्रती पत्र मंबाजी पाठवी । तुकोबा गोसावी शुद्र वाणी ॥ २ ॥
कथा करितसें देऊळीं सर्वदा । द्विज त्याच्या पदा लागताती ॥ ३ ॥
रामेश्वरभट्ट अति योगी थोर । तेही नमस्कार त्यांसी करिती ॥ ४ ॥
आम्हांसीं अन्याय हाची थोर वाटे । होत असें खोटें वेद-वाक्य ॥ ५ ॥
तुम्ही थोर आहां दंड करावया । बांधोनीया तया न्यावें तेथें ॥ ६ ॥
आणिक ही एक स्त्री-पुरुष आहेती । तेही म्हणविती शिष्य त्याचे ॥ ७ ॥
म्हणविती ब्राह्मण आहेती सोनार । कुळकर्णींहीं फार मान्य केलें ॥ ८ ॥
स्वधर्माचा लोप होतसे देखोन । धाडिलें लिहोन म्हणोनीया ॥ ९ ॥
याचा कीं अपमान न करितां जाण । राज्यही बुडोन जाय तरी ॥१०॥
डोंबाळें मांडून स्वधर्म लोपला । पाहिजे रक्षिला स्वामीराजें ॥११॥
बहिणी म्हणे ऐसें पत्र पाठविलें । चोरोनी लिहिलें घरामाजीं ॥१२॥

अभंग ५०

आपाजी गोसावी वाचोनिया पत्र । क्रोधें फार नेत्र भोवंडीत ॥ १ ॥
शुद्र होवोनिया नमस्कार घेत । पाप हें अद्भुत होत असे ॥ २ ॥
सोनाराच्या जाती म्हणविती ब्राह्मण । तयांचें दर्शन घेऊं नये ॥ ३ ॥
शुद्राचा अनुग्रह घेताती ब्राह्मण । भ्रष्टाकार पूर्ण होत असे ॥ ४ ॥
त्यासी शिक्षा द्यावी दोष नाहीं यासी । ऐसा निश्चयेसीं नेम केला ॥ ५ ॥
बहिणी म्हणे याचें प्रत्युत्तर लिहिलें । होय यथाकालें कार्यसिद्धी ॥ ६ ॥

अभंग ५१

मंबाजी गोसावी द्वेष करी जीवें । म्हणे तुम्हीं जावें येथोनिया ॥ १ ॥
तेणें फार चिंता वाटतसे मनीं । विघ्न कां भजनीं ओढवलें ॥ २ ॥
कोणाचें न घेतां न बोलतांही कांहीं । नसोनि अन्यायी द्वेष कांहीं ॥ ३ ॥
देवासी आठवी चिंतोनी मानसीं । साक्ष तूंचि यासी पांडुरंगा ॥ ४ ॥

माझें अंतरींचें जाणतोसी तूंचि । चित्तीं या द्वेषासी थार नाहीं ॥ ५ ॥
विघ्न हें आणिलें त्यासी तूं निवारीं । तुकोबाचें शिरीं आहेस तूं ॥ ६ ॥
भक्ति करी त्यासी पीडीसी अंतरीं । निष्ठा नानापरी लक्षीसी तूं ॥ ७ ॥
बहिणी म्हणे देवा संचितासारिखें । नाना सुखदुःखें प्राप्त होती ॥ ८ ॥

अभंग ५२

कोल्हापुरीं गाय होती जे सांगातें । कांहीं ते दुग्धातें देत होती ॥ १ ॥
गाय ते बांधोनी घातली घरांत । सोटेही मारीत तयेलागीं ॥ २ ॥
पाहों गाय तंव न दिसे पहातां । तुकोबासी व्यथा तेचि झाली ॥ ३ ॥
पाहातोसी काय होत असे कष्टी । तीन रात्री खुंटीं बांधलीसे ॥ ४ ॥
नाहीं तृण पाणी मारिलेंसें फार । धांवण्यासी थार नाहीं दिसे ॥ ५ ॥
तुकोबा जागृत झाले तंव पाठ । सुजेली ती नीट होयेची ना ॥ ६ ॥
सोटे अंगावरी दिसती तुकोबा । आठवी विठोबा नानापरी ॥ ७ ॥
देखोनि तयासी कष्ट होती जनां । सांगितलें स्वप्नांतील सर्व ॥ ८ ॥
तुकोबा अंतरीं आठवुनी देवा । धांव रे माधवा सोड म्हणे ॥ ९ ॥
कोणें गाय कोठें बांधिली कळेना । धांव नारायणा गाय रक्षीं ॥१०॥
तंव अकस्मात तयाचिये गृहीं । अग्नि लागे तोहि महाथोर ॥११॥
धांवोनिया लोक विझविती अग्नि । गाय ते निमग्न बैसलीसे ॥१२॥
जे गाय पहाती आजी तीन दिवस । चांडाळें तियेस बांधिलेंसें ॥१३॥
गाय सोडोनिया आणिली बाहेरी । तंव पाठीवरी मारिलेंसें ॥१४॥
भ्रतार आपुला बोलावोनी पाहे । गाय सांभाळीं हें ब्राह्मणा तूं ॥१५॥
तुकोबा धांवोनी करी प्रदक्षिणा । नमस्कारी गुणा धन्य तुझे ॥१६॥
दाखविलें स्वप्न मज माय तुवां । न कळेचि धांवा केला माझा ॥१७॥
तुझा माझा एक आत्मा सर्वांगत । ते साक्ष निश्चित आली मज ॥१८॥
ऐसा तुकोबानें केला फार धांवा । तंव माझ्या जीवा दुःख झालें ॥१९॥

मजही तैसेची क्लेश झाले फार । साक्ष हें अंतर विठ्ठलाचें ॥२०॥
तुकोबाचे पाठीं पहाताती जन । गायही देखोन थोर कष्टी ॥२१॥
बहिणी म्हणे ऐसे वर्तलें हें जाण । गायीचें निर्वाण हरी जाणे ॥२२॥

अभंग ५३

रामेश्वरभट्टें ऐकिला वृत्तांत । धांवोनि त्वरीत तेथ आला ॥ १ ॥
तुकोबाचें तींहीं घेतलें दर्शन । गाय तेहि पूर्ण पाहियेली ॥ २ ॥
दोहीचें पाठीचा दिसे एक भाव । रुदनीं ते सर्व प्रवर्तले ॥ ३ ॥
तुकोबाचा पार वर्णीलसा कोण । कलियुगीं जाण प्रल्हाद हा ॥ ४ ॥
सर्वांतर साक्षी करोनिया स्तुती । स्वसुखें रमती आपुलिया ॥ ५ ॥
बहिणी म्हणे लोक बोलती सकळ । तुकोबा केवळ पांडुरंग ॥ ६ ॥

अभंग ५४

महादाजी कुळकर्णी तयाचिये घरीं । असोनि निर्धारीं काळ क्रमूं ॥ १ ॥
येताती हेलावे दुःखाचे अनेक । लक्ष्मीनायक जाणतसे ॥ २ ॥
घालोनी संकटीं देवावरी भार । असों निर्विकार एकनिष्ठ ॥ ३ ॥
तंव तये काळीं झाली ये[1] प्रसूत । कन्या झाली तेथ आपणांसी ॥ ४ ॥
काशीबाई तिचें ठेवियेलें नांव । दाखविला भाव पूर्ण कांहीं ॥ ५ ॥
बहिणी म्हणे वत्स मेलें कोल्हापुरीं । तेंचि आलें उदरीं ऐसें वाटे ॥ ६ ॥

अभंग ५५

देवगांव माझें माहेर साजणी । शाखा वाजेसनी मौनस गोत्र ॥ १ ॥
तयाचिये कुळीं घेतलें शरीर । स्त्रीरूपें व्यवहार दावावया ॥ २ ॥
जयाचिये कुळीं गुरुपरंपरा । नाहींच सादरा श्रवण कांहीं ॥ ३ ॥
बहिणी म्हणे जन्म अंतरींचा नेम । हें तो जाणे वर्म नारायण ॥ ४ ॥

अभंग ५६

लोकांचीया मुली खेळती बोळकीं । वाटे घ्यावें मुखीं मज नाम ॥ १ ॥
आणिक नावडे खेळ ते बालिश । नेणें तो विश्वास प्रगटला ॥ २ ॥

---

१ ही

नावडे फुगडी टिपरीयाचा खेळ । असावें निश्चळ वाटे मना ॥३॥
बहिणी म्हणे पूर्वी होतें जें पदरीं । तेंची या संसारीं प्रगटलें ॥४॥

अभंग ५७

मातापितयानें लग्न संपादिलें । कन्यादान केलें गौतमगोत्रीं ॥१॥
झाला चार दीस लग्नाचा सोहळा । न कळे देवाचा हेत आनु ॥२॥
मायबापें माझीं दरिद्री पिडीलीं । उपद्व्यापें जालीं कासावीस ॥३॥
देशत्याग झाला मिरासीच्या भयें । तव गंगा जाय दोही थड्या ॥४॥
सांगातें घेतलें माझिया स्वामीस । आले परदेशास महादेवीं ॥५॥
मायबाप बंधु भ्रतारासहित । बहिणी म्हणे तेथ स्थिर जाले ॥६॥

अभंग ५८

चालले पंढरीं महादेवाहूनी । संतांचे दरुषणीं सुख वाटे ॥१॥
संतसमागम जिवाहुनी गोड । परि भय दृढ भ्रताराचें ॥२॥
जमदग्नीचा क्रोध ऐकियला कानीं । भ्रतार तो जनीं तेची रूप ॥३॥
बहिणी म्हणे झालें वरुषें एकादश । क्षणही जिवास सुख नाहीं ॥४॥

अभंग ५९

वैदिक व्यवहार स्वामी[१] उदरार्थ । करितसे तेथ देव कैंचा ॥१॥
वेद पाठ कांहीं नावडेची भक्ती । पराधीन युक्ती न चले माझी ॥२॥
वय तो लहान लौकीक तो वेडा । वेदाचिया भिडा उभी राहे ॥३॥
बहिणी म्हणे माझें चित्त कासावीस । संसाराचा त्रास बहु झाला ॥४॥

अभंग ६०

स्त्रियेचें शरीर पराधीन देह । न चाले उपाव विरक्तीचा ॥१॥
पडिलें अंतर विवेकाचें बळें । काय निर्मियेलें राघोबानें ॥२॥
तापलें शरीर त्रिविध तापानें । वाटतसे मनें प्राण द्यावा ॥३॥
न घडे हरीची भक्ति अणुमात्र । शत्रु इष्टमित्र संसाराचे ॥४॥

---

१ पति; नवरा

शरीराचे भोग वाटताती वैरी । माझी कोण करी चिंता आतां ॥५॥
बहिणी म्हणे जैसा वोकियला वोक । तैसे हे मायीक वाटे मना ॥६॥

अभंग ६१

हरण सांपडें जैसें वाघुरेंत । अंध अरण्यांत पडे जैसा ॥१॥
तैसें मज झालें पुसूं कोणा हित । होय माझें चित्त कासाविस ॥२॥
जलावीण मत्स्य गाईविण वत्स । मृगीवीण पाडस जयापरी ॥३॥
बहिणी म्हणे देवा ऐसीया संकटीं । करीं कृपादृष्टी दीनावरी ॥४॥

अभंग ६२

विरक्तीचें मूळ प्रपंचाचा त्याग । पहातांची एक ग्रहशैल ॥१॥
संकट मांडिलें धांव तूं झडकरीं । विवेक-उत्तरीं बोधीं चित्त ॥२॥
भ्रतार त्यागितां वेदासी विरुद्ध । परमार्थ तो शुद्ध सांपडेना ॥३॥
द्वाराशीं भुजंग प्रहजळे अंगीं । जीव त्या प्रसंगीं केवीं राहे ॥४॥
वेदाचें वचन त्यागूं नये धर्म । माझें तंव प्रेम हरिभक्ती ॥५॥
बहिणी म्हणे ऐसीं संकटें दाटती । क्लेश ते वाढती काय सांगू ॥६॥

अभंग ६३

वेद हांका देती पुराणें गर्जती । स्त्रियेच्या संगतीं हित नोहे ॥१॥
मी तों सहज स्त्रीयेचाची देह । परमार्थाची सोय आतां कैंची ॥२॥
मूर्खत्व ममता मोहन मायिक ! संगची घातक स्त्रियेचा तो ॥३॥
बहिणी म्हणे ऐसा स्त्रीदेह घातकी । परमार्थ या लोकीं केवीं साधे ॥४॥

अभंग ६४

काय पाप केलें पूर्वील ये जन्मीं । आतां पुरुषोत्तमीं अंतरलें ॥१॥
लाधलें नरदेह स्त्रियेचेनी रूपें । असंख्यात पापें फळा आलीं ॥२॥
अधिकार नाहीं वेदार्थश्रवणीं । गायत्री ब्राह्मणीं गुप्त केली ॥३॥
करूं नये मुखें प्रणवाचा उच्चार । बीजाचा संचार ऐकों नये ॥४॥
बोलों नये बोल पराचिया संगें । भ्रतार तो अंगें जमदग्नी ॥५॥
बहिणी म्हणे होतो जीव कासावीस । नये देवाजीस करुणा माझी ॥६॥

अभंग ६५

नामाचा विटाळ आमुचिये घरीं । गीताशास्त्र वैरी कुळीं आम्हां ॥ १ ॥
देव तीर्थ यात्रा नावडती हरी । ऐसीयांचे घरीं संग दिला ॥ २ ॥
संतसमागम राघवाची भक्ति । नावडती श्रुती शास्त्र कथा ॥ ३ ॥
बहिणी म्हणे माझ्या पापाचा संग्रहो । तुटोनीया राहो चित्त स्थिर ॥ ४ ॥

अभंग ६६

अनुतापें तापलें बहुत मानसी । नये देवाजीसी करुणा कैसी ॥ १ ॥
वाटे देह आतां घालूं अग्नी-आंत । किंवा ही करवत घालूं माथा ॥ २ ॥
वाटे जीव द्यावा नदीचे प्रवाहीं । किंवा दिशा दाही उल्लंघाव्या ॥ ३ ॥
वाटे अरण्यांत घेऊनी धरणें । बैसावें; पारणें करूं नये ॥ ४ ॥
बहिणी म्हणे माझा जीव हा तळमळी । कारे वनमाळी मोकलीसी ॥ ५ ॥

अभंग ६७

गांजविसी देह भ्रताराचे हातें । माझिया तों चित्तें नेम केला ॥ १ ॥
न सोडी भजन प्राणही गेलीया । आतां देवराया दीनबंधु ॥ २ ॥
पहातोसी काय आतां माझा अंत । होतसे देहांत पती-हातें ॥ ३ ॥
करूं काय मज मांडलें सांकडें । नाहीं देहाकडे हेत माझा ॥ ४ ॥
पडो देह परी राहतसे हेत । पहावा अनंत ज्ञानदृष्टीं ॥ ५ ॥
करावी हे भक्ति स्वधर्म-आचारें । तुज ज्ञानद्वारें ओळखावें ॥ ६ ॥
राहिल हें काय शरीर पिडेनें । का रे हें वचन नायकसी ॥ ७ ॥
हेत राहे तया जन्म घडे पुन्हा । वेदाच्या वचना आयकिलें ॥ ८ ॥
आतां या संकटीं तुझें शिरीं हत्त्या । राखावी अपत्त्या आपुलीया ॥ ९ ॥
बहिणी म्हणे हरी बहिरा आंधळा । का रे विश्वपाळा झालासी तूं ॥१०॥

अभंग ६८

सखा सहोदर तूंची एक हरी । दीनांचा कैवारी पांडुरंग ॥ १ ॥
तुझी भक्ती घडे पतिव्रताधर्म । ऐसें मेघश्याम विचारावें ॥ २ ॥

वेदासी विरुद्ध नव्हे तो परमार्थ । म्हणोनी हा अर्थ विचारावे ॥३॥
बहिणी म्हणे दोन्ही घडतील हरी । हेत हा झडकरीं विचारावा ॥४॥

अभंग ६९

मातापिता बंधु प्रपंचाचे सखे । होती महा दुःखें माझ्या संगें ॥१॥
देवासी सांगता जाणसी अंतर । सांगावया थार नाहीं मज ॥२॥
सांगती न कोणी स्वहितविचार । नाहीं तो शेजार सज्जनाचा ॥३॥
एकली एकट पडियेलें वनीं । क्षुधा तृषा मनीं आठवेना ॥४॥
बोलावें न ऐसें वाटे कोणासवें । विचार केशवें करावा हा ॥५॥
बहिणी म्हणे नाम तुझें जाणें एक । कोणासी आणिक सांगूं हरी ॥६॥

अभंग ७०

सोसियले क्लेश जिवें बहू फार । जाली हे अपार दीन सख्या ॥१॥
चित्तीं समाधान केलें असें एक । प्रारब्धें हें दुःख आलें भागा ॥२॥
भोगणें न चुके ब्रह्मादिकां दुःख । इतर हे रंक कोण तेथें ॥३॥
बहिणी म्हणे माझ्या देहाचें प्रारब्ध । ऐसिया गोविंद काय करी ॥४॥

अभंग ७१

देहाचिया माथां सुखदुःख आलें । पाहिजे भोगिलें आवश्यक ॥१॥
परिहार माझा होतसे पापाचा । लाभ हाचि साचा मानियला ॥२॥
अंतरींचा हेत नामसंकीर्तनीं । शरीर पीडेनें पीडियलें ॥३॥
बहिणी म्हणे माझ्या संचितीं जें आहे । तंव पीडा काय कवणावरी ॥४॥

अभंग ७२

प्रारब्धाची गती न संडी सर्वथा । व्यर्थ आतां चिंता कोण वाहे ॥१॥
निश्चय निर्धारीं धरियला मनीं । आतां चक्रपाणी पांडुरंग ॥२॥
शरीराचे क्लेश निवारे न कोणा । अगा नारायणा कळों आलें ॥३॥
बहिणी म्हणे आतां केशवा शरण । नको माझें मन पाहूं हरि ॥४॥

अभंग ७३

तुटलें संचीत जालें शुद्ध चित्त । अंतरींचा हेत ओळखिला ॥१॥
कृपा केली देवें इंद्रायणीतीरीं । देहुग्रामीं थोर भक्तिपंथ ॥२॥
तेथें पांडुरंग देवाचें देऊळ । रहावया स्थळ प्राप्त झालें ॥३॥
तुकाराम संत संताचें कीर्तन । तिन्ही काळ तीन दृष्टीपुढें ॥४॥
नमस्कार तया न घडे पतिभयें । परि चित्त राहे सदा पायीं ॥५॥
बहिणी म्हणे ऐसे मास झाले सात । अवघेंची संचित सरों आलें ॥६॥

अभंग ७४

आनंदवोवरी होती तये ठायीं । वाटे तेथें कांहीं बसावेंसें ॥१॥
करूनिया ध्यान लावावे लोचन । करावें स्मरण विठोबाचें ॥२॥
तुकारामा तंव देखतां देखत । आलें अकस्मात मृत्युरूप ॥३॥
बहिणी म्हणे तेथ पुसोन मातेसी । क्रमियल्या निशी तीन तेथें ॥४॥

अभंग ७५

नेणें जप तप नेणें अनुष्ठान । घालावें आसन कळेना तें ॥१॥
ध्यानाचें लक्षण इंद्रियाचा रोध । नाहीं याचा बोध ऐकियला ॥२॥
पाषाणप्रतिमा विठोबाचें ध्यान । हृदयीं चिंतन राममुद्रा ॥३॥
तुकारामकथा करावी ती द्वारीं । ऐसा हा अंतरीं हेत होता ॥४॥
टाळ्या चिपोळ्यांचा ध्वनी आयकतां । आनंद हा चित्ता समावेना ॥५॥
लावियले नेत्र निद्रेंत जागृती । तुकाराममूर्ति देखियली ॥६॥
ठेवियला हस्त मस्तकीं बोलून । दिधलें वरदान कवित्वाचें ॥७॥
बहिणी म्हणे नेणें स्वप्न कीं जागृती । इंद्रियांच्या वृत्ती वोसरल्या ॥८॥

अभंग ७६

आनंदें सद्गद जाहलीं इंद्रियें । तुकाराम पाय आठवले ॥१॥
होऊनी सावध उघडिले नेत्र । आठवला मंत्र षडक्षरी ॥२॥
ठसावला ध्यानीं मनाचिये ठायीं । आणिक तें कांहीं आठवेना ॥३॥
बहिणी म्हणे हात घातला मस्तकीं । देह तो या लोकीं आढळेना ॥४॥

अभंग ७७

तें सुख सांगतां वाचे पडे मौन । जाणतां तें धन्य गुरुभक्त ॥१॥
झालासे आनंद इंद्रियाचे द्वारीं । बैसलें शेजारीं चैतन्याचे ॥२॥
घट हा बुडावा जैसा डोहा-आंत । न फुटतां ओतप्रोत पाणी ॥३॥
बहिणी म्हणे तैसें झालें माझे मना । तुकाराम खुणा ओळखी त्या ॥४॥

अभंग ७८

वाटे उठों नये जीव जाय तरी । सुख तें अंतरीं हेलावलें ॥१॥
आनंदें निर्भर होऊनिया मन । करूं आलें स्नान इंद्रायणी ॥२॥
घेतलें दर्शन पांडुरंगमूर्ती । तंव झाली स्फूर्ति वदावया ॥३॥
तुकोबासी तेथें करूनि नमस्कार । आलें मी सत्वर बिन्हाडासी ॥४॥
बहिणी म्हणे जैसा लोटला समुद्र । हृदयकाशीं इंद्र बोले वाचा ॥५॥

३. निर्याणपर

अभंग ७९

रुक्मीणीची आम्हीं केली बोळवण । आम्हांसी प्रयाण त्याच मागें ॥१॥
पाठवावें पत्र गोदेसी सत्वर । पडेल अंतर पुत्रपणा ॥२॥
टाकोनी सकळ काम धाम धंदा । मरण सर्वदा वाट पाहे ॥३॥
म्हणोनीया पत्र लिहित तांतडी । मरणाची गुढी उभी पुढें ॥४॥
तेराविया दीशीं ब्राह्मणभोजन । निघणें करोन अति त्वरें ॥५॥
पडेल आक्षेप वाटेसी खोळंबा । टाकोनी विठोबा[१] त्वरें येईं ॥६॥
पांच दिवस पुढें देहांतसमये । रोधोनिया पाहे वाट वायू ॥७॥
आश्विनाची शुद्ध जाणावी प्रतिपदा । मरणमर्यादा सांगितली ॥८॥
बहिणी म्हणे पुत्रपणाचें उत्तीर्ण । होसील म्हणोन त्वरा करीं ॥९॥

अभंग ८०

बैसलों[२] समस्त शुक्लेश्वरापासीं । देखीलें पत्रासी अकस्मात ॥१॥
वाचिलें सत्वर निघालों तांतडी । केली घडामोडी मनामाजीं ॥२॥
आणावी जाऊन गोदातीरा माय । ऐसा ये उपाय करूं आतां ॥३॥
पाहोनिया स्थळ समाधीकारण । आलों मी धांवून दर्शनासी ॥४॥

अभंग ८१

ऐकोनिया पत्र आलासी तांतडी । घालोनिया उडी पुत्रराया ॥१॥
तेरावा दिवस केला रुक्मिणीचा । सद्गदित वाचा कंठ दाटे ॥२॥
झालासी उत्तीर्ण तूंचि गा सर्वांचा । मनें काया वाचा सर्वभावें ॥३॥
देखोनिया तुज संतोष वाटला । प्रेमें दाटियला कंठ माझा ॥४॥
मृत्यूचा संकल्प आश्विन शुद्ध प्रतिपदा । ऐक बा प्रसिद्ध सांगितला ॥५॥
खेद तो अंतरीं न धरावा कदा । सांगतां मर्यादा नुलंघावी ॥६॥
पुत्रपण तुझें आलें आजी फळा । माझे अंतकाळा पावलासी ॥७॥

---

१ विठोबा हें बाईच्या मुलाचें नांव असावें असें वाटतें.
२ हे अभंग बहुतेक बहिणाबाईच्या मुलाचे असावेत असें वाटतें.

*अभंग ८२

अंतरींची साक्ष जाणीजे अंतरीं । माय तूं निर्धारी सद्‌गुरुही ॥ १ ॥
देखियेलें स्वप्न कचेश्वरीं माये । विमान हें पाहे तुज आलें ॥ २ ॥
शंख भेरी नाना वाजताती वाद्यें । गर्जती आनंदें नामघोषें ॥ ३ ॥
शंख चक्र गदा अंकित वैडूर्य । करिती उत्सव नाना परी ॥ ४ ॥
मृदंग वाजती टाळघोळ कथा । पताका अनंता गरुडटके ॥ ५ ॥
ब्राह्मणाचा थाट पुढें मागें लोक । माळा गळां देख तुळसीच्या ॥ ६ ॥
मिरवती विमान देखीयेलें स्वप्नीं । आनंद हा मनीं थोर वाटे ॥ ७ ॥
उदबत्ती बुका गंधाक्षता होती । ब्राह्मणाच्या पंक्ती नाना परी ॥ ८ ॥
देखियले जन्म उत्सव या मना । थोर झाला स्वप्नामाजीं पाहे ॥ ९ ॥
उठुनी प्रात:काळीं आली मना साक्ष । स्वप्न हें प्रत्यक्ष नव्हे मिथ्या ॥१०॥
बैसलों समस्त कचेश्वरापासीं । देखिलें पत्रासी अकस्मात ॥११॥
वांचोनी सत्वर निघालों तांतडी । केली घडामोडी मनामाजीं ॥१२॥
आणावी जाऊनी गोदातीरा माय । ऐसाची उपाय करूं आतां ॥१३॥
वंदुनी चरण उभा असें पुढें । मनांतील कोडें जाणसी तूं ॥१४॥
शुक्लेश्वरापाशीं मागितलें स्थळ । आज्ञा ते केवळ तुझी आतां ॥१५॥

अभंग ८३

ऐकियलें तुझें वचन सादर । तुवां जो निर्धार केला असे ॥ १ ॥
मानलें माझिया स्थळ जाण चित्ता । परि ऐक पां आतां एक माझें ॥ २ ॥
नाहीं गा अवकाश तें स्थळीं जावया। मृत्यूच्या समया लागों पाहे ॥ ३ ॥
प्रतिपदीं आम्हां टाकणें शरीर । आजि तों साचार त्रयोदशी ॥ ४ ॥
यालागीं निश्चय सांगतसें एक । तीर्थ आम्हां देख प्रणित असे ॥ ५ ॥
रावणेंही एथें केलें अनुष्ठान । शंकर प्रसन्न येथें झाला ॥ ६ ॥
वाहियेलीं शिरें नवही पुजेसी । सहस्र अठ्यायसी ऋषी आले ॥ ७ ॥
ब्रह्मादिक देव यज्ञाच्या सन्निध । तीर्थ हें प्रसिद्ध शिवपूर ॥ ८ ॥

* हा अभंग बहुतेक बहिणाबाईचा मुलाचा असावा असें वाटतें.

अवभृथस्नानीं वरद तयांचा । समूह तीर्थांचा असे येथें ॥ ९ ॥
प्रणिता तीर्थाऐसें तीर्थ भूमंडळीं । नाहीं चंद्रमौळी बोलिलासे ॥१०॥
काशी, गया तीर्थ सर्व याचि स्थळीं। मानोनी सकळीं स्नान कीजे ॥११॥
आमुचें मनींचा निर्धार हा खरा । माझिया अंतरा साक्ष आली ॥१२॥
तुवां हें वचन वंदूनी मस्तकीं । असावें स्वस्थ कीं होवोनिया ॥१३॥
बहिणी म्हणे पुत्रा सांगितलें मनीं । धरोनी वचनीं सिद्ध राहे ॥१४॥

अभंग ८४

तीर्थ देव यात्रा वर्ततां स्वधर्म । तुझे माझे जन्म गेले बारा ॥ १ ॥
तेरावा हा जन्म पुत्रपणें झाला । नाहीं तुझी तुला आठवण ॥ २ ॥
तेरा जन्म तुझा माझा असे संग । अद्वय अभंग एकनिष्ठ ॥ ३ ॥
पतिव्रता धर्म आमुचा सांगाती । बोलतां ते गति ग्रंथ वाढे ॥ ४ ॥
ज्ञानेश्वरी पूर्ण पहावी हे झाली । आतां ते उरली दशा थोडी ॥ ५ ॥
संभवतां तुज मज जाली कृपा । वोळखी ते बापा सांगितली ॥ ६ ॥
बहिणी म्हणे आतां नाहीं जन्म घेणें । उठलें धरणें वासनेचें ॥ ७ ॥

अभंग ८५

गोदा भागीरथी यमुना सरस्वती । तापी भोगावती सर्व तीर्थें ॥ १ ॥
येती प्रणितेसी माझे अंतःकाळीं । अंतरीं निश्चळ राहे पुत्रा ॥ २ ॥
कृष्णा, तुंगभद्रा, भीमा, फल्गु रेवा । पुष्करें हीं सर्वा पृथिवीची ॥ ३ ॥
देव तेही सर्व येती तये वेळीं । मृत्यु अनुभवेल तुज तेव्हां ॥ ४ ॥
ऋषिगण सर्व पांडुरंग उभा । जेव्हां मृत्युसभा येईल तें ॥ ५ ॥
बहिणी म्हणे तुज वाटेल असत्य । सांगेन तें तथ्य ऐक आतां ॥ ६ ॥

अभंग ८६

आत्मज्ञाना ऐसें कोण तीर्थ दुजें । ज्ञानिया उमजे पूर्व पुण्यें ॥ १ ॥
जेथें हें मानस केलें असें शुद्ध । तीर्थ हें प्रसिद्ध वेदशास्त्रीं ॥ २ ॥
तयाच्या मज्जनें जन्म गेले बारा । शुद्ध तें अंतरा करावया ॥ ३ ॥

तेरावा हा जन्म लाधलें साधनें । तया तीर्थीं स्नानें जन्म नाहीं ॥ ४ ॥
केले वो प्रयास साधनाचे कष्ट । होतें योगभ्रष्ट म्हणोनिया ॥ ५ ॥
वासना मलिन शुद्ध जाली येथें । ज्ञानियासी तीर्थ तेंची सत्य ॥ ६ ॥
वृत्ति शुन्य होय मानस तें ज्ञानी । तीर्थ सर्वांहूनी श्रेष्ठ तेंची ॥ ७ ॥
विचारोनी बरें पाहे तूं अंतरीं । बाह्य तीर्थांतरीं हेत नाहीं ॥ ८ ॥
बहिणी म्हणे वृत्ति जालीया निमग्ना । तीर्थाची ते संज्ञा तेची खरी ॥ ९ ॥

अभंग ८७

अंतकाळ वेळ होईल निरभ्र । दिशा होती शुभ्र पाहे बाळा ॥ १ ॥
घेईं याची साक्ष आपुले अंतरीं । राहोनी निर्धारीं आपुलीया ॥ २ ॥
देव निघालेती तीर्थासी विमान । हेलावे ते जाण तीन येती ॥ ३ ॥
दग्ध जालियानें अस्तंगत देह । पुत्रा तूंची पाहे मनामाजीं ॥ ४ ॥
बहिणी म्हणे तुम्ही धरोनी विश्वास । पहा साक्ष यास तुकाराम ॥ ५ ॥

*अभंग ८८

ऐक ऐक माते संदेह मानसीं । वाटला तयासी कोण फेडी ॥ १ ॥
गणगोत आम्हां मायही सद्गुरू । मनींचा निर्धारू जाणसी तूं ॥ २ ॥
बारा जन्म मागें साधलीया ज्ञान । आतां माझें मन स्थिरावलें ॥ ३ ॥
याचें मज कांहीं नकळेचि सर्वथा । आशंका हे आतां फेडीं माझी ॥ ४ ॥
जाणसी अंतर मानसींचा हेत । असेंचि या चित्त साक्ष तुझें ॥ ५ ॥
पूर्वानुक्रमेंशीं जन्म ते सांगिजे । माते कृपा कीजे एक वेळां ॥ ६ ॥

अभंग ८९

ऐक सावधान पुत्रा तूं वचन । बोलों नये मौन सांगतसें ॥ १ ॥
न बोलावें कोणा न सांगावें गुज । साक्ष माझी मज़ जाण आली ॥ २ ॥
न सांगतां तुज खेद हो वाटेल । हेतही तुटेल अंतरींचा ॥ ३ ॥
बहिणी म्हणे कदा न सांगावें जनां । ऐकोनिया मना हेत फेडीं ॥ ४ ॥

---

* हा अभंग विठोबाकृत आहे.

अभंग ९०

बेटाऊद तापी-तीरीं एक वैश्य । सांभवाचा दास केदार होता ॥ १ ॥
त्यासी नसे पुत्र कन्येचें संतान । केलें अनुष्ठान महाउग्र ॥ २ ॥
शंकरा प्रसन्न करोनिया तेणें । स्वप्नगत येणें जालें हरा ॥ ३ ॥
पुत्र नाहीं तुज होईल संतान । एक कन्या जाण रूपवंती ॥ ४ ॥
वारुणी हें नाम ठेवावें तियेसी । वांचेल सायासीं वर्षें तेरा ॥ ५ ॥
केदार वैश्यस्त्री रुपवंती नाम । स्त्रिया ती उत्तम पतिव्रता ॥ ६ ॥
पतीचें वचन तियेसी प्रमाण । शांभवी तें जाण दीक्षा तीची ॥ ७ ॥
रूपवंती गर्भ धरी तिये वेळां । जन्म मज दिला महारुद्रें ॥ ८ ॥
पूर्वील संस्कार होता कांहीं शुद्ध । जन्मतां प्रसिद्ध कळों आला ॥ ९ ॥
जन्मलिया मज वर्षांचिया पोटीं । पहातांची दृष्टीं वदन माझें ॥१०॥
आणिला सद्गुरु केदारें आपुला । तयातें दाविला भाव माझा ॥११॥
नाहीं लग्न करूं दिधलें आपण । माझा सहज गुण ओळखिला ॥१२॥
दिधली ते दीक्षा शंकराचा मंत्र । जपे अहोरात्र खेळतांही ॥१३॥
खेळतां देउळीं शंकराची मूर्ती । करितसे भक्ति प्रेमरसें ॥१४॥
नावडेची कांहीं आणिक सर्वथा । चित्ता अखंडता लागलीसे ॥१५॥
ऐसीं तेरा वर्षें होतांची संपूर्ण । जालें तें दर्शन तुझें तेथें ॥१६॥
सद्गुरु आमुचा तेथें तूं सेवक । जैसे एक रंक पोटासाठीं ॥१७॥
माझे मुखें पुत्र घेतलें रे तुज । अंत देख मज जाला तेव्हां ॥१८॥
त्यापुढें दुसरा जन्म म्यां घेतला । ऐक बा वहिला एक चित्तें ॥१९॥
बहिणी म्हणे पहिल्या जन्माचें हें मूळ । आणिक केवळ सांगतसें ॥२०॥

अभंग ९१

आणिक सांगेन पूर्वील वृत्तांत । सावधान चित्त असो तुझें ॥ १ ॥
एक जन्म तुज सांगितला आतां । पुढिली व्यवस्था सांगेन तें ॥ २ ॥
'कूर्म-चक्र-ग्राम' फल्गुचिये तिरीं । सात्विकाचे घरीं जन्म आम्हां ॥ ३ ॥
स्वधर्मी तो वैश्य शंकराचा भक्त । अत्यंत विरक्त आत्मवेत्ता ॥ ४ ॥

तयाचा सद्‌गुरु सुवर्मा ब्राह्मण । आगमीचें पूर्ण ज्ञान तया ॥ ५ ॥
मंत्रविद्येमाजीं असोनि प्रविण । आत्मज्ञानीं पूर्ण हेत तया ॥ ६ ॥
तयाचा तूं शिष्य सात्विकसा भोळा । पुत्र ते तयाला सात होते ॥ ७ ॥
कन्येसाठीं थोर उद्विग्न मानसीं । सद्‌गुरुनें तयासी सांगितलें ॥ ८ ॥
अनुष्ठान विधि मंत्र उपासना । सांगेन ते धारणा वैष्णवीची ॥ ९ ॥
ते वेळीं स्वप्न होवोनी तात्काळ । कन्या ते सुशील सदैव घेईं ॥१०॥
तिचे हातें तुज सांपडेल धन । न करोनी लग्न जाईल ते ॥११॥
अठ्ठावीस वर्षे क्रमील तुजपाशीं । आगर भक्तीसी करोनिया ॥१२॥
मग तेथें जन्म घेतला आपण । तुझा संग जाण तेथें होतां ॥१३॥
गुरुबंधु मज तेथें जोडळासी । सहवासें अससी निरंतर ॥१४॥
बहिणी म्हणे ऐसा जन्म हा दुसरा । आणिक तिसरा पुढें सांगें ॥१५॥

अभंग ९२

सांगेन ते ऐक जन्मांतर कथा । जेणें तुज चित्ता सुख वाटे ॥ १ ॥
गोदावरी जेथें प्रगट ब्रह्मगिरि । वैश्य तो अवधारीं तेथें होता ॥ २ ॥
नाम हें तयाचें वर्धमान शेटी । धनवंत कोटी दान पुरुष ॥ ३ ॥
तयाची हे भाजा भामिनी सुंदरा । पतिव्रता खरा धर्म तिचा ॥ ४ ॥
तीन पुत्र तिशीं चौथा तूं पालक । होउनी बालक असती तेथें ॥ ५ ॥
धन धान्य द्रव्य गायींची गोठणें । नसें कांहीं उणें घरीं तया ॥ ६ ॥
वर्धमान शेटी सर्वांमाजीं श्रेष्ठ । जाला स्थानभ्रष्ट एक वेळां ॥ ७ ॥
येवोनी पंचाळीं करी अनुष्ठान । यज्ञ तो संपूर्ण वाड केला ॥ ८ ॥
तयाचा हा हेत कन्या व्हावी मज । भामिनी सहज रूपवंती ॥ ९ ॥
तियेचिया पोटीं जालें मी निर्माण । माझें नाम जाण हेमकला ॥१०॥
तयासी संतोष देखोन वाढला । दान धर्म केला यथाक्रमें ॥११॥
ल विवंचना करी वर्धमान । तंव जालें स्वप्न भामिनीसी ॥१२॥
करू नको लग्न इये कन्यकेचें । रूप विरक्तीचें हेमवंती ॥१३॥

राग कला नाम ब्राह्मणाची सेवा । आठवी केशवा सर्व काळ ॥१४॥
तेथेंही संगती जाली तुझी मज । अंतरींचें गूज तुज सांगे ॥१५॥
वर्ष तें चोवीस आयुष्यमर्यादा । सारोनी स्वानंदा देह गेला ॥१६॥
ऐसे तीन जन्म वैशाचिये याती । घेवोनी विरक्ति वर्तियले ॥१७॥
बहिणी म्हणे आतां चौथा जन्म ऐक । करोनी विवेक सुखें राहे ॥१८॥

अभंग ९३

चौथा जन्म सांगेन पांचवा सहावा । आणिक सातवा योगभ्रष्ट ॥ १ ॥
गौळियांचें घरीं कन्याची होऊनी । गाई संरक्षणीं वर्ततसें ॥ २ ॥
नाम संकीर्तनीं काळाची क्रमणा । संगतीं ते जाणा वैष्णवाची ॥ ३ ॥
आवडती देव तीर्थ क्षेत्र यात्रा । ब्राह्मणां सर्वत्रां पूजीतसे ॥ ४ ॥
गायीचें रक्षण अरण्यांत वास । जाला सहवास संन्याशाचा ॥ ५ ॥
देखोनी तयासी करी नमस्कार । जाणोनी संस्कार कृपा केली ॥ ६ ॥
सातवे जन्मींचा सांगेन वृत्तांत । मागिलाचा प्रांत सांडियेला ॥ ७ ॥
गौळियांचें घरीं गायींचें रक्षण । करोनी कीर्तन देह पोषी ॥ ८ ॥
मग भेटलें ते सिद्ध आत्मज्ञानी । तिहीं वोळखोनी नेलें मज ॥ ९ ॥
म्हणती योगभ्रष्ट आहे ही विरक्त । दासत्वें सारीत बहुकाळ ॥१०॥
विरक्तीचें अंग ज्ञानाचा अभ्यास । करि रात्रंदिस एकनिष्ट ॥११॥
सासष्ट वरुषें सातविये जन्मीं । क्रमोनीया धर्मीं प्रवर्तलें ॥१२॥
अभ्यास करोनी टाकिलें शरीर । तुज हा प्रकार सांगितला ॥१३॥
बहिणी म्हणे जन्म पुढें उरले साही । प्रसंगेंची तेही सांगतसें ॥१४॥

अभंग ९४

सांगेन तो जन्म आठवा रे ऐक । धरोनी विवेक निश्चयाचा ॥ १ ॥
वेरुळ तें तीर्थ शिवालय क्षेत्र । शास्त्रज्ञ समर्थ ब्रह्मवेत्तां ॥ २ ॥
तयाचें तें नाम धर्मदत्त क्षेत्रीं । पूज्य तो सर्वत्रीं जनांमाजीं ॥ ३ ॥
तयाची सुंदरा पतिव्रता भली । कीर्ति फार केली पातिव्रत्यें ॥ ४ ॥

तयांचिये पोटीं जाला मज जन्म । कन्येचा उत्तम शांतिरूप ॥ ५ ॥
अठरा वर्षें क्रमिलीं आपण । करुनी श्रवण भागवत ॥ ६ ॥
लग्न केलें परी भ्रतार नासला । हितावह झाला तोही मज ॥ ७ ॥
नववे ये जन्मीं तेथेंची जन्मलें । नव वरुषें केलें स्थान तेंची ॥ ८ ॥
तेंचि मातापिता तेचि बंधुवर्ग । अनुष्ठान सांग तेंचि आम्हां ॥ ९ ॥
दहाविया जन्मीं कौशिक ब्राह्मण । अग्नीचें सेवन त्याचे घरीं ॥१०॥
नित्य हरिकथा वेदांतश्रवण । नित्य करी स्नान शिवालयीं ॥११॥
देवाचें दर्शन नित्य सेवाविधी । आत्मज्ञानबोधीं शांत देह ॥१२॥
कन्येचिया रूपें जन्म म्यां घेतला । क्रमिलिया काला कांहीं तेथें ॥१३॥
पितयानें लग्न केलें कन्यादान । पाहोनी ब्राह्मण शुक्ल दीक्षा ॥१४॥
ब्राह्मणाची भिक्षा करितां कोरान्न । गायींचें पालन घरीं तया ॥१५॥
बेचाळीस वर्षें आयुष्य घातलें । तेथें पुत्र जाले तीन मज ॥१६॥
पहिला पुत्र तेथें तूंचि गा जालासी । आणिक विशेषीं दोन पुत्र ॥१७॥
तुझा माझा गुरु संन्यासी केशव । तेणें विद्या सर्व प्रबोधिली ॥१८॥
तयावरी तेथें ठेविलें शरीर । दहा जन्म-सार सांगितलें ॥१९॥
बहिणी म्हणे आतां तीन जन्म शेष । सांगेन परीस ज्ञानवंता ॥२०॥

अभंग ९५

आणिक आईक अकरावा जन्म । प्रवरासंगम गंगातीर ॥ १ ॥
तेथें माध्यंदिन ब्राह्मण तो भला । तेणें वास केला गंगातीरीं ॥ २ ॥
अयाचित वृत्ति आलियासी अन्न । घालितसें जाण यथाकाळीं ॥ ३ ॥
गोकर्ण हें नाम तयाचें उत्तम । शांति दया धर्म क्षमादिक ॥ ४ ॥
तयाची वल्लभा भली पतिव्रता । सगुणाद्भूता नाम तिचें ॥ ५ ॥
तयांचिये पोटीं होऊनी मी कन्या । नाम हें सौजन्या ठेवियेलें ॥ ६ ॥
साता वर्षांतरीं केलें कन्यादान । पाहोनी निधान अति ज्ञानी ॥ ७ ॥
अत्यंत विरक्त योगाभ्यासी पूर्ण । घालोनी आसन योग साधी ॥ ८ ॥

नाम तयाचें कीं योगेश्वर ऐसें । सिद्धि त्या मानसें वोळगल्या ॥ ९ ॥
सेवेनें तयासी तोषविलें बहू । त्याचा माझा जीऊ एक झाला ॥१०॥
सांगितलें मज योगाचें आसन । धरोनी ध्यान खेचरीचें ॥११॥
गुरु तो भ्रतार सर्वस्वें आमुचें । घेतलें सेवेचें सौख्य तेथें ॥१२॥
गुरु बंधु पुत्र सांगातीं मागील । तूं होसी कैवल्य जन्मोजन्मीं ॥१३॥
क्रमोनिया तेथें वर्षें त्रेचाळीस । राहिला हव्यास ब्रह्मनिष्ठ ॥१४॥
बहिणी म्हणे आतां जन्म तो बारावा । सांगेन धरावा हृदयांमाजीं ॥१५॥

अभंग ९६

तुझें मनोगत जाणोनी अंतरीं । बोलिली वैखरी जन्म नाना ॥ १ ॥
ऐकावा बारावा सांगेन तांतडी । मृत्युची हें थोडी वेळ आहे ॥ २ ॥
लाखणी हें स्थळ अगाधचि तोये । लक्ष तीर्थ पाहे तये स्थळीं ॥ ३ ॥
शिवनद पाहे औट नदांतील । संगमीचें स्थळ महा उग्र ॥ ४ ॥
तेथें अनुष्ठानीं होतां एक द्विज । नाम तया साजे रामचंद्र ॥ ५ ॥
तयाची वल्लभा जानकी पवित्र । तया घरीं पुत्र दोघे होती ॥ ६ ॥
थोर ब्रह्मज्ञानी शांतीचा आगर । तीर्थाचें माहेर तीर्थरूप ॥ ७ ॥
तयाचिया पोटीं कन्येचिये रूपें । जन्मोनिया तपें साधियलें ॥ ८ ॥
धरोनिया मौन वर्ततसें जनीं । बोलती वचनीं वाचा नसे ॥ ९ ॥
करोनिया लग्न दिधलें ब्राह्मणा । ज्योतिषी तो जाणा महा थोर ॥१०॥
तयासी प्रसन्न गणेश प्रत्यक्ष । बोलतसे साक्ष तयासी तो ॥११॥
तयाचिये गेहीं निराहार देहीं । सेवासुख पाहीं घेतलें म्यां ॥१२॥
विरक्त मानस विषयभोगीं त्रास । सदा मज ध्यास आत्मनिष्ठा ॥१३॥
रामचंद्र पिता राम-उपासक । अत्यंत विवेक ज्ञान तया ॥१४॥
माझे अंतरींचा जाणोनिया हेत । केलें माझें चित्त स्थिर तेणें ॥१५॥
लावोनी समाधी बैसवी संन्निध । अंतरीं तो बोध ठसावला ॥१६॥
स्वधर्मे गौरवें देउनिया पती । सेवा आत्मस्थिती करी त्याची ॥१७॥

कोठें चित्त आणुमात्रही न वसे । सदा निजध्यासें देह वर्ते ॥१८॥
पडिलें शरीर छत्तिसा वर्षांत । व्हावें परी मुक्त शेष राहे ॥१९॥
बहिणी म्हणे जन्म बारावा तो ऐसा । तेराव्याची दशा सांगिजेल ॥२०॥

अभंग ९७

ऐक सावधान सांगेन आणिक । मागील तें देख सांगितलें ॥ १ ॥
कित्येक संदेह राहिले सांगतां । त्वरा जाली चित्ता अंतकाळीं ॥ २ ॥
विवेक तें शास्त्र अनुभव अंगींचा । असेल तो साचा अर्थ जाणे ॥ ३ ॥
अवघेचि ते जन्म आठवती मज । अंतरींचें गूज मृत्यु-वेळां ॥ ४ ॥
आदर्शांत जैसें दिसे प्रतिमुख । तैसे जन्म देख दिसती डोळां ॥ ५ ॥
लटिकेचि शब्द व्यवहारीं मानीती । मूर्ख तयांप्रती बोलों नये ॥ ६ ॥
कस्तूरीचा वास घेईल काऊळा । तरिच ते कळा कळे तया ॥ ७ ॥
तेरा जन्मां पूर्वीं आठवें समस्त । परी तैसा हेत नाहीं मज ॥ ८ ॥
मुंगीचा तो मार्ग सांपडे न वाघा । जरी तो थोर गा जाला बहू ॥ ९ ॥
बहिणी म्हणे देव कृपा करी जेव्हां । सर्व हित तेव्हां कळे मनीं ॥१०॥

अभंग ९८

तेरावा तो जन्म देह वर्ते हाची । सांगेन तयाची मूळ कथा ॥ १ ॥
देवगांवीं शाखा 'वाजसनीय' जाण । लेखक प्रविण एक सांगों ॥ २ ॥
मौनस कुळींचा ब्राह्मणाचा भक्त । भोळा ज्ञानवंत भाग्यनिधी ॥ ३ ॥
तयाची वल्लभा जानकी ते नाम । माता ती उत्तम पतिव्रता ॥ ४ ॥
तयाचिये घरीं कन्या मी जालीये । लग्न केलें तये स्थळीं जाण ॥ ५ ॥
गौतम कुळींचा भ्रतार पाहीला । अत्यंत शोभला ज्योतिषी तो ॥ ६ ॥
तयाचिये घरीं 'शक्ति' उपासना । तयाचि कामिना केली मज ॥ ७ ॥
कांहीं एक योगें दक्षिणीं कोल्हापुर । तेथें तो भ्रतार वास करी ॥ ८ ॥
माझी माता पिता बंधु भगिनीशीं । तयाचे भेटीसी सर्व गेलों ॥ ९ ॥
तेथें तो 'जयराम' कृष्णदास संत । महिमा अद्भुत सिद्धि त्यासी ॥१०॥
तया संगतीनें क्रमोनिया काळ । जाला तो दयाळ कृपानिधी ॥११॥

सांगितलें मज पतीचें सेवन । तीर्थ तें घेवोन नित्य राहें ॥१२॥
गीतेचें पठण करीं मी सर्वदा । वेदाची मर्यादा नुलंघोनी ॥१३॥
वाटलें भ्रतारा जावें स्वदेशासीं । त्वरें कुटुंबेंशीं निघाले गा ॥१४॥
आलों इंद्रायणी देहु-गांव स्थळा । कोंडाजी भेटला पंत तेथें ॥१५॥
ब्राह्मण म्हणोनी घातलें भोजन । तेथें गर्भ जाण तुझा होता ॥१६॥
देखियलें तेणें मग कुटुंबासी । म्हणे या स्थळासी रहा तुम्ही ॥१७॥
आहे गरोदर तुमची स्त्री जाण । प्रसूत होवोन जाणें पुढें ॥१८॥
देईन मी धान्य तुम्हा जें लागेल । क्रमोनिया काळ जावें स्थळां ॥१९॥
मागुतीं राहिलों विचारोनी मनीं । नामसंकीर्तनीं काळ सारूं ॥२०॥
पांडुरंग देव तुकाराम साधु । सर्वदा आनंदूं हरिकथा ॥२१॥
नमस्कार करूं तुकाराम यासी । चित्त पायापासीं विठोबाच्या ॥२२॥
आनंद वोवरी देखियली मग । देव पांडुरंग तयापासीं ॥२३॥
वाटलें मानसीं बैसावें एकांतीं । तीन अहोरात्री तये स्थळीं ॥२४॥
भ्रतार क्रोधाचा पुतळा सर्वही । एकांत तो पाहे केवीं साधे ॥२५॥
तंव अकस्मात कार्याच्या उद्देशें । भ्रतार आवेशें पुण्या गेला ॥२६॥
पुसोनी मातेसी इंद्रायणीस्नान । केलें पैं दर्शन विठोबाचें ॥२७॥
मनासी आवेश सत्त्वाचा लोटला । आनंद दाटला आसनीं हो ॥२८॥
तीन अहोरात्री क्रमिल्या ते ठायीं । आनंद तो देहीं थोर जाला ॥२९॥
दुसरिया दिवशीं तुकारामरूपें । मंत्र तीन सोपे सांगितले ॥३०॥
तेरावा हा जन्म लाधलीस आतां । पूर्वीं योगपंथा सिद्ध केलें ॥३१॥
आतां तुज पुढें नाहीं जन्म योनी । पतीच्या भजनी राहीं सुखें ॥३२॥
तुझीये वो पोटीं आला असे पुत्र । ते तुवां एकत्र तेरा जन्म ॥३३॥
तोही आत्मनिष्ठ होईल ज्ञानिया । पुढें जन्म तया पांच होती ॥३४॥
बोलोनिया ऐसें जाला तो अदृश्य । लाविला अंगुष्ठ भ्रूवोमध्यें ॥३५॥
मग म्यां बाहेरी केलें गंगास्नान । घेतलें दर्शन विठ्ठलाचें ॥३६॥
पांच पदें एक आरती लिहून । विठ्ठला ध्याऊन समर्पिली ॥३७॥

बाहत्तरी वर्षें आयुष्य मर्यादा । आजी झाली सिद्धासनीं पूर्ण ॥३८॥
अंतकाळ आतां आला रे सन्निध । सांगितला बोध जन्म तेरा ॥३९॥
सोळा प्रहर शेष राहिले आतां । सावधान चित्ता करीं बा रे ॥४०॥
अंतकाळ वेळ पांचही असावी । तें मना पुसावी मृत्यु वेळीं ॥४१॥
बहिणी म्हणे तेरा जन्माचें सर्वही । सांगीतलें कांहीं गुरु-कृपा ॥४२॥

अभंग ९९

तेरा जन्म तुज सांगीतले आज । दृश्य माझे मज सर्व होती ॥ १ ॥
आज याचि परी समयो पाहोनी । तुज रे निर्वाणीं सांगितले ॥ २ ॥
अठरा दिस मृत्यु पुढें कळों आला । परि नाहीं कथिला ऐक सांगे ॥ ३ ॥
रुक्मिणीसी आधीं मृत्यु जाल्यावरी । जावें गोदावरी उत्तरकार्या ॥ ४ ॥
अठरा दिस मृत्यू जाला अगोदर । रुक्मिणी सादर पतिव्रता ॥ ५ ॥
माझा मृत्यु तुज सांगतांची खेद । न जावेंचि गोदे क्रियाकर्म ॥ ६ ॥
यालागीं अंत सांगितला नाहीं । धरोनी हृदयीं सावधान ॥ ७ ॥
तुज गेलियानें नागरिक सर्व । सांगितला भाव अंतरींचा ॥ ८ ॥
तेरावा दिवस रुक्मिणीचा जेव्हां । तुम्हीं पत्र तेव्हां पाठवावें ॥ ९ ॥
पांच दिवस मृत्यु तेथोनी उरला । हेत सांगितला नागरिकां ॥१०॥
आठविलीं तीं तीं लिहविलीं पदें । पाहोनिया शुद्धें लिहिलीं पुढें ॥११॥
बहिणी म्हणे देव बोलवी जे वाणी । असत्य जो मानी नर्क तया ॥१२॥

अभंग १००

मृत्यूचे प्रसंगीं असावें सावध । आत्मनिष्ठ बोध राखोनिया ॥ १ ॥
ऐसें गीतेमाजी बोलिला भगवंत । आज तो वैकुंठ असे आम्हां ॥ २ ॥
अग्नीचें तें बळ आहे आजी देहीं । ज्योती तें हृदयीं सावधान ॥ ३ ॥
दिवसाचि मृत्यु शुक्लपक्षीं आहे । सांगितलें पाहे विचारोनी ॥ ४ ॥
नाहीं एक आजी उत्तरायण खरें । सद्गुरुनिर्धारें काय काज ॥ ५ ॥
उत्तराभिमुख घालोनी आसन । धैर्य सावरोन प्राण रोधीं ॥ ६ ॥

सद्गुरुस्मरणीं पांचही ते योग । आम्हांसी ते सांग फळा आले ॥ ७ ॥
बहिणी म्हणे तुज सांगितलें वर्म । पुढीलही क्रम पाहे डोळां ॥ ८ ॥

अभंग १०१

प्रपंचीं विन्मुख जालियानें चित्त । उत्तरायण सत्य तेंचि आम्हां ॥ १ ॥
नाहीं काज तया उत्तरायणाचें । सांगितलें साचें पुत्रराया ॥ २ ॥
प्रपंचाभिमुख मानस सर्वदा । दक्षिण प्रसिद्धा जाण तेची ॥ ३ ॥
बहिणी म्हणे वेदशास्त्राचे संमत । सांगितलें मत स्वानुभवें ॥ ४ ॥

अभंग १०२

मागीलही जन्म आठवती कांहीं । त्वरा जाली देहीं मृत्युवेळीं ॥ १ ॥
यालागीं राहिलें सांगणें मागील । साधनें प्रबळ होतीं खरीं ॥ २ ॥
देह प्राक्तनाचें भोगिलें संचित । स्वस्वरूपें चित्त भूमिका क्रमीं ॥ ३ ॥
सत्यही भूमिका वैराग्य सांगातीं । स्वधर्में विरक्ति संपादिली ॥ ४ ॥
विदेहि अवस्था भूमिका सातवी । तें येथें अनुभवीं साधियेली ॥ ५ ॥
सरलें संचित प्राक्तन देहाचें । माझी मज साचें साक्ष याची ॥ ६ ॥
तेरा जन्म सर्व भूमिका साधिल्या । वृत्तिही राहिल्या निमग्न त्या ॥ ७ ॥
बहिणी म्हणे कांहीं न धरीं संदेह । विवेकें विदेहदशा आली ॥ ८ ॥

अभंग १०३

मन हें विरक्त विषयीं सर्वदां । इंद्रियें गोविंदा समर्पिलीं ॥ १ ॥
तेंचि प्रायःश्चित घेतलें अंतरीं । सबाह्याभ्यंतरीं एकनिष्ठ ॥ २ ॥
मंत्रज्ञान सदा श्रीरामचिंतन । सद्गुरुभजन सर्वकाळ ॥ ३ ॥
दश दानें दशकां परेसीं समर्पूं । गोदानें संकल्पूं वासनेचीं ॥ ४ ॥
पंचगव्य तेंचि जाण अर्ध-मात्रा । सोहं या पवित्रा प्राशियेलें ॥ ५ ॥
ज्ञानगंगे स्नान मनाचें वपन । वृत्ति त्या निमग्न ब्रह्मरूपीं ॥ ६ ॥
हेंचि प्रायश्चित्त सदा सर्व काळ । मन हें अढळ निश्चयाचें ॥ ७ ॥
बहिणी म्हणे ऐसें केलें प्रायश्चित्त । शास्त्राचा संकेत शास्त्र जाणे ॥ ८ ॥

अभंग १०४

हेत तो प्रमाण जन्मासी कारण । अनुभव खूण हेचि आम्हां ॥ १ ॥
ऐसें जाणोनिया हेत निर्दाळीला । अद्वय तो जाला हेत चित्ता ॥ २ ॥
इंद्रियां आणोनी दिलें प्रायश्चित्त । ज्ञानमहातीर्थ आत्मनिष्ठा ॥ ३ ॥
विषयवासना भोगिली बहुसाल । तयाचें निर्मूळ आजि केलें ॥ ४ ॥
सद्गुरुवचनीं धरोनिया निष्ठा । वासना त्या भ्रष्टा शुद्ध केल्या ॥ ५ ॥
बहिणी म्हणे मना दिलें प्रायश्चित । आतां जालें मुक्त आत्मबोधें ॥ ६ ॥

अभंग १०५

तीन शतें आणि वरुषें एकावन्न । आयुष्य निर्माण तेरा जन्मीं ॥ १ ॥
घातलें स्त्रीरूपें साधनें हरीच्या । निमाल्या मनाच्या वृत्ती जंव ॥ २ ॥
आतां निश्चयानें सांगेन निर्धार । जालें निर्विकार चित्त माझें ॥ ३ ॥
बहिणी म्हणे पुढें कांहीं नाहीं हेत । स्वरूपीं निवांत चित्त माझें ॥ ४ ॥

अभंग १०६

हा देह जोंवरीं आहे तुझा जाण । तोंवरी तूं ज्ञान साधिसील ॥ १ ॥
यापुढें तुज जन्म होती श्रेष्ठ । असती योगभ्रष्ट जन्म नाना ॥ २ ॥
तीन जन्म तुझा काशी क्षेत्रीं वास । वैराग्य मानस होईल तें ॥ ३ ॥
ऐक तूं जन्मसी संन्यासी नेमस्त । चित्त कांहीं स्वस्थ होय तेथें ॥ ४ ॥
पांचविये जन्मीं अठरा वर्षीं तुज । विदेहत्व पूज्य होसी खरा ॥ ५ ॥
तयां पुढें जन्म घेणें नाहीं कदा । सांगतेस धंदा नको आतां ॥ ६ ॥
बहिणी म्हणे तुझें जाणवेल तुज । कृपा करे बुझ गुरु-खुणें ॥ ७ ॥

अभंग १०७

आपलें आपण देखिलें मरण । तो जाला शकून स्वानंदासी ॥ १ ॥
उभारिली गुढी मनाच्या शेवटीं । जाली मज भेटी आत्मारामीं ॥ २ ॥
केला प्राणायाम सोहं धारणेसी । मिळाली ज्योतीशीं ज्योत तेणें ॥ ३ ॥

सरलें संचित आयुष्य देहाचें । क्रियमाण अंतींचे रामरूप ॥ ४ ॥
उठति रात्रंदिनीं कामक्रोध माया । म्हणे अहा! अहा! यम धर्म ॥ ५ ॥
वैराग्याच्या श्रेणी लाविल्या देहाला । ज्ञानाग्नि लाविला ब्रह्मत्वेंसी ॥ ६ ॥
जाला प्रेतरूप शरिराचा भाव । देखियेला ठाव स्मशानींचा ॥ ७ ॥
फिरविला घट फोडिला चरणीं । महावाक्य ध्वनी बोंब झाली ॥ ८ ॥
दिली तिलांजुली कुळ नाम रूपासी । शरीर ज्याचें त्यासी समर्पिलें ॥ ९ ॥
बहिणी म्हणे रक्षा जाली त्रिपुरेची । तुकारामें साची कृपा केली ॥ १० ॥

अभंग १०८

शेष प्राक्तनाची रक्षा करूनिया । नेली तें अद्वयानंदतीर्थी ॥ १ ॥
त्रिकोण वेदिका त्रिगुणाचा देह । सिंपोनी विदेह रूप केलें ॥ २ ॥
निर्गुणाचें भाव येती जे आठही । गोमुत्र तें पाहीं तयावरी ॥ ३ ॥
लाविल्या पताका सात्विक भावना । मंत्राची धारणा ब्रह्मनिष्ठा ॥ ४ ॥
ऐसा सिंचनविधी संपादिला येथें । पुढें मोक्षपंथ क्रिया योग ॥ ५ ॥
बहिणी म्हणे क्रिया करितां स्वदेहाची । माझी मीच साची होउनी ठेलें ॥ ६ ॥

अभंग १०९

प्रथमदिनादारभ्य आरंभिली क्रिया । पिंडीं पिंड पहा निवेदिला ॥ १ ॥
दुसरिया दिवशीं द्वैत हरपलें । अद्वैत बिंबलें परब्रह्मीं ॥ २ ॥
तिसरिया दिवशीं त्रिगुणाची शांती । पिंडाची समाप्ती त्याचिपरी ॥ ३ ॥
चवथिया दिवशीं चौदेहातीत । उवडा संकेत वोळखिला ॥ ४ ॥
पांचविया दिवशीं केलें पिंडदान । पांचही प्राण बोळविलें ॥ ५ ॥
सहाविया दिवशीं षडूर्मी निमाल्या । वृत्ती स्थिरावल्या आत्मरूपीं ॥ ६ ॥
सातविया दिवशीं सप्तधातू आंत । राहे अखंडित अद्वयत्वें ॥ ७ ॥
आठविया दिवशीं नाश अष्ट भावा । अद्वयानुभवा सुखें राहे ॥ ८ ॥
नवमी नवांक भक्ति नवविधा । सरल्या आत्मबोधामाजों आल्या ॥ ९ ॥

दहाविया दिवशीं इंद्रीयें दहाही । बोळवण देहीं केली त्याची ॥१०॥
अश्मा तो उत्तरीं पंचधा विषये । ज्ञानगंगें पाहे योग त्याचा ॥११॥
अकरावे दिवशीं अकरावें मानस । परब्रह्मीं त्यास निवेदिलें ॥१२॥
वृषोत्सर्ग केला भव विरक्तीचा । विजनीं तयाचा वास केला ॥१३॥
होम केला सर्व शेष प्राक्तनाचा । हेत सुतकाचा पुढें नाहीं ॥१४॥
सपिंडीचें कर्म बाराव्या दिवसांत । वासनेचा प्रांत होय तंव ॥१५॥
व्हाया निर्वासना बाराव्या दिवशीं । अद्वय सरसीं परब्रह्म ॥१६॥
माया अविद्येचें जाळिलें बिंबलें । असि-पदीं आलें ऐक्य चित्ता ॥१७॥
सच्चिदानंद दृश्य द्रष्टा तें दर्शन । ध्येय ध्याता ध्यान विसरलें ॥१८॥
त्रिपुटीचा नाश तोचि रे बारावा । ब्रह्मत्व या जीवा केलें तेणें ॥१९॥
बिंब प्रतिबिंबीं हरपलें तेंचि । बाराव्यासी हेंचि साच संज्ञा ॥२०॥
सोहं हंस याची केली बोळवण । बारावा तो दिन आजी खरा ॥२१॥
उल्लंघोनी कळा चालिलें द्वादश । तेंचि बारामास श्राद्ध केलें ॥२२॥
चंद्राचिया कळा सोळाच्या उपरमा । न्युनाधिक सीमा तेचि आम्हां ॥२३॥
ज्ञान तेचि गंगा सांगे गुरु क्रिया । साक्षात्कार गया तेचि आम्हां ॥२४॥
मंगल श्राद्ध करूं गुरूचिया वचनीं । ब्रह्मचि होऊनी ब्रह्मदेवा ॥२५॥
ऐसी जाण क्रिया केली या शरीरें । विवेकें निर्धारें आपुलिया ॥२६॥
बहिणी म्हणे आतां असो देहभाव । आमुचा दृढ भाव हाचि खरा ॥२७॥

अभंग ११०

बोलावा ब्राह्मण मंत्रस्नान करूं । दानविधि सारूं अंतकाळीं ॥ १ ॥
घ्यावें प्रायश्चित वेदाचिया मतें । आमुचीं दैवतें द्विज तुम्ही ॥ २ ॥
दश दानें देऊनी केला नमस्कार । आतां कृपा फार असों द्यावी ॥ ३ ॥
सात प्रहर शेष उरला अंतकाळा । दिंडी टाळ घोळा कथाभारें ॥ ४ ॥
ज्ञानेश्वरी ग्रंथ संपला प्रजन्य? । करावे ब्राह्मण सिद्ध उभे ॥ ५ ॥
वाद्याचिये ध्वनी वाजती अंबरीं । दशनाद भीतरीं आयकां रे ॥ ६ ॥

घालोनी आसन बैसोनी ध्यानस्थ । पाहें मी प्रशस्त गुरु-खुणें ॥ ७ ॥
शंख चक्र गदा तुळसीच्या माळा । ब्राह्मणांच्या गळां शोभताती ॥ ८ ॥
सावधान तुम्ही म्हणा ज्ञानेश्वर । विठ्ठल निर्धार नाम जपा ॥ ९ ॥
सांगेन तें तुम्हीं ऐकावें सर्वही । अंतकाळ देहीं जवळ आला ॥१०॥
बहिणी म्हणे आतां पांचही ते योग । पाहों पा प्रसंग येचि क्षणीं ॥११॥

अभंग १११

आसनीं बैसोन उत्तराभिमुख । सहजासनीं देख अंतकाळीं ॥ १ ॥
सूर्योदयापूर्वी घटिका तीन जाण । आसनीं बैसोन ध्यान मुद्रे ॥ २ ॥
तंई तुवां पुत्रा बैसोनी पाठीसी । सावध मानसीं आत्मनिष्ठे ॥ ३ ॥
बाह्य ध्वनि कानीं पडती तुज कांहीं । ध्यान तें हृदयीं धरीं तेथें ॥ ४ ॥
करावा गजर नामकीर्तनाचा । दीस आनंदाचा महा थोर ॥ ५ ॥
लावीन रे हात जाण जये स्थानीं । जाण तूं तें मनीं प्राण तेथें ॥ ६ ॥
तीन आणि तेरा सोळा घटिका जाण । आसनीं बैसोन ध्यान मुद्रे ॥ ७ ॥
नव घटिका नाम न सांडी उच्चार । चित्ताचा निर्धार सांगितला ॥ ८ ॥
सात घटिका पुढें तयाची लोडणी । इंद्रियें गोठणीं सर्व येती ॥ ९ ॥
चार घटिका ध्यानीं राहेन तटस्थ । तुवां मन स्वस्थ असों द्यावें ॥१०॥
ऐसिया घटिका तेरा गेलियानें । सद्गुरुस्मरणें वदे जिव्हा ॥११॥
तुकाराम मुखीं गंगाधरस्मरण । आठवण जाण मालिकेची ॥१२॥
नंतर त्या पुढें नासिकाग्रीं दृष्टी । वळोनिया मुष्टी हात दोन्ही ॥१३॥
माळ तेव्हां कंठीं घालीन स्वहस्तें । करोनी प्रशस्त चित्त राहे ॥१४॥
एकाग्रता सर्व वायूचा उपरम । उदानीं संभ्रम योग त्याचा ॥१५॥
हृदयीं धरोन नारायण ध्यान । राहे समरसोन चित्त तेव्हां ॥१६॥
अखंड अद्वय हृदय व्यापक । स्मरण तें एक अद्वयाचें ॥१७॥
बहिणी म्हणे ऐसी अंतकाळस्थिती । सांगितली गति निश्चयेंसी ॥१८॥

अभंग ११२

सद्‌गुरू वोवळा वोवाळा । उजाळोनी निज ज्योतिज्वाळा ॥ १ ॥
पिंड हरपला पिंडीं । तेज व्यापिलें ब्रह्मांडीं ॥ २ ॥
शांतिसुखाचें आसन । अद्वय बोधाचें पूजन ॥ ३ ॥
चिद्धन चिदानंदगाभा । सच्चिदानंद निज प्रभा ॥ ४ ॥
तेज प्रकाशलें लोचनीं । बहिणी हरपली चिद्धनीं ॥ ५ ॥

अभंग ११३

घट फुटलियावरी । नभ नभाचेभीतरीं ॥ १ ॥
ऐसा देह गेलियानें । उरे स्वरूप चिद्धन ॥ २ ॥
जळ आटलिया जाण । प्रतिबिंब म्हणे कोण ॥ ३ ॥
लागली कापुरासी । अग्निरूप नाहीं ह्मसी ॥ ४ ॥
बहिणी ऐसें नाम माया । गेलें ध्याऊनी अद्वया ॥ ५ ॥

अभंग ११४

शेवटीं ते आतां सांगतसें लोकां । मनीं धरा निका सत्य भाव ॥ १ ॥
घरोघरीं संत जाले कलीमाजीं । केज्यावरी भाजी तैशापरी ॥ २ ॥
बहिणी म्हणे येथें आपुला सद्भाव । तारील सर्वां सर्व हेंचि जाणा ॥ ३ ॥

अभंग ११५

ऐकोनिया पत्र आलासी तांतडी । घालोनिया उडी पुत्राराया ॥ १ ॥
तेरावा दिवस केला 'रुक्मिणी'चा । सद्गदित वाचा कंठ दाटे ॥ २ ॥
जालासी उत्तीर्ण तूंचिरे सर्वांचा । मनें काया वाचा सर्व भावें ॥ ३ ॥
देखोनिया तुज संतोष वाढला । प्रेमेंचि दाटला कंठ माझा ॥ ४ ॥
मृत्यूचा संकल्प अश्विन शुद्ध प्रतिपदा । ऐक तूं प्रसिद्धा सांगितला ॥ ५ ॥
खेद तो अंतरीं धरावा न कदा । सांगतां मर्यादा नुल्लंघावी ॥ ६ ॥
पुत्रपण तुझें आजी आलें फळा । माझ्या अंतकाळ पावलासी ॥ ७ ॥
बहिणी म्हणे आतां विचारिजे बाळा । साशंकता खळा नको ठेवों ॥ ८ ॥

संत बहिणाबाईचे चि. संत विठ्ठलमहाराज यांचे अभंग

अभंग ११६

उदर भराया केलें असें ढोंग । घरोघरीं बोंब उपदेशाची ॥१॥
आपणा कळेना लोकां सांगे ज्ञान । धरोनिया ध्यान बकाऐसें ॥२॥
स्वयें बुडोनिया लोकां बुडविती । हात धरुनी जाती यमलोका ॥३॥
विठा म्हणे त्यांच्या काय करूं कपाळा । पापाचा कंटाळा न करिती ॥४॥

४. मनःपर

अभंग ११७

सद्‌गुरूचे पाय धरीन हृदयांत । राहीन ध्यानस्थ सर्व काळ ॥ १ ॥
मग मना तुझें काय तेथें उरे । ध्यानाचे वागुरे सांपडसी ॥ २ ॥
सद्‌गुरुवचनीं धरीन विश्वास । प्रेम अविनाश होय तेथें ॥ ३ ॥
सद्‌गुरूचा सर्वदा होईन मी दास । सर्वस्वीं उदास होउनीया ॥ ४ ॥
देह वाचा मन समर्पिन पायीं । सद्‌गुरु हृदयीं सांठवीन ॥ ५ ॥
बहिणी म्हणे मना सांडीं रे मीपण । जाय तूं शरण सद्‌गुरूशी ॥ ६ ॥

अभंग ११८

सर्व साधनांच्या माथा गुरुसेवा । जे करी या जीवा ब्रह्मरूप ॥ १ ॥
तयाचिया पायीं जाऊनी राहेन । तेथें मना कोण तुज पुसे ॥ २ ॥
शास्त्रवेद नाना दर्शनां वरिष्ठ । सद्‌गुरु हा श्रेष्ठ सर्वां परी ॥ ३ ॥
बहिणी म्हणे स्वामी सद्‌गुरूची कृपा । दाखवील सोपा मार्ग मना ॥ ४ ॥

अभंग ११९

बचनागाचे झाडीं विष कोण घाली । इंद्रावनातळीं कडूपण ॥ १ ॥
तैसें मना तुज विषय हे अंगींचे । तुझे तुज रुचे गुळापरी ॥ २ ॥
दुर्गंधी त्या घाली विष्ठेमाजीं कोण। कावळ्यासी गुण विष्ठा भक्षी ॥ ३ ॥
बहिणी म्हणे मना विषय तुझें मूळ । तेथें तूं अचल वृत्तिदास ॥ ४ ॥

अभंग १२०

तृण अरण्यांत पेरावया जावें । ऐसें कोणी जीवें आदरीना ॥ १ ॥
तैसें मना तुज विषय भोगकरी । सांगेन विचारी नलगे कोणा ॥ २ ॥
नाना वृक्षयाती डोंगरीं लागती । स्वभावतां क्षितीं वाढी तया ॥ ३ ॥
पशुपक्ष्यांप्रती कोण सांगे काम । ज्याचें जें जें कर्म तें तो करी ॥ ४ ॥
बहिणी म्हणे मना तुज ही धारणा । विषयाची वासना कल्पकोटी ॥ ५ ॥

अभंग १२१

निंबा कडुपण देत असे कोण । इक्षु गोडपण कोण करी ॥ १ ॥
बिजाऐसें फळ गोडीचा निवाडा । हा अर्थ उवडा दिसतसे ॥ २ ॥
इंद्रावनामुळीं कोण घाली विष । अमृत आम्रास कोण देई ॥ ३ ॥
बचनागाअंगीं विष कोण लावी । सुगंधता द्यावी नलगे पुष्पा ॥ ४ ॥
तीक्ष्ण मोहरी करितसे कोण । खारीक निर्माण मधुर कां हो ॥ ५ ॥
बहिणी म्हणे बीजाऐसें येत फळ । उत्तम ओंगळ परीक्षावें ॥ ६ ॥

अभंग १२२

शुकरा आणि श्वाना गर्दभासी जाणा । विष्ठेच्या भक्षणा कोण सांगे ॥ १ ॥
ज्याचा तो संस्कार घेउनिया उठे । लोकां दुःख वाटे कासयासी ॥ २ ॥
दंश करीं ऐसें कोण सांगे सर्पा । विंचवाच्या कोपा लोक कष्टी ॥ ३ ॥
व्याघ्रवृकादिकां कोण सांगे कानीं । राहोनिया रानीं जीव मारा ॥ ४ ॥
गोचीड ढेकूण हे रक्त भक्षिती । तयां हे सांगती लोक कायी ॥ ५ ॥
बहिणी म्हणे पूर्व संस्कार जीवाचा । प्रवर्तवी साचा न सांगतां ॥ ६ ॥

अभंग १२३

केळी आणिक या नारळी पोफळी । कोण घाली मुळीं दुग्ध तयां ॥ १ ॥
बीज तैसें फळ येत असे गोड । जाणती निवाड संत याचा ॥ २ ॥
फणस आणि आंबा सिताफळें नाना । मुळींचिया गुणा गोड होती ॥ ३ ॥
बहिणी म्हणे बीज गोड त्याचें फळ । उत्तम केवळ सेव्य सर्वां ॥ ४ ॥

अभंग १२४

मना तुझा संस्कार संग हा पूर्वील । विषयाचें बळ तुझे अंगीं ॥ १ ॥
म्हणोनी प्रार्थना करितसें तुझी । इंद्रियांसी राजी केलें असें ॥ २ ॥
नायकसी माझें सांगितलें जरी । शरिराची उरी उरों नेदीं ॥ ३ ॥
करीन उपवास कोंडोनिया श्वास । पंचाग्नीचा वास उष्णकाळीं ॥ ४ ॥
धूम्रपानें देह पीडीन सर्वथा । हिंडवीन तीर्थां सर्व पृथ्वी ॥ ५ ॥

साधोनिया योग बैसेन आसनीं । राहीन निर्वाणीं उपोषणें ॥ ६ ॥
घालीन कर्वतीं देह हा आपुला । तेथें मग तुला प्राप्त काय? ॥ ७ ॥
बहिणी म्हणे मना सांगतसें ऐक । नाहीं तरी भीक मागशील ॥ ८ ॥

अभंग १२५

विवेक वैराग्य सांपडलें मज । आतां मना तुज कोण पुसे ॥ १ ॥
धरोनी आणीन करीन ध्यानस्थ । होईल तों अस्त इंद्रियांचा ॥ २ ॥
तुझाच तुजला करीन पारखी । मना तूं विलोकीं आपणासी ॥ ३ ॥
बहिणी म्हणे मना यश घेतां हित । आहे तूं निवांत पाहें ऐसें ॥ ४ ॥

अभंग १२६

विवेकाचें बळें वैराग्य साधलें । तेथें तुझें केलें काय चाले ॥ १ ॥
म्हणोनी आपुल्या ठायीं तूं आपण । पाहें विचारून मनामाजीं ॥ २ ॥
काम क्रोध लोभ मद हा मत्सर । तुजसवें वैर चालवीती ॥ ३ ॥
बहिणी म्हणे मंत्री विवेकासारिखा । जोडिला हा निका निश्चयाचा ॥ ४ ॥

अभंग १२७

म्हणशील मना इंद्र म्यां ठकिला । ब्रह्मयाचा केला मानभंग ॥ १ ॥
तुझा तेथें काय पाड असे मूढा । मनाचा पवाडा वेदशास्त्रीं ॥ २ ॥
नारदाची केली नारदी आपण । माझे ठायीं पण बोलों नये ॥ ३ ॥
शिवासी आपण हिंडवीलें रानीं । विष्णु करी ध्यानीं वृंदा वृंदा ॥ ४ ॥
व्यासा ठकविलें ऋषी नागवीले । मज मनावेगळें काय असे ॥ ५ ॥
बहिणी म्हणे ऐसा मनाचा प्रतिशब्द । ऐकोनीया स्तब्ध चित्त झालें ॥ ६ ॥

अभंग १२८

इंद्राचा संकेत होता लग्नकाळीं । भोगीन मी बळी अहिल्येसी ॥ १ ॥
हेत होता त्याचा तरी तो काय कळे । हेतींच बांधीलें ज्याचें तया ॥ २ ॥
नारदेंही तेंच मागितलें दान । हेतींच बंधन पावला तो ॥ ३ ॥
ब्रह्मयाचा हेत भवानी सुंदर । अंगुष्ठें विकार आणियेला ॥ ४ ॥

शिवासी कामाचा हेत सर्वकाळ । म्हणोनी चपळ बांधी तया ॥ ५ ॥
व्यासही तैसाची निष्काम तो नाहीं । तो पडे अपायीं नवल कोण ॥ ६ ॥
बहिणी म्हणे हेत गुंतला ते ठायीं । घालिसी अपायीं सत्य मना ॥ ७ ॥

अभंग १२९

आम्ही तों निर्हेत साक्षी ऐसी येत । भोगांमाजीं चित्त क्षणू नाहीं ॥ १ ॥
आतां मना येथें काय तुझें चाले । निर्हेत पाउलें विठोबाचीं ॥ २ ॥
मनांत पाहिलें बुद्धींत गाइलें । चित्तांत ध्याइलें विठ्ठलासी ॥ ३ ॥
वासना गाळिली सर्वही चाळिली । शांति स्थिरावली विठ्ठलीं हे ॥ ४ ॥
काम क्रोध लोभ मत्सराचें अंग । झाला पांडुरंग आपणची ॥ ५ ॥
बहिणी म्हणे मना हेतूंचा उगाणा । करूनी निर्वाणा पहातसें ॥ ६ ॥

अभंग १३०

ब्रह्मचर्य आणि संन्यास घेइजे । वानप्रस्थ कीजे याचिलागीं ॥ १ ॥
निर्वासना साधे हेत हा निरसोन । विषयांचा मन वीट धरी ॥ २ ॥
योगयाग तपें व्रतें अनुष्ठान । सेवावें अरण्य याचिलागीं ॥ ३ ॥
बहिणी म्हणे हेत विषयांचा निरसला । तरी मना तुला कोण पुसे ॥ ४ ॥

अभंग १३१

दमुनी इंद्रियें आणिला विवेक । दाखवील सुख आत्मयाचें ॥ १ ॥
मना तुझें मग काय चाले तेथें । राहे पैं निवांत आपणची ॥ २ ॥
काम तो निष्काम करील विवेक । शांतीपाशीं देख क्रोध राहे ॥ ३ ॥
लोभ तो निर्भास ठकोनी राहील । मोहारी जाळील ज्ञानानळीं ॥ ४ ॥
शुद्ध सत्त्व गुण तिन्ही अहंकार । घालील निर्धार धरीं मना ॥ ५ ॥
आशा मनसा तृष्णा इच्छा हे वासना । आधीन आपणा करील ते ॥ ६ ॥
सांगितलें तेंची इंद्रियें वर्तती । विवेकसंपत्ती ब्रह्मनिष्ठ ॥ ७ ॥
बहिणी म्हणे मना विवेक तो सार । तरी तो विचारा आत्मवंता ॥ ८ ॥

अभंग १३२

विवेक सांगाती जयासी जोडला । थारा तो मोडला पातकांचा ॥ १ ॥
तो आम्हीं विवेक केलासे कैवारी । मना तुझी करी कोण चिंता ॥ २ ॥
विवेक वैराग्य जोडेल निश्चित । भक्ति हो अंकित विवेकाची ॥ ३ ॥
बहिणी म्हणे मना विवेक हा खरा । तुझिया व्यापार कोण पुसे ॥ ४ ॥

अभंग १३३

विवेकें श्रवण करीन वेदांत । साधीन अद्वैत ब्रह्मनिष्ठा ॥ १ ॥
तुजपुढें बोलें हाचि पण मना । धरीं तूं धारणा आत्मयाची ॥ २ ॥
श्रवणाचें सार्थक मनन होय जाण । निजध्यासीं खूण विश्रांतीची ॥ ३ ॥
बहिणी म्हणे मना होईं तूं सुमन । कासया भांडण होय पुढें ॥ ४ ॥

अभंग १३४

दहा इंद्रियें हीं गोंविन हरिपदीं । मग तुझी बुद्धि हरपेल ॥ १ ॥
यालागीं मना तूं इंद्रियांसमवेत । होय शरणागत अच्युताचा ॥ २ ॥
निश्चयेंसी बुद्धि चित्त अहंकार । संकल्पें निर्धार आत्मयाचा ॥ ३ ॥
बहिणी म्हणे होय पायीं ओळंगणा । विषयीं वासना सांडोनिया ॥ ४ ॥

अभंग १३५

मना तुझीं सर्व वाहनें हिरोनी । नेलीं तीं बांधोनी विवेकें हो ॥ १ ॥
बैसोनी हृदयीं होय तूं ध्यानस्थ । संकल्पाचा हेत वंचुनिया ॥ २ ॥
दहा इंद्रियें हीं होऊनी पारखीं । विवेकाचीं सखीं सर्व झालीं ॥ ३ ॥
बहिणी म्हणे तुज रूप नाहीं नांव । मना तुझी धांव पारुषली ॥ ४ ॥

अभंग १३६

नयन गोंविले ध्यानीं केशवाचे । श्रवण हरीचे कीर्तनीं हो ॥ १ ॥
विवेकें इंद्रियां दावोनिया सुख । गोंविलीं आणिक नाठवती ॥ २ ॥
वाचा हे गोंविली नामसंकीर्तनीं । सेवा मुक्त पाणी केशवातें ॥ ३ ॥
पाय तीर्थयात्रा देवाच्या दर्शना । कर्मेंद्रिय-खुणा वोळखाव्या ॥ ४ ॥

दहाही इंद्रियें विवेकें गोंविलीं । मना तूं निर्बली याचियोगें ॥ ५ ॥
बहिणी म्हणे मना विषयसेवनीं । येती न नेमोनी टाकिलीं तीं ॥ ६ ॥

अभंग १३७

चित्त नाहीं शुद्ध जयाचें अंतर । विषयीं तत्पर सर्व काळीं ॥ १ ॥
तया ज्ञान साधे असें तों घडेना । ज्ञानावीण जाणा मोक्ष कैंचा ॥ २ ॥
नाहीं ज्या अपेक्षा साधनाची चाड । दोषाचा तो घड ओतलासे ॥ ३ ॥
बहिणी म्हणे ज्ञान संतसंगें होय । चित्त जरी राहे सदा पायीं ॥ ४ ॥

अभंग १३८

माझिया रे मना सखया सज्जना । ऐक तूं प्रार्थना विनवितें ॥ १ ॥
सांडीं हें मीपण अहंतालक्षण । निवांत आपण सुखी राहें ॥ २ ॥
किती वणवण करीसी भ्रमण । व्यर्थ वायां शीण श्रम देहीं ॥ ३ ॥
मायामृगजलापाठीं कां लागसी । कष्ट कां भोगसी चौऱ्याशींचे ॥ ४ ॥
येणें काय हित घडे पाहे तुज । धरीं कांहीं लाज सज्जनांची ॥ ५ ॥
बहिणी म्हणे गेले संत जया वाटां । पावले ते निष्ठा सुखरूप ॥ ६ ॥

अभंग १३९

शुक वामदेव व्यास पराशर । गेले थोर थोर जेणें पंथें ॥ १ ॥
जेणें पंथें सुखी जाले पैं निर्भय । मना तेचि सोय धरीं बापा ॥ २ ॥
वसिष्ठ अरुंधती सनकादिक पाहें । गेले लवलाहें जेणें पंथें ॥ ३ ॥
बळी बिभीषण प्रल्हाद वाल्मीक । पावले ते सुख जेणें पंथें ॥ ४ ॥
ऐसे किती सांगों बहु वर्णांतरीं । जाले ते संसारीं सुखरूप ॥ ५ ॥
बहिणी म्हणे मना धरीं रे धारणा । लागलें चरणां निजभावें ॥ ६ ॥

अभंग १४०

मना तूंचि माझें संचितक्रियमाण । भाग हें भोगणें सुखदुःख ॥ १ ॥
तुझेनीच मज बंध मोक्ष जाण । येऱ्हवीं पुसे कोण मजलागीं ॥ २ ॥
मी माझें हें द्वैत वाढवी विकल्प । पुण्य आणि पाप तुझे देठीं ॥ ३ ॥

निश्चलता तुज जरी हे असती । सुखदुःखप्राप्ति कोणालागीं ॥ ४ ॥
जीवशिव नामें वाढली उपाधी । तुझेनीच बुद्धि मना जाण ॥ ५ ॥
बहिणी म्हणे मना भाकितसें करुणा । सोडवीं मज दीना काळाहातीं ॥ ६ ॥

अभंग १४१

काळ आणि वेळ घटि तास पळ । तुझेनी हें मूळ गणनेलागीं ॥ १ ॥
जेथें नाहीं काळ तेथें कैंची वेळ । उपाधीचें मूळ तूंचि मना ॥ २ ॥
अणूचें प्रमाण सूक्ष्मब्रह्मपणा । एवढी गणना तुझेमुळें ॥ ३ ॥
पंचमहाभूतें वर्तती आपण । चंद्रसूर्य जाण दिनमासीं ॥ ४ ॥
अवघी हे गणना ब्रह्मांडरचना । मना तुजवीण नाहीं नाहीं ॥ ५ ॥
बहिणी म्हणे ऐसें काळचक्र चाले । ऐसे तुझे चाळे दिसती बापा ॥ ६ ॥

अभंग १४२

मना तूं व्यापकापरीस व्यापक । ब्रह्मांड हे देख व्यापियलें ॥ १ ॥
तेथें निजसुख कैंचे जीवालागीं । म्हणोनी तुजलागीं विनवीतसें ॥ २ ॥
जेथवरी मना फिरे तुझा वारा । तेथवरी थारा सुखा नाहीं ॥ ३ ॥
जेथवरी मना तुझा बा पसार । सुखाचा विचार तेथें नाहीं ॥ ४ ॥
तुझी कृपा होये तरी सुख लाहे । म्हणोनिया पाय धरीतसें ॥ ५ ॥
बहिणी म्हणे तुवां ठकिलें बहुवस । तेणें कासावीस जीव माझा ॥ ६ ॥

अभंग १४३

विधाता एवढा तपोनिधि होता । त्यासी त्वां तत्वतां ठकियेलें ॥ १ ॥
ऐसे तुझे खेळ खेळसी तूं लगट । भोगविसी कष्ट जीवांलागीं ॥ २ ॥
विष्णु ठकवोनी नारद ठकियेला । शंकराचा केला लिंगपात ॥ ३ ॥
बहिणी म्हणे ऐसें सांगतां अपार । मना तुझे चार कळती न ॥ ४ ॥

अभंग १४४

तुजसाठीं मना धरिती धारणा । योगमुद्रा जाणा नानापरी ॥ १ ॥
ऐसे तपोनिधी साधिती साधना । नाकळसी मना काय सांगों ॥ २ ॥

एक प्राणापान निरोधूनी द्वारें । ब्रह्मांडविवरें वायू नेती ॥ ३ ॥
उघडे बोडके जटाळ सुडके । होऊनिया मुके हिंडताती ॥ ४ ॥
एक भूमीमार्जी पुरोनिया घेती । वनीं विचरती अन्नावीण ॥ ५ ॥
बहिणी म्हणे ऐसीं नाना मतें सांग । हिंडती वैराग्यें मनासाठीं ॥ ६ ॥

अभंग १४५

तुज साधावया एकचि कारण । फार पुण्य जया गांठीं वसे ॥ १ ॥
तेव्हां निजमन वश पै आपण । जैसें केलें जाण तैसें होय ॥ २ ॥
तपाचिया राशी वसे ज्याचे गांठीं । तेव्हां मन हातीं गवसे पां ॥ ३ ॥
बहिणी म्हणे मग मन तेंचि तृण । पाहीजे कारण पुण्यप्राप्ती ॥ ४ ॥

अभंग १४६

वश मन झालें मग काय उरलें । ब्रह्मांड घातलें पालथें जेणें ॥ १ ॥
ऐसें पुण्य करा मनासी या वरा । सद्गुरूचे धरा पाय आधीं ॥ २ ॥
मन वश होतां साधनें साधितां । ब्रह्मसायुज्यता रोकडी ती ॥ ३ ॥
मन जंव नाकळे मग केविं कळे । वायांचि सोहळे साधनांचे ॥ ४ ॥
मन नाहीं ठायीं सोंस घेउनी कायी । अज्ञानासी पाही झकवाया ॥ ५ ॥
बहिणी म्हणे येथें केलें तें आपण। जेवत्याची खूण वाढिता जाणे ॥ ६ ॥

अभंग १४७

तुजसाठीं मना जाईन येथोनी । राहीन चरणीं सद्गुरुचे ॥ १ ॥
मग तुझें काय चाले पाहें तेथें । येतां तुज तेथें हाल होती ॥ २ ॥
तुजसाठीं मना घेईन देसवटा । धरीन मी निष्ठा गुरूपायीं ॥ ३ ॥
बहिणी म्हणे मना ब्रह्मांडासगट । भरीन तुझा घोट गुरुकृपे ॥ ४ ॥

अभंग १४८

विषयाचा लंपट जरी तूं नसतासी । तरी मना तुशीं काय संबंध ॥ १ ॥
निज सुख मग सहज तूं आपण । साधनांचा शीण कोणासाठीं ॥ २ ॥
सांडोनी प्रवृत्ति असतास निवृत्ति । तरी भोगप्राप्ती कोणालागीं ॥ ३ ॥
बहिणी म्हणे मना विषयाचे सांगातीं । एवढी आटाआटी करिसी जीवा॥ ४ ॥

अभंग १४९

सद्गुरुकृपेनें साधीन तव कळा । वासना अबला दंडीन मना ॥ १ ॥
केंविलवाणें मुख करिसील मग । तुझें तूंचि सुख नेणसी घेऊं ॥ २ ॥
अनाथाची परी होईल तुजलागीं । ऐसें वीतरागी करीन क्षणीं ॥ ३ ॥
बहिणी म्हणे तुझ्या सांडवीन खोडी । विवेकाची बेडी जडीन पायीं ॥ ४ ॥

अभंग १५०

निंबोळियाभरें निंब बहरला । सुकाळ जाहला वायसांसी ॥ १ ॥
कावकाव तेणें मदें ओरडती । परी ते नेणती चवी कैसी ॥ २ ॥
तैसें नको मना मातूं कामभरें । हित होय बरें तेंचि करीं ॥ ३ ॥
मुक्ताफळें हंस सेविती पक्षीया । हासती ते तयां काग कैसे ॥ ४ ॥
परी त्याची गोडी नेणती विचारें । मुखें अनिवार भरले फांटा ॥ ५ ॥
जो जेथें रातला तो तेथें मातला । पूर्ण ब्रह्मकळा-चवी नेणे ॥ ६ ॥
विष्ठा पैं कस्तूरी केंवि ते समान । बहिणी म्हणे ज्ञान दुर्लभ हें ॥ ७ ॥

अभंग १५१

ज्याचे गांठीं फार पुण्याचे हे सांठे । मन त्याचें विटे विषयभोगीं ॥ १ ॥
मग तो दैवाचा सांगाती निजाचा । सखा तो आमुचा प्राणदाता ॥ २ ॥
आत्मसुखालागीं सर्वस्व त्यागिलें । विरक्तीसी केलें साह्य जेणें ॥ ३ ॥
संसाराचा त्रास ज्या मनीं उपजला । निज सुखा झाला धनी तोची ॥ ४ ॥
उरलेनि प्रारब्धें आयुष्य घालविती । स्वरूपाची स्थिति अखंडत्वें ॥ ५ ॥
बहिणी म्हणे मना सोडीं मज आतां । ब्रह्मसायुज्यता सुख देईं ॥ ६ ॥

५. भक्तिपर

अभंग १५२

भक्ति हें कारण साधन वरिष्ठ। रोकडें वैकुंठ हातीं वसे ॥ १ ॥
स्थिर करीं चित्त प्रेम अखंडित। पावसी अच्युतपद पाहें ॥ २ ॥
भक्तीपाशीं ज्ञान वैराग्य आंदण। सर्व हीं साधनें लया जाती ॥ ३ ॥
बहिणी म्हणे भक्ति विरक्तीचें मूळ। चित्त हें निश्चळ करीं बारे ॥ ४ ॥

अभंग १५३

संताचे वचनीं दृढ जया भाव। भक्ति अभिनव हेचि खरी ॥ १ ॥
सांगितली खूण आयके जो मनीं। पावेल निर्वाणीं तोचि एक ॥ २ ॥
संताचें वचन शास्त्राचे आधारें। भक्तिचें निर्धारें दृढ होई ॥ ३ ॥
बहिणो म्हणे संत-पायीं जया आर्त। हाचि भक्तिपंथ वोळखावा ॥ ४ ॥

अभंग १५४

नामसंकीर्तन सर्व काळ जया। भक्तिवंत तया म्हणों आम्ही ॥ १ ॥
क्षण एक नाहीं नामाविण वाचा। सोंस हा भक्तीचा सर्वकाळ ॥ २ ॥
नेत्रीं हरिध्यान मुखीं तें कीर्तन। सर्वदां श्रवण मोक्षशास्त्रें ॥ ३ ॥
सेवा घडे हातीं पायीं प्रदक्षिणा। विश्रांति धारणा आत्मयाची ॥ ४ ॥
आठही प्रहर नाहीं आराणूक। संतावरीं रंक होउनी ठेला ॥ ५ ॥
बहिणी म्हणे भक्ति खरी मोक्षदाती। पाहिजे संगतीं संतसेवा ॥ ६ ॥

अभंग १५५

जलावीण मासा जैसा तळमळी। चातक भूतळीं मेघ इच्छी ॥ १ ॥
तैसें भक्तीलागीं कळवळे मन। भक्ति हे निर्वाण तेच खरी ॥ २ ॥
एकुलता पुत्र सांपडे वैरिया। कुरंग हा ठाया पारधीचे ॥ ३ ॥
पतिव्रता पतिवियोगें तडफडी। भ्रमर प्राण सोडी पुष्पावीण ॥ ४ ॥
तृषाक्रांत जैसा इच्छित जीवन। चकोर हा जाण चंद्रामृता ॥ ५ ॥
बहिणी म्हणे तैसी आवडे हरिभक्ति। तेव्हां चित्तवृत्ति वोळखावी ॥ ६ ॥

अभंग १५६

भक्तीविण काय वांचोनिया व्यर्थ । अंतरला स्वार्थ देखतांची ॥ १ ॥
नये त्याचें तोंड पाहण्या सर्वथा । कासयासी माता तया व्याली ॥ २ ॥
न करी सेवन न पूजी सज्जन । न करी श्रवण मनामाजीं ॥ ३ ॥
बहिणी म्हणे जया न घडे हरिभक्ति । मग त्या विरक्ति केविं साधे ॥ ४ ॥

अभंग १५७

चित्तशुद्धि होय भक्तिचेनि योगें । होईल वाउगें दृश्यजात ॥ १ ॥
वैराग्य संचरे मनामाजीं जाण । जैसें हें वमन सर्व तैसें ॥ २ ॥
विषय असत्य रोहिणीचें जळ । वाटतें सकळ भ्रांतिरूप ॥ ३ ॥
बहिणी म्हणे जंव चित्तशुद्धि नाहीं । प्रपंच तंव कांहीं न सुटेची ॥ ४ ॥

अभंग १५८

विषयाचा संग नावडे जयासी । वैराग्य मानसीं संचरल्या ॥ १ ॥
मग काय उणें सुखालागीं तया । सर्वदा सुखीया तोचि होय ॥ २ ॥
नावडे ज्या संग स्त्रिया पुत्रधन । इंद्रियाचरण नावडेची ॥ ३ ॥
नावडे पहाणें बोलणें ऐकणें । नावडे मिष्टान्न भोग भोगूं ॥ ४ ॥
नावडे संपत्ती गणगोत कांहीं । नावडेचि देहीं अहंपण ॥ ५ ॥
बहिणी म्हणे होईल उदास मानस । प्रपंचाची आस तैंच तुटे ॥ ६ ॥

अभंग १५९

भ्रतार गांवासी गेलीयानें सतीं । भोग ते लागती विषाऐसे ॥ १ ॥
अनुताप तैसा संचरे शरीरीं । आत्मा हा अंतरीं वोळखतां ॥ २ ॥
अपूर्ण हा काम जालिया कामुका । भोग सर्व विखापरी होती ॥ ३ ॥
धनलोभियाचें धन नेतां चोरीं । क्षणही अंतरीं सुख नाहीं ॥ ४ ॥
मीन जलांतुनी काढिलियावरी । विष सर्वांपरी होत तया ॥ ५ ॥
बहिणी म्हणे तैसें ब्रह्मप्राप्तीवीण । जाय एक क्षण युगाऐसा ॥ ६ ॥

अभंग १६०

परलोक नावडे इंद्राची संपत्ती । इहलोक चित्तीं विष भासे ॥ १ ॥
तो एक विरक्त ज्ञानासी अधिकारी । ब्रह्मप्राप्ति खरी होय तया ॥ २ ॥
सर्व सिद्धि येतां घरासी सर्वथा । नावडती चित्ता विरक्तीनें ॥ ३ ॥
रंभा तिलोत्तमा उर्वशी मेनका । नावडती एका हरीवीण ॥ ४ ॥
चंदन आगरू नाना उपचार । गमती विखार हरीविण ॥ ५ ॥
बहिणी म्हणे पूर्ण विरक्ति मानसीं । ज्ञान हें तयासी वोळंगण ॥ ६ ॥

अभंग १६१

प्रपंच असत्य कळों आला जया । विषय हे तया नावडती ॥ १ ॥
उदासीनापरी वर्ततो प्रपंचीं । आस हें मनाची सांडोनिया ॥ २ ॥
मनाचा स्वभाव संकल्प विकल्प । होय साक्षिरूप तयांचा ही ॥ ३ ॥
बुद्धीचा निश्चय अनुसंधानीं चित्त । अहंकारीं हेत अहंतेचा ॥ ४ ॥
सर्वही मायिक व्यवहार जाणती । निश्चय अद्वैतीं ठेवोनिया ॥ ५ ॥
बहिणी म्हणे माया सत्य ना असत्य । श्रीगुरूनें तथ्य सांगितलें ॥ ६ ॥

६ सद्गुरूची थोरवी

अभंग १६२

असत्य हे माया म्हणों जातां दिसे । सत्य म्हणतां नसे ज्ञानदृष्टी ॥ १ ॥
ऐसा हा संदेह निवारी सद्गुरु । विवेकनिर्धारू करोनिया ॥ २ ॥
ब्रह्महरिहर मायेचे त्रिगुण । माया ब्रह्मीं जाण बोलों नये ॥ ३ ॥
माया काल्पनीक अकल्पित ब्रह्म । कळे न हें वर्म कोणेपरी ॥ ४ ॥
माया हे सावेव किंवा निरावेव । न कळे याचा ठाव कोणेपरी ॥ ५ ॥
बहिणी म्हणे याचें वर्म कळावया । वोळंगावें पायां सद्गुरूच्या ॥ ६ ॥

अभंग १६३

ब्रह्मापासोनिया जाली म्हणे माया । उपाधी हे तया केवीं घडे ॥ १ ॥
करावा निवाडा सद्गुरुवचंन । भेद निरसोन विकल्पाचा ॥ २ ॥
माया ब्रह्मीं नाहीं ऐसें म्हणों जरी । स्वतंत्रता तरी म्हणों नये ॥ ३ ॥
बहिणी म्हणे ऐसा संदेह मायेचा । निरसी जो साचा तोचि गुरु ॥ ४ ॥

अभंग १६४

ब्रह्म तों अद्वय श्रुतीचें संमते । वेगळी माया ते म्हणों कैसी ॥ १ ॥
कोणासी पुसावें मायेचें ठिकाण । सद्गुरूवांचोन सत्य जाणा ॥ २ ॥
सुवर्णकांचन नांव मात्र भिन्न । ज्ञानें एकपण वोळखावें ॥ ३ ॥
तोय आणि तरंग भेद नाममात्र । ऐक्य हें सर्वत्र ज्ञानदृष्टी ॥ ४ ॥
सूत वस्त्र दोन्ही ऐक्यता सहजें । ज्ञानदृष्टीवोजें पाहिलिया ॥ ५ ॥
बहिणी म्हणे ऐसा पहातां विवेक । सहजची ऐक्य मायाब्रह्मीं ॥ ६ ॥

अभंग १६५

असत्य हे माया म्हणतां प्रत्यक्ष । मायेचा हा पक्ष दृश्य आघवें ॥ १ ॥
काय तें धरावें काय तें सोडावें । रहावें अनुभवें कोण्यापरी ॥ २ ॥
विधिहरिहर नाम अवतार । मायेचा बडिवार दिसतसे ॥ ३ ॥
बहिणी म्हणे माया असत्य म्हणतां । गुणांच्या अवस्था दिसताती ॥ ४ ॥

अभंग १६६

सत्य म्हणों माया ज्ञानें निरसत । अनुभवें अद्वैत होउनी ठेलें ॥ १ ॥
सत्य म्हणों जातां नसे हे सर्वथा । आतां काय चित्ता बोध करूं ॥ २ ॥
सूर्यापुढें काय अंधकार राहे । विवेक हा ठाये न दिसे इच्या ॥ ३ ॥
बहिणी म्हणे सत्य म्हणों नये कदा । संत आत्मबोधा पावलिया ॥ ४ ॥

अभंग १६७

गुरुकृपा पूर्ण जयासी लाधली । माया ही निरसली तया मनीं ॥ १ ॥
येर तें अज्ञान पडिलें भ्रमणीं । संसार-जाचणी अनिवार ॥ २ ॥
जयांचा विकल्प निरसला निश्चित । तेचि ब्रह्मीभूत होउनी ठेले ॥ ३ ॥
जयांची वासना निमाली अंतरीं । तेचि निर्विकारी सहज जाले ॥ ४ ॥
जयांचा हा हेत निरसला देहींचा । रावो ब्रह्मांडींचा तोचि एक ॥ ५ ॥
बहिणी म्हणे काय सांगावें कवणा । मायेचा देखणा विरळा असे ॥ ६ ॥

अभंग १६८

सूर्यचिये घरीं रहाणें जयासी । अंधार तयासी स्वप्नीं नाहीं ॥ १ ॥
तैसा स्वानुभवीं देखे न तो माया । ब्रह्म तों अद्वयानंद अंगें ॥ २ ॥
परीस तो जाणे काय सोनें लोह । निर्ममते मोह कदा नोहे ॥ ३ ॥
बहिणी म्हणे न लागे तृषा ते जीवना । पूर्णत्वें भावना भावशुद्धी ॥ ४ ॥

अभंग १६९

सूर्याचिये अंगीं भासे मृगजळ । सूर्य तो केवळ नेणे तया ॥ १ ॥
तैसी जाण माया ब्रह्मींच आभासे । परी स्पर्श नसे ब्रह्मत्वासी ॥ २ ॥
चुंबकासंन्निध लोहासी भ्रमण । सूर्यसत्ते जन वर्ततसे ॥ ३ ॥
बहिणी म्हणे ऐसा अनुभव पाहिजे । स्वसुखीं राहिज्रे निरंतर ॥ ४ ॥

अभंग १७०

दृश्य आणि द्रष्टा दर्शनें समवेत । ब्रह्म सदोदित सर्वकाळ ॥ १ ॥
काय घेऊं काय सांडूं कोणीकडे । अनंत ब्रह्मांडें रोमरंध्रीं ॥ २ ॥

ध्येय ध्याता ध्यान ज्ञेय ज्ञप्ति ज्ञान । साध्य तो साधन आपण झाला ॥ ३ ॥
बहिणी म्हणे द्वैत स्वप्नामाजीं नसे । अवघाची प्रकाशे राम माझा ॥ ४ ॥

अभंग १७१

कैंची माया आणि अविद्या कल्पना । कैंची हे वासना पहातोसी ॥ १ ॥
जगदाकारें ब्रह्म अखंडित सर्व । पाहें हा अनुभव निश्चयाचा ॥ २ ॥
कैंचे मन बुद्धि कैंचा अभिमान । सर्व नारायण अंतर्बाह्य ॥ ३ ॥
बहिणी म्हणे अवघे गुणाचे विकार । ब्रह्म निर्विकार स्वयंसिद्ध ॥ ४ ॥

अभंग १७२

त्रिगुणीं हें जाण व्यापिलेंसें जग । यामाजीं श्रीरंग वेगळाची ॥ १ ॥
विश्वाकार तोची पाहे अनुभव । येथील गौरव सद्‌गुरु जाणे ॥ २ ॥
उफराटी दृष्टी पाहिलियावरी । सौख्य हें अंतरीं होय तेव्हां ॥ ३ ॥
बहिणी म्हणे गुण मायेचे अंकुर । ब्रह्म परात्पर अद्वयत्वें ॥ ४ ॥

अभंग १७३

सत्त्वगुण साधी ज्ञानाचिये सिद्धी । स्थिर होय बुद्धि आत्मरूपीं ॥ १ ॥
कासया रज तम जगीं दिसे अंगीं । वाढविसी संगीं पापरूप ॥ २ ॥
काय एक नाहीं सत्त्वगुणापासीं । पाहे तूं मानसीं आपुलिये ॥ ३ ॥
सत्त्वगुणें स्वर्ग साधेल मोक्षही । विचरोनी देहीं पाहे पां रे ॥ ४ ॥
सत्त्वगुण आणि संताची संगती । कर्माची निवृत्ति होय तेणें ॥ ५ ॥
बहिणी म्हणे सत्त्व मोक्षासी कारण । पाहिजे तें ज्ञान शुद्ध अंगीं ॥ ६ ॥

अभंग १७४

स्नान संध्या जप नित्य अनुष्ठान । करीं सावधान आत्मनिष्ठे ॥ १ ॥
फलाशा सांडोनी अहं करी व्यक्त । मोक्ष तो आयता असे तेथें ॥ २ ॥
स्वधर्माचरण आपुलाले वर्ण । यज्ञ आणि दान करीं सर्व ॥ ३ ॥
बहिणी म्हणे ऐसा साधील तो जरी । सत्त्व जों अंतरीं प्रवेशला ॥ ४ ॥

अभंग १७५

दुधाचिये चाडें गायीचें सेवन । आंब्याचें पालन फळांसाठीं ॥ १ ॥
तैसें कर्म करी फलाशा धरोन । रजोगुणी जाण वोळखावा ॥ २ ॥
द्राक्षाचिया मुळा दुधाची घागरी । समर्थाचे घरीं आमंत्रणें ॥ ३ ॥
बहिणी म्हणे ऐसी क्रिया जयापाशीं । ज्ञान तयापाशीं नये कदा ॥ ४ ॥

अभंग १७६

वेदशास्त्र जया नाहींची प्रमाण । अशुची तो जाण अंतर्बाह्य ॥ १ ॥
तामसी तो खरा वोळखावा नर । तयासी अघोर कल्पकोटी ॥ २ ॥
वेदाचें प्रमाण तें तें अप्रमाण । भल्यासीही मान नाहीं जेथें ॥ ३ ॥
बहिणी म्हणे ऐसा अंगींचा दुर्जन । त्यासी संभाषण करों नये ॥ ४ ॥

अभंग १७७

जन्मजन्मांतरीं वासनेचा भ्रष्ट । मोक्षा हा वरिष्ठ केवीं साधे ॥ १ ॥
जैसी काउळ्याची अमंगलीं प्रीती । राजहंसपंक्ती कैंची तया ॥ २ ॥
कुकर्म आवडे अधर्मीं प्रवृत्ती । अंध तम छत्रीं घेत असे ॥ ३ ॥
बहिणी म्हणे त्याचें तोंड पाहों नये । नरकाचा तो ठाये एक जाणा ॥ ४ ॥

अभंग १७८

गुणाची वागुरा मांडीलीसे जीवा । सुटेल केधवां केशीराजा ॥ १ ॥
ऐसा अनुताप होईल अंतरीं । मोक्ष होय तरी प्राणियासी ॥ २ ॥
कामक्रोधलोभ वैरी हे भोंवतें । करावी अनंतें कृपा आतां ॥ ३ ॥
बहिणी म्हणे धन्य ते एक संसारीं । पूर्ण जयांवरी गुरुकृपा ॥ ४ ॥

अभंग १७९

न लगती वेद शास्त्राचें पठण । परमार्थाची खूण वेगळीच ॥ १ ॥
सद्‌गुरुशी जाई शरण सर्वभावें । मग तूं स्वभावें ब्रह्मरूप ॥ २ ॥
न लगती तपें व्रतें अनुष्ठान । आत्मत्वाची खूण वेगळीच ॥ ३ ॥
न लगती देव तीर्थ क्षेत्र यात्रा । आगमींच्या मंत्रा धांडोळावें ॥ ४ ॥
न लगती योग याग प्राणायाम । साधनाचें वर्म वेगळेंच ॥ ५ ॥

नलगे ब्रह्मचर्य गृहस्थ संन्यास । व्रताचे हव्यास व्यर्थ तेही ॥ ६ ॥
न लगती पंचाग्नी धूम्राचें प्राशन । आकाश वसन नलगे कांहीं ॥ ७ ॥
बहिणी म्हणे एक सद्‌गुरूवांचोनी । मोक्ष ना गहनीं प्राप्त होय ॥ ८ ॥

अभंग १८०

शब्दाचें बोलणें दृश्य हें तोंवरी । अदृश्य वैखरी हारपली ॥ १ ॥
तेथें हा सद्‌गुरु बोधील समर्थ । दाखवोनी अर्थ श्रुति शास्त्रें ॥ २ ॥
बुद्धीचें बोधक चित्ताचें चिंतन । अदृश्य हें जाण हारपलें ॥ ३ ॥
इंद्रियांचें सर्व आकारीं बोलणें । निराकारीं जाणें हारपलें ॥ ४ ॥
बहिणी म्हणे जेथें अनिर्वाच्य बोली । सद्‌गुरु माऊली तेची दावी ॥ ५ ॥

अभंग १८१

प्रारब्धाआधीन शरीर लागलें । आत्मत्व निराळें वेगळेंचि ॥ १ ॥
सुखदु:ख याचें नाणावें अंतरीं । पूर्ण साक्षात्कारी स्थिर राहे ॥ २ ॥
बहिणी म्हणे त्याचें सांगेन विंदान । सद्‌गुरुचरण पाहें पां रे ॥ ३ ॥

अभंग १८२

पिंड ब्रह्मांडासी करोनी ऐक्यता । हो या परता साक्षीरूप ॥ १ ॥
सर्व तूंचि होसी सर्वांही वेगळा । ऐसी साध कळा सद्‌गुरुमुखें ॥ २ ॥
हिंग हिरण्यासी ऐक्य करोनिया । जाय तूं अद्वया ब्रह्मपदा ॥ ३ ॥
आशा तृष्णा माया एकरूप दोनी । करोनिया जनीं वर्तें सुखें ॥ ४ ॥
सर्वही प्रपंच ऐक्यतेसी आणी । तूंचि जनीं वनीं होउनी राहें ॥ ५ ॥
बहिणी म्हणे सर्व हारपली मुळी । तें रूप न्याहाळी ज्ञानदृष्टीं ॥ ६ ॥

अभंग १८३

काळे-गोरेपण धुतलिया जाय । दाहकपण काय अग्नि सांडी ॥ १ ॥
तैसें तें प्राक्तन न सोडी सर्वथा । ज्ञानियाच्या माथा साट वाजे ॥ २ ॥
शीतलता उदक काय सांडी गुण । चंचलत्व मन केविं सांडी ॥ ३ ॥
बहिणी म्हणे याचें होईल निरसन । सद्गुरुचरण पाहलिया ॥ ४ ॥

*अभंग १८४

गुरु अवघे जाले उपदेश मांडिले ।
सद्गुरुकृपेचा न कळे महिमा कोणासी ॥ १ ॥
नानापरीचें ज्ञानध्यान । सांगती जपतपानुष्ठान ।
परि तें सद्गुरुलक्षण अगम्य जाणा वो ॥ २ ॥
आगमनिगमधारी । एक तें जारणाधिकारी ।
चुकोनी जाले वैरी । देवाचे कैसे ॥ ३ ॥
नाना मंत्र उपासना । सांगती ते यंत्रधारणा ।
परी ते सद्गुरुचरणा । न पावती कोणी ॥ ४ ॥
बहिणी म्हणे आतां काया । जतन कां करावी वायां ।
भजावें श्रीगुरूच्या पायां । सर्वही सिद्धि रे ॥ ५ ॥

अभंग १८५

गुरुपरंपरा आम्हां चैतन्य बळी ।
तयाचे स्मरणें आम्ही वैकुंठीं बळी ॥ १ ॥
नमस्कार हा तया साष्टांग माझा ।
वोवाळूं जीवें साधु चैतन्य राजा ॥ २ ॥
चैतन्य हा सर्वगत व्यापक सद्गुरू ।
प्रगटला हा 'तुकाराम'वेषें दातारू ॥ ३ ॥
तयाचें हें ध्यान सदा माझीये अंतरीं ।
अंतरींचें ध्यान 'तुका' सबाह्याभ्यंतरीं ॥ ४ ॥
नेणें स्नान दान जप आसन मुद्रा ।
सदा सर्व काळ ध्याऊं चैतन्यपदा ॥ ५ ॥
बहिणी म्हणे मुक्त आम्हीं सद्गुरूचे ध्यानें ।
प्रेमें भक्ति-भावें तपा वोवाळूं प्राणें ॥ ६ ॥

---

* हें पद असून याला चाल 'रामदासी पदाची' असें मुळांत म्हटलें आहे (संग्राहक).

अभंग १८६

आतां सद्गुरु स्वामी राणा । माझिया प्राणा ॥ ध्रु. ॥
ठेविन मी मस्तक ह्याचे चरणीं । लाविल मज स्मरणीं ।
ध्याईन मी निश्चल अंतःकरणीं । निज दाविल नयनीं ॥ १ ॥
ज्याचे दर्शनीं द्वैत निरसे । माया न स्पर्शे ।
अमृतवृष्टि ज्यावरि वर्षे । आनंदें हर्षे ॥ २ ॥
खंती वाटे त्याची मजगे । किती सांगूं मी तुज गे ।
सांगेल मुक्तीचें बीज गे । बहिणी म्हणे मग गे ॥ ३ ॥

७. अनुतापपर

अभंग १८७

अनुताप-अग्नि लागला अंतरीं । आतां कृपा करीं जगन्नाथा ॥ १ ॥
तापत्रयें फार पीडिलें शरीर । नलगे संसार स्वर्ग तोही ॥ २ ॥
पेटलीं इंद्रियें धडाडीत अंगें । कृपा करी वेगें पांडुरंगा ॥ ३ ॥
बहिणी म्हणे सुख तेंचि झालें दुःख । ऐसा हा विवेक संचरला ॥ ४ ॥

अभंग १८८

पाहें परतोन मी हा येथें कोण । देह तोही जाण नाशवंत ॥ १ ॥
इंद्रियाचरण होतसे कैसेंनी । सृष्टीचा तो धनी कोण येथें ॥ २ ॥
पृथ्वी आप तेज वायू हें गगन । सर्वही निर्माण जालें कोठें ॥ ३ ॥
बहिणी म्हणे याचा करावया शोध । होउनी सावध विचारिजे ॥ ४ ॥

अभंग १८९

आपुलीये मनीं विचारोनी सर्व । पुसावया ठाव पहातसें ॥ १ ॥
जेथें पुसे तेथें संदेह तुटेना । करि स्थिर मना कोण ऐसा ॥ २ ॥
शास्त्रासीं पुसावें थोडें तों आयुष्य । कर्म तें अवश्य कर्मीं गोंवी ॥ ३ ॥
बहिणी म्हणे ऐसी चिंता साधकासी । कैसी भवपाशीं मुक्त होऊं ॥ ४ ॥

अभंग १९०

जेथें पुसों जावें तेथें अभिमान । आपुलेंची ज्ञान प्रतिष्ठी तो ॥ १ ॥
जाणोनि अंतरीं न सांगेची कोणी । कोणाचे वचनीं स्थिर राहों ॥ २ ॥
लय हें लक्षण सांगती धारणा । नाना उपासना नाना मंत्र ॥ ३ ॥
एक ते सांगती पंच मुद्रा जप । एवं खटाटोप आसनाचा ॥ ४ ॥
एक ते सांगती तीर्थ तप व्रत । एक ते अनंत पूजाविधि ॥ ५ ॥
बहिणी म्हणे आतां नव्हे स्थिर मन । जेथें तेथें रण अविद्येचें ॥ ६ ॥

अभंग १९१

कामाचे विकिले क्रोधाचे जिंकिले । लोभाचे अंकिले सर्व भावें ॥ १ ॥
तयांसी पुसतां काय देती सुख । अंतरीं विवेक नाहीं जयां ॥ २ ॥
आशेलागीं जया आंदण दिधलें । ममतेचे जाले सेवक ते ॥ ३ ॥
बहिणी म्हणे तेचि ग्रासिले मायेनें । आम्हां सोडवणें केवीं होती ॥ ४ ॥

अभंग १९२

दुजियाच्या दुःखें शिणें ज्याचें चित्त । तोचि एक संत वोळखावा ॥ १ ॥
तयासी पुसतां हरील तो शीण । दुःख घे हिरोन रोकडेंची ॥ २ ॥
परोपकार जया जालासे विभागी । शांती हे सर्वांगीं डोलतसे ॥ ३ ॥
बहिणी म्हणे नाहीं आपुलें पारिखें । वर्ततो विवेकें ज्ञानदृष्टी ॥ ४ ॥

अभंग १९३

चंदन सर्वांगें झिजोनिया जाय । जेणेंपरी होय तोष प्राण्या ॥ १ ॥
तैसें साधु जन मनें वाचें कायें । सुख देतां नोहे उदासीन ॥ २ ॥
उदक तें जैसें संतोषवी जनां । उपकार तो तृण आदि करुनी ॥ ३ ॥
बहिणी म्हणे संतीं अवतार घेतले । जनहित केलें सर्व परीं ॥ ४ ॥

अभंग १९४

अनुतापें विरक्त होईल मानस । विषयाचा ध्यास तुटेल तैं ॥ १ ॥
वाटेल जैं चित्ता नावडती जन्म । इंद्रियासी नेम होय तेव्हां ॥ २ ॥
स्वर्ग संसाराची तुटेल आवडी । होय देशोधडी काम क्रोध ॥ ३ ॥
बहिणी म्हणे ऐसें होय जैं अंतर । तैंच तेथें वर सद्गुरूचा ॥ ४ ॥

अभंग १९५

इहलोक सत्य मानितांचि जाण । आली नागवण घरामाजीं ॥ १ ॥
निश्चय विवेक करुनी निर्धार । शाश्वत हें सार घेई मूढा ॥ २ ॥
इहलोक पहातां क्षणांतचि नासे । येथील हव्यास धरूं नको ॥ ३ ॥
बहिणी म्हणे देह प्रपंच असत्य । मनांतील तथ्य सांगितलें ॥ ४ ॥

अभंग १९६

असत्य प्रपंच म्हणोनि सांडिसी । नागवण परियेसी तेही बापा ॥ १ ॥
असत्यचि सत्य साधला जाणिजे । विवेक पाहिजे आपुलीया ॥ २ ॥
असत्य शरीर तयाचेनि जाण । साधिती निर्वाण ब्रह्मनिष्ठ ॥ ३ ॥
सोहागी असत्य परी एकवटी सोनें । लोखंड भूषणें घडवीत ॥ ४ ॥
नाग तो विखार सेवितां तो हित । महाविषें मृत्यु न बाधती ॥ ५ ॥
बहिणी म्हणे सत्य असत्यचि साधे । सद्गुरुचिया बोधें वर्तलिया ॥ ६ ॥

अभंग १९७

आणिलें उसनें पांचांचें शरीर । साधावया सार मोक्षपंथ ॥ १ ॥
येथें तुवां जरी मांडिला आळस । होईल तरी नाश स्वहिताचा ॥ २ ॥
भाड्याचिये घोडे करोनि आणिले । पाहिजे साधिलें कार्य त्वरें ॥ ३ ॥
बहिणी म्हणे ज्याचें नेईल तो धनी । होईल ते हानि स्वहिताची ॥ ४ ॥

अभंग १९८

पृथ्वी आप तेज वायु आणि नभु । ब्रह्मांडीं स्वयंभु वर्तती ते ॥ १ ॥
आणियेले अंश नांव करावया । भव तारावया स्वहित ते ॥ २ ॥
अस्थिमांसत्वचा नाडी आणि रोम । पांच हे उत्तम धरित्रीचे ॥ ३ ॥
लाळ मूत्र स्वेद शुक्र हें शोणीत । आणिले हे सत्य उदकाचे ॥ ४ ॥
क्षुधा तृषा निद्रा आलस्य मैथुन । मागितले गुण तेजापाशीं ॥ ५ ॥
चलनवलन अकुंचन निरोधन । प्रसरण हे जाण वायूपाशीं ॥ ६ ॥
राग द्वेष भय लज्जा मोह पाहे । निःसंदेह गुण हे पांचापाशीं ॥ ७ ॥
ऐसे हे पांचांचे गुण पंचवीस । आणिले सायास करोनिया ॥ ८ ॥
शंभर वर्षांचा करोनिया नेम । आणिले उत्तम गुण तिन्ही ॥ ९ ॥
चाऱ्ही वेदयासी आउलें ठेविलें । बळीसी दिधलें बलिदान ॥१०॥
बहिणी म्हणे नाम भवसिंधुतारक । निर्मिलें अनेक जीवमात्र ॥११॥

अभंग १९९

सत्त्वाचिये धाटी घालुनी चालिली । ते जाण पावली स्वर्ग लोका ॥ १ ॥
चिंतिलिये ठायास जाइजे चिंतितां । हित तें तत्त्वतां विचारावें ॥ २ ॥
रजाचिये धाटी चालियेलें जरी । भूलोकाभीतरीं पाववी ते ॥ ३ ॥
तमोगुणी धाटी घालोनी चालिली । अधोगती गेली तेचि नाव ॥ ४ ॥
शुद्ध सत्त्वीं नाव लोटलिया जाण । पावती निर्वाण ब्रह्मपदीं ॥ ५ ॥
बहिणी म्हणे तारी मारी नाव हेची । वासना जयाची तयापरी ॥ ६ ॥

अभंग २००

सत्य सत्य श्रुति धर्मासी चालवी । तापसी तो दैवी संपत्तीचा ॥ १ ॥
तो जाय स्वर्गासी सत्याचिया बळें । त्यजोनी सकळ कर्मपंथा ॥ २ ॥
दयाक्षमा भूतकृपा जयापाशीं । निष्कामता तैसी शुद्ध बुद्ध ॥ ३ ॥
निश्चय सबल अंगीं जया धैर्य । वचनीं माधुर्य अवंचक ॥ ४ ॥
संतोषी सर्वदां नुल्लंघोनी वेद । अंतरीं आनंद सर्वकाळ ॥ ५ ॥
संतांची संगती सद्‌गुरुसेवन । नाहीं दुजेपण जयामध्यें ॥ ६ ॥
वैराग्यीं वर्तत प्रपंच्याचा साक्षी । आलियाचें रक्षीं चित्त जो कां ॥ ७ ॥
बाहिणी म्हणे ऐसा स्वर्गा जाय नर । आत्मज्ञानशूर जाय मोक्षा ॥ ८ ॥

अभंग २०१

कर्म करी देहीं धरोनी फळाशा । द्वैताचा वळसा जयापाशीं ॥ १ ॥
तयासी हा जाण प्राप्त मृत्यु लोक । रजोगुणी एक वोळखावा ॥ २ ॥
गर्व जयापाशीं क्रोध सर्वकाळ । निद्रा ते जवळ ठेविलीसे ॥ ३ ॥
मोहाचिये माळा सर्वकाळ कंठीं । परस्त्रिया दृष्टीं न्याहाळीत ॥ ४ ॥
आलियानें घरां इंद्राची संपत्ती । समाधान चित्तीं नाहीं जया ॥ ५ ॥
पापिया निष्ठुर विषयांचा ध्यास । जया अविश्वास सर्वकाळ ॥ ६ ॥
चुंबक निंदक भूतमात्रीं द्रोह । नाहीं निःसंदेह चित्त ज्याचें ॥ ७ ॥
बहिणी म्हणे ऐसा वर्ते जो मानसीं । मृत्युलोकीं त्यासी जन्म घेणें ॥ ८ ॥

अभंग २०२

विधिहीन वर्ते वेदांसी न मानी । श्रेष्ठ अव्हेरोनी वर्ततसे ॥ १ ॥
तया दुर्जनासी नर्कयोनीं जन्म । जाणावा अधम तमोगुणी ॥ २ ॥
करितसे घात विश्वास देउनि । हिंसक अवगुणी मंदबुद्धि ॥ ३ ॥
अखाद्य भक्षण अच्योष्य चोषण अपेयाचें पान सुखें जया ॥ ४ ॥
न धरीं भय मनीं नर्काचिये बीज । वर्तणें सहज पापबुद्धि ॥ ५ ॥
बहिणी म्हणे ऐसा जाणा तमोगुणी । पडेल पतनीं हीनमती ॥ ६ ॥

अभंग २०३

त्रिगुणाचें जाण शरीर ओतलें । देहीं क्रिया चाले गुणापरी ॥ १ ॥
म्हणोनिया साक्षी होय तूं गुणाचा । मग तुज कैचा द्वैतभाव ॥ २ ॥
त्रिगुणाचें भय ब्रह्मादिकां असे । त्रिगुणाचे फांसे घातकी हे ॥ ३ ॥
त्रिगुण सांकळी जीवासी जडली । तयाचेनी झाली बाधकता ॥ ४ ॥
त्रिगुणाचा सर्प झोंबला जयासी । मरण तयासी साच आलें ॥ ५ ॥
बहिणी म्हणे गुण निवारील ऐसे । एक कृपा वसे सद्‌गुरूची ॥ ६ ॥

अभंग २०४

त्रिगुणापरतें आहे तेंची एक । भावने भाविक जाणती ते ॥ १ ॥
सर्वांमाजीं असे सर्वांही वेगळें । इंद्रियां नाकळे अखंडत्वें ॥ २ ॥
दृश्य म्हणों तरी न दिसेची डोळां । नाहीं तो आगळा भास याचा ॥ ३ ॥
बहिणी म्हणे नाहीं नामरूप गुण । सर्वांठायीं पूर्ण सदोदित ॥ ४ ॥

अभंग २०५

जाला वासनेचा अंत । तेंचि जाणावें ललित ॥ १ ॥
ऐसें जाणती सज्जन । साक्षी जया आलें मन ॥ २ ॥
आला विषयांचा त्रास । पुढें जाले सावकाश ॥ ३ ॥
चित्त झालें पाठमोरें । एक आपुल्या निर्धारें ॥ ४ ॥
ज्ञानें जाळिलें संचित । हेत राहिला निवांत ॥ ५ ॥
बहिणी म्हणे स्थिर बुद्धि । हेचि अखंड समाधि ॥ ६ ॥

अभंग २०६

रूप असोनिया डोळियांसी दिसे । तेजही प्रकाशे नेत्रांमाजीं ॥ १ ॥
तें रूप चोरटें ओळखें बा चित्ता । बुद्धीचा आरुता पैस जेथें ॥ २ ॥
सगुण निर्गुण लक्षातीत वस्तु । जाला तेथ अस्तु इंद्रियांचा ॥ ३ ॥
बहिणी म्हणे शब्दीं न सांपडे तरी । शब्द त्या भीतरीं अंतर्बाह्य ॥ ४ ॥

अभंग २०७

पृथ्वीचा तो गंध उदकींचा रस । तेजामाजीं अंश आत्मयाचा ॥ १ ॥
परी तो न दिसे ज्ञानचक्षूवीण । पाहिजे अंजन गुरु-कृपा ॥ २ ॥
वायूमाजीं ज्याचें वसतसे रूप । नभीं असें दीप आत्मयाचा ॥ ३ ॥
बहिणी म्हणे सर्व सर्वांही आगळा । ज्ञानाचिया डोळां पाहें पां रे ॥ ४ ॥

अभंग २०८

पहावयां जातां पहाणेंची सरे । विज्ञान तें विरे जयांमाजीं ॥ १ ॥
तें रूप डोळिया पाहतां न दिसे । जयाचेनी अंशें श्रेष्ठाश्रेष्ठ ॥ २ ॥
लक्षूं जातां लक्ष हारपलें जेथें । परेचाही प्रांत तेथ जाला ॥ ३ ॥
बहिणी म्हणे तेथें व्यवहार राहिला । जे वेळीं पाहिला देवराणा ॥ ४ ॥

अभंग २०९

बोध नंद बुद्धि यशोदा गोकुळीं । जन्म झाला कुळीं गवळियाचे ॥ १ ॥
तें रूप सांवळें पहा डोळेभरीं । बाह्य अभ्यंतरीं ओतप्रोत ॥ २ ॥
नवविध नवमास पूर्ण जाले तेथ । कृष्ण अखंडित जन्मला तो ॥ ३ ॥
बहिणी म्हणे रूप सांवळें सुकुमार । राक्षसांचा भार उतरिला ॥ ४ ॥

अभंग २१०

आकाशींचा सूर्य जळांत बिंबला । तरी काय बुडाला तयामाजीं ॥ १ ॥
तैसा या शरीरीं अलिप्तचि असें । इंद्रियसमरसें असोनिया ॥ २ ॥
चुंबकदर्शनें लोखंडा चलन । आत्मा देहीं जाण तैसा असे ॥ ३ ॥
पूर्ण चंद्र होतां सिंधूसी भरतें । तैसा देह वर्ते आत्मयानें ॥ ४ ॥

आलिया वसंत येती पुष्पें फळें । तैसा देह चळे आत्मसत्ता ॥५॥
बहिणी म्हणे आत्मा सर्वांही अतीत । अनुभवें पदार्थ सर्व कळे ॥६॥

अभंग २११

कोणे ठायीं असे कोणे ठायीं नसे । ऐसें तो मानसें चोजवेना ॥१॥
यालागीं सद्गुरु बोलती जें भावें । आत्मा तो स्वभावें कळावया ॥२॥
कोण याचें गांव कोण याचा ठाव । न कळे स्वयमेव काय धरूं ॥३॥
कोण याचें कुळ कोण याचें स्थळ । कवळायासी बळ कळेचिना ॥४॥
कोण याची माता कोण याचा पिता । अमूकची तत्त्वतां कोण जाणे ॥५॥
बहिणी म्हणे कोणा पुसों याची कथा । ऐसें विवंचितां कल्प गेले ॥६॥

अभंग २१२

सत्य म्हणतां माया ज्ञानें लया जाय । असत्य तरी नोहे कदा काळीं ॥१॥
जाणती अनुभव ज्ञान दृष्टिरूप । मायेचें अमूप रूप वाढे ॥२॥
आकारलें जें जें मायिक तें खरें । शब्द तो निर्धारें मायारूप ॥३॥
ज्ञान तेंही माया ध्यान तें मायाचि । मायेवीण कैंची दृष्टि वाढे ॥४॥
जोंवरी हें द्वैत मनामाजीं वसे । तोंवरी मायांशें लोकत्रय ॥५॥
बहिणी म्हणे माया लटकी म्हणों नेदी । करोनी वेदादि पहा बरें ॥६॥

अभंग २१३

घट भंगलियावरी । नभ नभाचे भीतरीं ॥१॥
तैसा देह गेलियानें । जीव शिव मिथ्या बाणे ॥२॥
जळ आटलियावरी । प्रतिबिंबा कैंची उरी ॥३॥
बहिणी म्हणे भासे द्वैत । जाण उपाधीनें येथ ॥४॥

अभंग २१४

चालतां पाऊल पंढरीच्या वाटे । ब्रह्मसुख भेटे रोकडेंची ॥१॥
दिंडी ध्वजा भार चालती अपार । मृदंग-गंभीर-स्वरश्रुति ॥२॥
हमामा हुंबरी घालिती परवडी । होवोनी उघडी विष्णुदास ॥३॥
बहिणी म्हणे ऐसा आनंद वाटेचा । कोण तो दैवाचा देखे डोळां ॥४॥

८. संतवर्णनपर

अभंग २१५

गर्व जयापाशीं नाहीं अणुमात्र । सर्वांगें पवित्र संतवृत्ति ॥१॥
तेचि एक साधु तारितील जन । भ्रांतीसी हिरोन ज्ञान देती ॥२॥
अंतर्बाह्य शुद्ध सूर्याचिये परी । ज्ञान कर्में करी बाह्यात्कारें ॥३॥
रत्न कीं कर्पूर शुद्ध अंतर्बाह्य । मनांतील गुह्य सांगे जनीं ॥४॥
कृपा जयापासीं होउनी आंदण । आनंदीं निमग्न सदा राहे ॥५॥
बहिणी म्हणे मनीं भूतकृपा पूर्ण । तेचि वोळखण संतजनां ॥६॥

अभंग २१६

तीर्थें इच्छितातीं तया साधुजनां । पुण्याची गणना कोण करी ॥१॥
ब्रह्मरूप स्वयें तारावया जन । अवतार घेवोन येथें आले ॥२॥
ब्रह्मादिका देव इच्छिताती भेटी । अमृताची वृष्टि क्रिया तैसी ॥३॥
बहिणी म्हणे ज्याचें बोलणें सहज । वेदांतींचें बीज हातीं वसे ॥४॥

अभंग २१७

गंगेच्या प्रवाहा सागरींच गति । बोलताती श्रुति ब्रह्मवरी ॥१॥
तैसी जाण बुद्धि चाले तोचिवरी । निश्चय शिखरीं विरुनी जाये ॥२॥
पतिव्रते काम वाढे तो भ्रतारीं । सूर्य तो अंबरीं प्रभा दावी ॥३॥
वहिणी म्हणे तैसें संतांचें बोलणें । साक्षात्कार मनें होय जीवा ॥४॥

अभंग २१८

सहज स्वभावें गोडी ते अमृतीं । पुष्पीं जाण अद्भुती अंगींच जो ॥१॥
तैसा तो स्वभाव क्रिया ते वर्तत । वेद मूर्तिमंत आकारला ॥२॥
परिसाचा गुण अंगीं साच खरा । रत्न गार हिरा सूर्य जैसा ॥३॥
बहिणी म्हणे तैसी सहज अंगीं शांति । संतांची संपत्ति सर्व कर्म ॥४॥

अभंग २१९

संतां असंतांचें शरीर सारिखें । भिन्नत्व वोळखें क्रियेपाशीं ॥१॥
काय सांगों फळ दोहींचें वेगळें । जाणत्यासी कळे ज्ञानदृष्टीं ॥२॥
परीस आणि गार सारिखें स्वरूप । तेल आणि तूप पाहें पारे ॥३॥
कांच आणि मणि पहातां समान । अंतरींचा गुण भिन्न असे ॥४॥
खरें आणि खोटें सारिखेंची नाणें । ताक दूध गुणें वेगळेंची ॥५॥
बहिणी म्हणे मैंद साधु वोळखून । पुढें त्याचे गुण अंगीकारीं ॥६॥

अभंग २२०

संतसंगें शुद्ध होय चित्तवृत्ति । लागेल प्रवृत्ति संतसंगें ॥१॥
यालागीं तयाचें करावें दासत्व । तेणें निजतत्त्व सांपडेल ॥२॥
संतसंगें दोष नासतील सर्व । संतसंगें गर्व जाईल तो ॥३॥
संतसंगें तुज सांपडेल निज । संतसंगें गुज प्रगट होय ॥४॥
संतसंगें दृष्टि पडेल स्वरूपीं । संतसंगें स्वल्पीं मोक्ष जोडे ॥५॥
बहिणी म्हणे संग धरावा निःसंग । साधनाचें अंग कळे तेव्हां ॥६॥

अभंग २२१

संतसंगें होय वैराग्य मनासी । देईल शांतीसी संतसंग ॥ १ ॥
संत सकलांचे शिरोमणि थोर । पाहिजे निर्धार एकनिष्ठ ॥ २ ॥
संतसंगें ज्ञान विज्ञान ठसावें । संतसंगें होये सुख देहीं ॥ ३ ॥
बहिणी म्हणे संतसंगाचा विचार । जाणती निःसार भक्तिवंत ॥ ४ ॥

अभंग २२२

संत महावैद्य भवरोग फेडीती । सांगेन ते गति ऐक त्यांची ॥ १ ॥
अर्ध मात्रा रस देउनिया जीव । रोग दूरी सर्व करितातीं ॥ २ ॥
विषयाचा त्याग सांगोनिया पथ्य । भाव यथा तथ्य सेववितीं ॥ ३ ॥
बहिणी म्हणे ऐसें जाणोनी अंतर । तैसाची प्रकार प्रेरितातीं ॥ ४ ॥

अभंग २२३

चंदनाचा संग लाधलिया वृक्ष । तैसेचि प्रत्यक्ष होती जाणा ॥ १ ॥
तैसी ही संगति साधूची जालिया । संत आपसया होती जीव ॥ २ ॥
गांवींचा ओहोळ मिळालिया गंगे । गंगारूप संगें होय जैसा ॥ ३ ॥
परिसाचा संग जालियानें लोह । होय तें विदेह सुवर्णची ॥ ४ ॥
वातीसी लाधला दीपकाचा संग । प्रकाश अभंग साध्य तया ॥ ५ ॥
बहिणी म्हणे संग सज्जनाचा करी । तोचि रे संसारीं धन्य एक ॥ ६ ॥

अभंग २२४

दुर्जनाचे संगें दुर्जनची होय । पाहे अभिप्राय सहज तो ॥ १ ॥
हिंगाची संगति लाधली कापुरा । स्वगुण तो खरा हारपला ॥ २ ॥
तक्राचे संगतीं नासलें तें दूध । भांग करी मुग्ध जीव क्षणीं ॥ ३ ॥
बहिणी म्हणे संग आपुलेंसें करी । म्हणोनी विचारीं साधुजनां ॥ ४ ॥

अभंग २२५

वोळखोनी करीं संग तूं निर्धारीं । सुख तें अंतरीं पावशील ॥ १ ॥
हा जाण निर्धार विवेकाची युक्ति । न धरावीं आसक्ति मनामाजीं ॥ २ ॥
सुपंथ जाणोनी सज्जनाचे संगें । पावसी सर्वांगें आनंदातें ॥ ३ ॥
बहिणी म्हणे शास्त्र केलें याचिलागीं । कळावया जगीं मार्गामार्ग ॥ ४ ॥

अभंग २२६

संतसंगतीचा महिमा अद्भुत । होती ज्ञानवंत सत्वगुणी ॥ १ ॥
यालागीं सेवावे संतांचे चरण । स्थिर होय मन एक क्षण ॥ २ ॥
संतांचें बोलणें ऐकतांचि कानीं । ब्रह्मरूप झणीं होय सर्व ॥ ३ ॥
बहिणी म्हणे संतदर्शनेंचि मोक्ष । अनुभव प्रत्यक्ष पाहें याचा ॥ ४ ॥

अभंग २२७

तीर्थें हिंडलिया काय होय फळ । अंतर निर्मळ नाहीं जंव ॥ १ ॥
यालागीं निर्मळ होय चित्त येणें । संतांचें दर्शन घेतलिया ॥ २ ॥

पाषाणप्रतिमा काय बोलतील । सुख हें देतील काय चित्ता ॥ ३ ॥
बहिणी म्हणे ज्याचे वचनीं निःसंदेह । होईल विदेह रोकडाची ॥ ४ ॥

अभंग २२८

प्रपंचीं असोन प्रपंचा अतीत । करताती संत सर्व कर्म ॥ १ ॥
यालागीं सेवावे संतांचे चरण । मोक्षासी कारण एक हेंची ॥ २ ॥
तक्रांतील लोणीं न मिळेचि पुनः । वेगळ्याची गुणां आंत आलें ॥ ३ ॥
पद्मिनीचें पत्र न मिळे उदकांत । असताही तेथ जन्मवरी ॥ ४ ॥
बहिणी म्हणे तैसें प्रपंचीं असोन । न बाधी खूण साधूपाशीं ॥ ५ ॥

अभंग २२९

संतकृपा झाली । इमारत फळा आली ॥ १ ॥
ज्ञानदेवें रचिला पाया । उभारिलें देवालया ॥ २ ॥
नामा तयाचा किंकर । तेणें रचिलें तें आवार ॥ ३ ॥
जनार्दन एकनाथ । खांब दिधला भागवत ॥ ४ ॥
तुका झालासे कळस । भजन करा सावकाश ॥ ५ ॥
बहिणी म्हणे फडकती ध्वजा । निरूपणा केलें *वोजा ॥ ६ ॥

अभंग २३०

संत होती खरे भवार्णवीं तारूं । जाणती उतारू प्राणियाचा ॥ १ ॥
कासे लाविताती निष्ठेचिया बळें । नेती ते कृपाळ पैल तीरा ॥ २ ॥
नामाची सांगडी बांधोनी बळकट । दाविताती तट सायुज्याचे ॥ ३ ॥
बहिणी म्हणे मागें उतरिले बहुत । येणेंपरी संत तारूं खरे ॥ ४ ॥

अभंग २३१

एका मतें संत धन्वंतरी जाण । मंत्रवादी पूर्ण भासताती ॥ १ ॥
वांचविले जीव सर्पदृष्टीपासांव । सामर्थ्य अपूर्व वाटतसे ॥ २ ॥
पंचमुखी अहि विष ज्या झोंबलें । लहरी येती बळें नानाविध ॥ ३ ॥
बहिणी म्हणे संत बघती ज्याकडे । विष त्याचें झडे नवल मोठें ॥ ४ ॥

---

* चांगल्या रीतीनें; सहज.

अभंग २३२

संतांपाशीं असे ज्ञानाची निजशक्ति । अज्ञाननिवृत्ति होय तेणें ॥ १ ॥
यालागीं संतासी जावें लोटांगणीं । रिघावें शरण मनोभावें ॥ २ ॥
संतांचिये कृपे विषयमळ-नाश । सांपडे अविनाश परब्रह्म ॥ ३ ॥
बहिणी म्हणे संत देव हे प्रत्यक्ष । कां न घेशी साक्ष मनामार्जी ॥ ४ ॥

अभंग २३३

संतसंगें योग संतसंगें याग । संतसंगें प्रयोग जोडे मना ॥ १ ॥
यालागीं आवडी धरावी संतांची । प्रत्यक्ष मोक्षाची वाट हेचि ॥ २ ॥
संतसंगें तीर्थ संतसंगें क्षेत्र । संतसंगें मंत्रसिद्धि जोडे ॥ ३ ॥
बहिणी म्हणे संतसंगें जोडे ज्ञान । संतसंगें मन स्थिर होये ॥ ४ ॥

अभंग २३४

संत देखतां दृष्टी । वृत्ति जाली उफराटी ।
हारपल्या अवघ्या गोष्टी । पडिलें मौन ॥ १ ॥
दृश्याचें लोपलें भान । द्वैताचें उठलें ठाण ।
ब्रह्मानंदसुखें गगन । भरोनी ठेलें ॥ २ ॥
मनासी जाहले ठक[१] । डोळीयां पडलें टक[२] ।
देखानि अखंड एक । स्वरूप डोळां ॥ ३ ॥
शब्द निःशब्द झाला । निवृत्तीसी सामावला ।
सुमनाचा ध्यास तुटला । जयाचे ठायीं ॥ ४ ॥
बहिणीस लाधतां संतसंग । संतप्रेमा अंतरंग ।
सकळाचा होऊनी भंग । अखंड ठेली ॥ ५ ॥

अभंग २३५

आजि माझा जन्म सफल गे माये । संतसज्जनांचे देखियले पाये ।
त्यांचे चरणरजें देहभार जाये । सुख हें होय अनिवार ॥ १ ॥

---

१ तटस्थपणा. २ एकाग्र दृष्टी.

आजि माझें भाग्य फळासी आलें । साधुसंतांचे पाय देखिले ।
सप्रेम या देहीं दाटलें । सुख सुखावलें सहजची ॥ २ ॥
एकपणें होतें अनेक झालें । पहातां विश्वाकार विस्तारलें ।
वटबीजन्यायें कैसें विरूढलें । सर्व होउनी ठेलें माझी मीच ॥ ३ ॥
आलें गेलें अवधान *नाथिला भ्रम । आजवरी प्रकृतीनें केला हा धर्म
रज्जुसर्पन्यायें मिथ्या जाला भ्रम । देखतां चरणरज नाचे ॥ ४ ॥
बहिणी म्हणे तेणें अहंपण माझें । संसारदु:ख उतरिलें वोझें ।
तुकाराम भेटला धन्य जिणें । कृतकृत्य जालें सहजची ॥ ५ ॥

---

*नाहींसा केला.

९. बोधपर

अभंग २३९

मरण न यो म्हणतो । रे! नर मरण न यो म्हणतो ।
स्वानुभविक सुख जया तोही विषयाशीं रमतो ॥ १ ॥
स्त्री सुत धन दुहिता प्रिय ज्यासी भ्रमर जसा भ्रमतो ।
आवडे मान प्रतिष्ठा लौकिक येथेंची जो रमतो ॥ २ ॥
राज्यसुखीं रति आर्त मूर्छना कामीं लुब्धक तो ।
जो व्यसनप्रिय मद्यपी स्त्रीलंपट तामस तो ॥ ३ ॥
वांच्छित इंद्रपद प्रमदासुख त्यास्तव याज्ञिक तो ।
बहिणी म्हणे अरे ये स्थितिचा नर मृत्युभयासि भितो ॥ ४ ॥

अभंग २४०

मृत्यु भया न भीं रे । ज्ञानी मृत्युभया न भीं रे ।
सिंधुवरी जसे बुडबुडे येती त्या वातें विलयो रे ॥ १ ॥
मायिक सर्व प्रपंच मिथ्या कैंचा त्या प्रळयो ।
स्वप्न जैसें प्रतिभासत मिथ्या देह तदन्वयो रे ॥ २ ॥
घृत जैसें थिजलें विघुरे मग तेंचि पुन्हा घट होये ।
हेमाचे नग आटुनि हेमचि काय तयासि भये रे ॥ ३ ॥
बहिणी म्हणे निज अनुभव ज्यासी, द्वैत तेथें न यो रे ।
देह पडो अथवा न पडो । अनुभवी परि ब्रह्मिच त्यासि लयो रे ॥ ४ ॥

अभंग २४१

थोरपणा दूरी टाकोनिया जाण । संतांसी शरण जाय वेगीं ॥ १ ॥
तुझी सर्व चिंता हरेल चित्ताची । स्थिरता मनाची होय तरी ॥ २ ॥
सर्वभावें शरण रिघतां संतांसी । ज्ञानाभिमानासी टाकोनिया ॥ ३ ॥
बहिणी म्हणे संत दयानिधि खरे । चित्ताचे निर्धारें सेवीं बापा ॥ ४ ॥

अभंग २४८

वरि वरि वेष संताचा । भींतरीं †धुमस इंद्रियांचा ॥ १ ॥
ऐसे संत जाले कळीं । बोले बोल तो न पाळी ॥ २ ॥
सभा देखोनी धरी मौन । एऱ्हवीं भुंके जैसें श्वान ॥ ३ ॥
तोंड देखोनी बरवे बोले । जगामागें झोंड चाले ॥ ४ ॥
बहिणी म्हणे हे भांड । यांसी कोठें व्याली रांड ॥ ५ ॥

(बोधपर अभंगांपैकीं २३९ ते २४१ व २४८ इतकेच घेतले आहेत.)

---

† चाळा.

१०. नाममाहात्म्यपर

अभंग ३९३

नामसंकीर्तन सदा सर्वकाळ । अखंड प्रेमळ देह ज्याचे ॥१॥
तयासीच भक्ति म्हणावी निर्धार । जाणती उत्तर ज्ञानवंत ॥२॥
क्षण एक काळ जाऊं नेदी रिता । आवडी हे चित्ता पांडुरंगीं ॥३॥
बहिणी म्हणे जीव जाईल सर्वथा । काळ जाऊं नेदी रिता नामाविण ॥४॥

अभंग ३९४

जलावीण मीना होय प्राण साटी[१] । तैसें नाम पोटीं आवडे ज्या ॥१॥
भक्ति हे तयासी सज्ञान बोलती । येर ते जल्पती वाउगेची ॥२॥
तृषाक्रांता जेवीं उदकाचा आवडी । तैसी जया ओढी संकीर्तनीं ॥३॥
बहिणी म्हणे वांझ इच्छिती बाळक । तैसें नामसुख आवडे त्या ॥४॥

अभंग ३९५

भक्ति नाहीं हाटीं घेईजे विकत । हिंडतां वनांत सांपडेना ॥१॥
चित्ताचिये साठीं भक्ति हे साधेल । आणिक जे बोल वायावीण[२] ॥२॥
भक्ति नाहीं पाहीं जाणिवेचे घरीं । धनाढ्यमंदिरीं सांपडेना ॥३॥
भक्ति नाहीं राजा-प्रधानाचे घरीं । भक्ति नाहीं पारीं चौधरीच्या ॥४॥
बहिणी म्हणे भक्ति साधावया एक । पाहिजे विवेक पूर्ण देहीं ॥५॥

अभंग ३९६

भाव तेथें भक्ति, भक्ति तेथें ज्ञान । ज्ञानें समाधान होय चित्ता ॥१॥
मग तूं सहज समाधि पावसी । चित्त नामापाशीं लीन होतां ॥२॥
संतसमागमीं असोनी श्रवण । सदा सावधान अनुक्रमीं ॥३॥
बहिणी म्हणे भक्ति पाहिजे कारण । मग त्या निर्वाणपदप्राप्ति ॥४॥

---

१ भय. २ व्यर्थ.

अभंग ३९७

भाव शुद्ध तरी मोक्ष तया शुद्ध । यासी ग्वाही वेद पहा तुम्ही ॥१॥
अशुद्ध तो भाव करी घात सर्व । अंगीं वसे गर्व तयाचिया ॥२॥
भक्ति हेचि मोक्ष भक्ति हीच मुक्ति । भक्ति ते विरक्ति सत्य खरी ॥३॥
बहिणी म्हणे भक्ति पाहिजे सुदृढ । मग तया गूढ कासयाचें ॥४॥

अभंग ३९८

गुरुमंत्र देव औषध भावार्थें । फळ एक चित्तें पाहें ऐसें ॥ १ ॥
याचिया निर्धारें भावार्थेंसी भज । हृदयींचें गूज सांगितलें ॥ २ ॥
पाषाणप्रतिमा भावें भजलीया । इच्छितसे तया फळ पावे ॥ ३ ॥
बहिणी म्हणे ज्याचा भावार्थ चोखट । तयासी वैकुंठ रोकडेंची ॥ ४ ॥

अभंग ३९९

भावार्थे वाल्मिका आला तो फळासी । जाले सप्तऋषि भावार्थेंची ॥ १ ॥
यालागीं भावार्थ असावा साधकां । करितसे रंकां राज्यनिधि ॥ २ ॥
कौशिकासी भाव फळा आला सत्य । भावार्थ अगत्य पाहिजे तो ॥ ३ ॥
बहिणी म्हणे भाव इच्छाफलदायी । पावसी निर्वाणीं मोक्षपदा ॥ ४ ॥

अभंग ४००

भक्तिबळें इच्छा पुरवितो देव । आला अनुभव पुंडलिका ॥ १ ॥
म्हणोनियां भक्ति असावें कारण । आहे नारायण भाव तेथें ॥ २ ॥
पक्क तुलसीपत्रा-आंत प्रवेशून । तुलेसी भगवान तुका नये ॥ ३ ॥
द्रौपदीचीं वस्त्रें स्वयें जाला देव । पोह्यासाठीं गांव सोनियाचा ॥ ४ ॥
भाजिचीया पानें तृप्त केले ऋषी । भावें गणिकेसी वैकुंठ तें ॥ ५ ॥
बहिणी म्हणे भाव तोचि आम्हां देव । नाहीं या संदेह अणुमात्र ॥ ६ ॥

अभंग ४०१

भावार्थाचें दावें देवाचिया गळां । तयासी मोकळा कोण करी ॥ १ ॥
विचारितां जन्म सोशी गर्भवास । द्वारपाळ त्यास करी बळी ॥ २ ॥

भावार्थाचे खुंटीं बांधिला हा देव । सोडी ऐसा राव कोण आहे ॥ ३ ॥
बहिणी म्हणे भावतंतु कोण सोडी । भावार्थ-परवडी देव जाणे ॥ ४ ॥

अभंग ४०२

पांचां विषयांचा समूह एकत्र । होउनी परत्र अंतरलें ॥ १ ॥
यालागीं सांगति उपाय ते भले । आपणही केले तरावया ॥ २ ॥
कुरंग तो जाण नादासी वेधला । प्राणासी मुकला क्षणामाजी ॥ ३ ॥
स्पर्श करोनियां सांपडला हस्ती । मारी नेम हातीं पहासी तूं ॥ ४ ॥
पतंग रूपासी भुलोनी दीपकीं । प्राणें गेला दुःखी होउनिया ॥ ५ ॥
रसनेचा लोभ धरोनिया मीन । न लागतां क्षण जीवें गेला ॥ ६ ॥
भ्रमर गुंतला कमलिनी-गंधें । गेला प्राण वेधें तये वेळां ॥ ७ ॥
बहिणी म्हणे पांचा विषय पांचजण । वेंचुनिया प्राण न सुटती ॥ ८ ॥

अभंग ४०३

नामेंविण क्षण जाऊं नेदी घडी । चित्तासी आवडी सर्वकाळ ॥ १ ॥
भजन हें तथा बोलिजे देवाचें । मनें कायावाचे समर्पिलें ॥ २ ॥
संतसमागमीं श्रवणाची आर्त । चित्तीं अखंडित प्रेमभाव ॥ ३ ॥
बहिणी म्हणे मन नेणे विषयसुख । नित्य ज्या हरिख नामपाठीं ॥ ४ ॥

११. ब्रह्मकर्मपर

अभंग ४०४

तपाचें सामर्थ्य आहे बहु मोठें । पाहीं तूं वरिष्ठे मागील ते ॥ १ ॥
विश्वामित्रें सृष्टि केलीसे दुसरी । जाण तपावरी गायत्रीच्या ॥ २ ॥
वसिष्ठें धरित्री दर्भाचिये अग्रीं । ठेविली सामुग्री तपाची हे ॥ ३ ॥
सूर्य-तेज आलें समक्ष साक्षीसी । तयाच्या तपासी कोण वर्णी ॥ ४ ॥
अगस्तीनें केलें आचमन सिंधूचें । तप हें तयाचें अति उग्र ॥ ५ ॥
बहिणी म्हणे तप जयापाशीं असे । तयासी सायास कासयाचे ॥ ६ ॥

अभंग ४०५

वर्णांमाजीं एक ब्राह्मण वरिष्ठ । ऐसें मार्गें श्रेष्ठ बोलियेले ॥ १ ॥
म्हणोनी ब्राह्मण पूजावे आदरें । मोक्षाचीं, तीं द्वारें प्राणियासी ॥ २ ॥
ब्राह्मणाचे मुखीं सदा वसे वेद । जाणताती भेद अर्थ त्याचा ॥ ३ ॥
बहिणी म्हणे देव वाहे ज्याची लाथ । हृदयीं विख्यात असे ठावें ॥ ४ ॥

अभंग ४०६

ब्राह्मणाचे मुखें तृप्त होय देव । पहा अनुभव रोकडा हा ॥ १ ॥
यालागीं ब्राह्मण वंदावें मस्तकीं । शास्त्रें समस्त कीं बोलताती ॥ २ ॥
ब्राह्मणाचे मंत्रें पाषाणीं प्रतिष्ठा । धरिलिया निष्ठा प्रगटे देव ॥ ३ ॥
बहिणी म्हणे देव कलियुगीं हेचि । ऐसी हे वेदाची असे साक्ष ॥ ४ ॥

अभंग ४०७

ब्राह्मणाचें तीर्थ प्राप्त होय जया । पृथ्वीचींही तया घडती तीर्थें ॥ १ ॥
यालागीं ब्राह्मण श्रेष्ठ सर्वांपरी* । जयाचिये द्वारीं सर्व सिद्धि ॥ २ ॥
ब्राह्मणाची कृपा होय जयावरी । कल्याण तो वरी कल्पकोटि ॥ ३ ॥
बहिणी म्हणे ज्याचे दर्शनेंचि पाप । जाय आपोआप जळोनियां ॥ ४ ॥

---

* पेक्षां

अभंग ४०८

ब्राह्मणाची सेवा घडे एक क्षण । इच्छा होय पूर्ण अंतरींची ॥ १ ॥
म्हणोनी तयासी भजावें पूजावें । आदरें घालावें लोटांगण ॥ २ ॥
ब्राह्मणाचे काजें वेंचलिया प्राण । इंद्रपदीं जाण वास तया ॥ ३ ॥
बहिणी म्हणे ऐसे ब्राह्मण हे थोर । मोक्ष हा किंकर तयांपाशीं ॥ ४ ॥

अभंग ४०९

ब्राह्मणाची आज्ञा देव वंदी शिरीं । मुक्ति आज्ञाधारी जयापाशीं ॥ १ ॥
यालागीं ब्राह्मण तारक कलियुगीं । धन्य तेचि जगीं सेविती त्या ॥ २ ॥
ब्राह्मणाचे देहीं मूर्त भगवान । वेद तो आपण मुखीं जया ॥ ३ ॥
बहिणी म्हणे त्यांचें काय वर्णूं एक । शरीर विवेकरूप त्यांचें ॥ ४ ॥

अभंग ४१०

चहुं वर्णांमाजीं वरिष्ठ ब्राह्मण । समीपता जाण मुक्ति त्यासी ॥ १ ॥
ब्रह्मची ब्राह्मण बोलताती श्रुति । वचन वंदिती लोकत्रय ॥ २ ॥
बाह्मण जालिया नाहीं अधोगति । देव सर्व ध्याती ब्राह्मणासी ॥ ३ ॥
बहिणी म्हणे जें हें गायत्रीचें स्थळ । पहा या केवळ देह ज्यांचे ॥ ४ ॥

अभंग ४११

ब्राह्मण कोणासी म्हणावें निश्चित । पहावा हा अर्थ विवेकेंची ॥ १ ॥
मग ते वंदावे भजावे सप्रेमें । मोक्षदानी नेमें वेदवाक्य ॥ २ ॥
जीव, देह, जाति, वर्ण कर्म, धर्म । पहावे तें वर्म शोधोनियां ॥ ३ ॥
बहिणी म्हणे ज्ञान पांडित्य ब्राह्मणीं । विवेकेंकरोनी पहा चित्तीं ॥ ४ ॥

अभंग ४१२

जीव हा ब्राह्मण म्हणावा इत्यर्थ । तरी येथें अर्थ सांपडेना ॥ १ ॥
सर्वांठायीं जीव सारिखाचि एक । पशु पक्षी देख चांडाळादि ॥ २ ॥
पुढें जीव होती मागें बहु झाले । ब्राह्मणत्व आलें नाहीं तया ॥ ३ ॥
बहिणी म्हणे जीव प्राणिमात्रीं एक । ब्राह्मणत्व देख म्हणों नये ॥ ४ ॥

अभंग ४१३

देहचि ब्राह्मग म्हणों जरी आतां । न घडे तत्त्वतां विवेकदृष्टि ॥ १ ॥
विचारोनी आधीं ब्राह्मण तो कोण । मग तूं भजोन सुखें राहें ॥ २ ॥
देह हे सर्वांचे एकचि जाणिजे । पंचभूतें सहजें सर्वांठायीं ॥ ३ ॥
तारुण्य वार्धक्य बालत्व देहासी । जाणावें जिवासी स्थान तेंचि ॥ ४ ॥
देह तेथें जीव जीव तेथें देह । ब्राह्मग तो काय म्हणों तया ॥ ५ ॥
बहिणी म्हणे सर्व योनींसी शरीरें । सारिखींचि बा रे विवंचितां ॥ ६ ॥

अभंग ४१४

जरा मृत्यु भय सर्वांसी समान । तरी ते ब्राह्मण म्हणों कैसे ॥ १ ॥
यालागीं विवेक धरोनी मानसीं । 'ब्राह्मण' पदासी वोळखावें ॥ २ ॥
मातापितयाच्या जाळिलें शरीरा । ब्रह्महत्या नरा कैविं नोहे ॥ ३ ॥
बहिणी म्हणे देह ब्राह्मग तो नव्हे । विवेक-वैभवें विचारितां ॥ ४ ॥

अभंग ४१५

आतां वर्ण हाची ब्राह्मग म्हणावा । तरी तो अनुभवा नये कांहीं ॥ १ ॥
ब्राह्मग वेगळा वर्णाही अतीत । पहातां निश्चित भासतसे ॥ २ ॥
श्वेत तो ब्राह्मग क्षत्रिय आरक्त । वैश्य वर्ण पीत नाहीं ऐसें ॥ ३ ॥
कृष्ण वर्ण शूद्र नाहीं ऐसा भेद । आयुष्याचा बांध सारिखाची ॥ ४ ॥
बहिणी म्हणे वर्ण ब्राह्मण तो नव्हे । विवेचूनि पाहें मनामाजीं ॥ ५ ॥

अभंग ४१६

आतां यातीलागीं म्हणावें ब्राह्मण । तरि तें निर्वाण नये चित्ता ॥ १ ॥
निरसोनी सर्व विचारा वेदांतें । उरे तें आयतें वोळखावें ॥ २ ॥
ऋषि शृंगी झाला मृगीचिये पोटीं । गौतम शेवटीं कुशास्तरणीं ॥ ३ ॥
जंबुक तो ऋषि जन्मला जांबुळीं । वाल्मीकाची कुळी वारुळीं ते ॥ ४ ॥
कैवर्तक-पोटीं व्यास तो जन्मला । विश्वामित्र जाला क्षत्रणीचा ॥ ५ ॥
वसिष्ठाचा जन्म उर्वशी-उदरीं । अगस्ति निर्धारीं कलशोद्भव ॥ ६ ॥

नारद प्रसिद्ध ठाउका सर्वांसी । दासी हे तयासी प्रसवली ॥ ७ ॥
बहिणी म्हणे याति नव्हेचि ब्राह्मण । ब्राह्मणाची खूण वेगळीच ॥ ८ ॥

अभंग ४१७

म्हणों जरी आतां ब्राह्मण पंडितां । न मानें तत्त्वतां मना तेंही ॥ १ ॥
जाणता विवेक निवडी तो बरा । ब्राह्मण तो खरा ज्ञानवंत ॥ २ ॥
क्षत्रिय वैश्य शूद्र ब्राह्मणादि सर्व । पांडित्य अपूर्व करिती सर्व ॥ ३ ॥
पद-पदार्थांचें करिती विवरण । सर्व वर्ण जाण काव्यअर्थ ॥ ४ ॥
अविंधादिक ही करिती पांडित्य । ब्राह्मण त्या तथ्य कोण मानी ॥ ५ ॥
बहिणी म्हणे ऐसें वोळखावें जनीं । ब्राह्मण निर्वाणीं कोण ऐसे ॥ ६ ॥

अभंग ४१८

आतां म्हणों जरी कर्म तें ब्राह्मण । चहूं वर्णीं जाण कर्म आहे ॥ १ ॥
म्हणोनी म्हणावें कर्मिक ब्राह्मण । आहे तेचि खूण वेगळीच ॥ २ ॥
आपुल्याचि कर्मीं वर्तताति वर्ण । तयासी ब्राह्मण म्हणों नये ॥ ३ ॥
बहिणी म्हणे कर्म विचारितां पाहे । ब्राह्मणत्व नोहे कर्मासी तें ॥ ४ ॥

अभंग ४१९

शास्त्रासी प्रमाण आपुलालें कर्म । वर्णाचा स्वधर्म आचरती ॥ १ ॥
तयांसी ब्राह्मण कैसेनि बोलिजे । विचार हा कीजे मनामार्जी ॥ २ ॥
कोणे वर्णीं कर्म शास्त्र न बोलेचि । आज्ञा समर्थाची सर्वांवरी ॥ ३ ॥
बहिणी म्हणे वेदाप्रमाणें चालती । सर्व त्या बोलती ब्राह्मण केवीं ॥ ४ ॥

अभंग ४२०

आतां धर्म यासी म्हणावें ब्राह्मण । तरि हें अप्रमाण दिसतसे ॥ १ ॥
ब्राह्मण ते भिन्न जाण ते जाणती । ज्ञानी ओळखती आत्मदृष्टीं ॥ २ ॥
ब्राह्मण-क्षत्रिय-वैश्य-शूद्रां जाण । धर्म हा प्रमाण सांगितला ॥ ३ ॥
अन्नदानद्रव्यगोदानादि सर्व । चहूंवर्णीं भाव सारिखाचि ॥ ४ ॥
बहिणी म्हणे धर्म नव्हे तो ब्राह्मण । ब्रह्मपरीक्षण वेगळेंची ॥ ५ ॥

अभंग ४२१

स्वर्गलोकप्राप्ति होय जयां धर्में । ब्राह्मण उत्तम तेही नव्हती ॥१॥
ब्रह्म जाणे तोचि ब्राह्मण बोलिजे । येर तें सहजें ब्रह्मबीज ॥२॥
नाना यज्ञ दान अनुष्ठान तप । ब्राह्मणाचें रूप तेंही नोहे ॥३॥
बहिणी म्हणे किती सांगावें मनासी । ओळखी हे कैसी ब्राह्मणाची ॥४॥

अभंग ४२२

ब्राह्मण तो एक सांगेन इत्यर्थ । जेणें हा वेदार्थ सांठविला ॥१॥
वेदांहीं प्रमाण तोच असे केला । वरिष्ठ तो भला गुरु सर्वां ॥२॥
थोर नाहीं दुजें ब्राह्मणावांचोनी । कैवल्य ज्याचेनी प्राप्त होय ॥३॥
मोक्ष अधिकारी जयाचेनि शब्दें । जळती प्रारब्धें दृष्टिमात्रें ॥४॥
ब्रह्म ब्राह्मणासी नसे अणु भेद । साधा हें निर्द्वंद्व तयापाशीं ॥५॥
बहिणी म्हणे चिन्ह कोण त्याचें जाणे । विवेकें शहाणे वोळखती ॥६॥

अभंग ४२३

गुणांत असोनी गुणांसी नातळे । क्रियेसी नाकळे अणुमात्र ॥१॥
तोचि गा ब्राह्मण वोळखावा जनीं । द्वैत जया स्वप्नीं आढळेना ॥२॥
षडूर्मीरहित षड्भाव नातळे । दोषांचेनि मेळें सांपडेना ॥३॥
बहिणी म्हणे सत्य न संडी सर्वथा । ब्राह्मण तत्त्वतां तोचि एक ॥४॥

अभंग ४२४

निर्विकल्प जया समाधि जोडली । चित्तासी अमोलीं परब्रह्मीं ॥१॥
तोचि एक खरा ब्राह्मण वेदार्थें । आणिक तीं मतें पाखंडाचीं ॥२॥
सर्वांभूतिं एक आत्मा देखियेला । शांतीचा वोतिला मूर्तिमंत ॥३॥
बहिणी म्हणे जैसें आकाश सर्वत्र । तैसा तो एकत्र जगामाजीं ॥४॥

अभंग ४२५

अंतर्बाह्य एक अखंड अद्वय । प्रत्यक्ष प्रमेय अनुभवें ॥१॥
तयासीच जाण म्हणावें ब्राह्मण । जयाचें निर्वाण परब्रह्मीं ॥२॥

अनपेक्षा जयाचें आंदण हें जाण । करतल विज्ञान हातीं वसे ॥ ३ ॥
बहिणी म्हणे काम क्रोध सर्व गेले । तेथेंचि राहिलें ब्राह्मणत्व ॥ ४ ॥

अभंग ४२६

शमदम सर्व साधिले नवगुण । संतोषें संपन्न सर्वदा जो ॥ १ ॥
ब्राह्मण वरिष्ठ श्रेष्ठाचाही श्रेष्ठ । जयाचेनि भ्रष्ट मोक्ष पावे ॥ २ ॥
तृष्णा मोह दंभ गेला अहंकार । वृत्ति निर्विकार सर्व कर्मी ॥ ३ ॥
बहिणी म्हणे ज्याची निमाली वासना । ब्राह्मण तो जाणा ब्रह्मनिष्ठ ॥ ४ ॥

अभंग ४२७

ब्रह्मभाव देहीं सदासर्वकाळ । ब्राह्मण केवळ तोचि एक ॥ १ ॥
श्रुति स्मृति साक्ष करोनि बोलिले । नाहीं म्यां ठेविलें गुज कांहीं ॥ २ ॥
ब्रह्मींच सर्वदा वर्तती इंद्रियें । ब्राह्मण तो होय याचि अर्थें ॥ ३ ॥
बहिणी म्हणेब्रह्मीं नांदे तो ब्राह्मण । यातीशीं प्रमाण नसे तेथें ॥ ४ ॥

अभंग ४२८

हरिकथा करी म्हणे हरिदास । संतवृत्ति त्यास संत म्हणती ॥ १ ॥
क्रियेपाशीं नाम आपण ठसावें । नलगे सांगावें सकळ लोकां ॥ २ ॥
सोन्याचे घडणार सोनार त्या म्हणती । वैद्य तो म्हणती वैद्यकीनें ॥ ३ ॥
बहिणी म्हणे तैसें ब्रह्म जेथें नांदे । ब्राह्मण तो वेदें प्रतिष्ठिला ॥ ४ ॥

अभंग ४२९

ब्रह्म नाणे तोचि बोलिजे ब्राह्मण । वेदाचें वचन साक्ष यासी ॥ १ ॥
पहा अनुभव आपुलिया देहीं । शास्त्राचिया ग्वाही करोनिया ॥ २ ॥
द्वादशकला या जया अंगीं तेज । सूर्य तो सहज न बोलतां ॥ ३ ॥
राजचिन्ह अंगीं राजा तोचि एक । करी जो कनक परीस तोचि ॥ ४ ॥
पुरवील काम तीच कामधेनु । वारील मरणु अमृत तें ॥ ५ ॥
बहिणी म्हणे तैसा ब्रह्माचा जाणता । ब्राह्मण तत्त्वतां तोचि एक ॥ ६ ॥

अभंग ४३०

ज्ञाननिष्ठ सदा लक्षी लक्षयुक्त । चित्त तें विरक्त विषयभोगी ॥ १ ॥
तोचि एक जगीं ब्राह्मण निर्धार । पहा चमत्कार मनामार्जी ॥ २ ॥
फलाचीही आस नाहीं मनामार्जी । वर्ततां सहजीं स्वधर्मेंचि ॥ ३ ॥
बहिणी म्हणे दुजें न देखे आणिक । ब्राह्मण तो एक वोळखावां ॥ ४ ॥

अभंग ४३१

भक्ति ज्ञान आणी वैराग्य मानसीं । वेद जाण त्यासी प्राप्त जाले ॥ १ ॥
तोचि रे ब्राह्मण जाण ब्रह्मवेत्ता । आणिक तत्त्वतां द्विजोत्तम ॥ २ ॥
विरक्ति हे सत्य जया अंगीं भार्या । ज्ञानाग्नि ज्ञानिया साग्निक जो ॥ ३ ॥
गुरुवचनीं सर्व नित्यनैमित्तिक । अखंड विवेक आत्मयाचा ॥ ४ ॥
शांति दया क्षमा भाव तो निजबोध । अपत्यें प्रसिद्ध जया हो तीं ॥ ५ ॥
बहिणी म्हणे ऐसें देखोनियां चिन्ह । तयासी ब्राह्मण वेद बोले ॥ ६ ॥

अभंग ४३२

सद्गुरूचें वाक्य तेंचि अग्निरूप । समिधास्वरूप वासना ते ॥ १ ॥
ऐसा तो साग्निक बोलिजे ब्राह्मण । विषयां मारून शेषभोक्ता ॥ २ ॥
अविद्या स्मृतीसी कामक्रोधयुक्त । होउनी यथोक्त आश्रमी तो ॥ ३ ॥
बहिणी म्हणे ऐसे ब्राह्मण ते सत्य । वेदार्थ निश्चित हाचि खरा ॥ ४ ॥

अभंग ४३३

सद्गुरुवचनीं ज्ञानाग्नि प्रगटला । हृदयीं राहिला जयाचिये ॥१॥
तयासीच जगीं ब्राह्मण म्हणावें । सांगितले स्वभावें मनाचिया ॥२॥
विषयांचा होम ज्ञानाग्नींत करी । पूर्णाहूति खरी मनाची ती ॥३॥
बहिणी म्हणे ऐशा चिन्हीं चिन्हांकित । ब्राह्मण निश्चित तोचि एक ॥४॥

अभंग ४३४

एक ते ज्योतिषी एक ते पाठक । अग्निहोत्री एक तीर्थाटनी ॥१॥
परब्रह्म जाणे तोचि कीं ब्राह्मण । देव तो आपण प्रत्यक्षचि ॥२॥

एक ते पंडित वैदिक ते एक । गायत्री नेटका ब्राह्मण ते ॥ ३ ॥
बहिणी म्हणे एक वीर्यमात्र बीज । ऐसें तें सहज सांगितलें ॥ ४ ॥

अभंग ४३५

पिंडब्रह्मांडासी करोनियां ऐक्य । मनीं महावाक्य-बोध झाला ॥ १ ॥
तयासी ब्राह्मण बोलिजे साचार । ब्रह्मसाक्षात्कार प्रत्यक्ष हा ॥ २ ॥
मी-तूंपणाचा सबलांश सांडिला । जीव शिव केला ऐक्य ज्ञानें ॥ ३ ॥
महाकारणादि देह चार पाहें । शोधोनियां जाये तूर्यपदा ॥ ४ ॥
सोहं हंस मंत्र अखंड उच्चार । समाधि साचार अखंडत्व ॥ ५ ॥
बहिणी म्हणे ब्रह्मवेत्ते हे ब्राह्मण । यांचिया दर्शनें मुक्ति जोडे ॥ ६ ॥

अभंग ४३६

एकाचा निश्चय गुरुवचनीं मुक्ति । एक ते मांडिती निर्गुणध्यान ॥ १ ॥
परि आहे मोक्ष वेगळाचि जाण । ज्ञानी ते निर्वाण साधिती हो ॥ २ ॥
सगुणचि मोक्ष एकाचिये मतें । आकाररहित मोक्ष म्हणती ॥ ३ ॥
एक ते भाविती मोक्ष भक्ति ज्ञान । वैराग्य साधन म्हणती मोक्ष ॥ ४ ॥
एक सिद्धीलाचि म्हणतात मोक्ष । शास्त्र तेचि मोक्ष म्हणती एक ॥ ५ ॥
एक ते स्वाचारें मोक्ष प्रतिष्ठिती । फलत्यागी म्हणती मोक्ष एक ॥ ६ ॥
मनोजय एक कल्पिताती मोक्ष । ध्यानाचा तो पक्ष मुक्ति म्हणती ॥ ७ ॥
एक महत्तत्त्व विचारें स्थापिती । मद्यमांस घेती मोक्षहेतु ॥ ८ ॥
एक ते इंद्रियें आचरती यथेष्ठ । तोचि मोक्ष स्पष्ट मानिताती ॥ ९ ॥
एक ते वेदाचे पठणेंचि म्हणती । मोक्ष एक म्हणती प्रपंचातें ॥ १० ॥
एक क्लेशें जाणा दंडिती देहासी । म्हणती मोक्षासी हेतु हाचि ॥ ११ ॥
एक ते पंचाग्नि धूम्रपान वनीं । मोक्ष हाचि जनीं स्थापिताती ॥ १२ ॥
एक ते संन्यासी जटिल तापसी । मोक्ष हा तयासी स्थापिती ते ॥ १३ ॥
एक पंचीकरणें पहाती सर्वदा । म्हणती मोक्षपदा हेंचि मूळ ॥ १४ ॥
एक मौनी जपी तपी अनुष्ठानी । भाविताती कोणी मोक्ष येणें ॥ १५ ॥

एक पंचमुद्रा लाविती आपण । म्हणती मोक्ष जाण येणें होय ॥१६॥
एक तीं दैवतें ध्याती नानापरी । मोक्ष हा अंतरीं मानिताती ॥१७॥
बहिणी म्हणे मोक्ष आहे तो निराळा। जाणती ते कला ज्ञानवंत ॥१८॥

अभंग ४३७

नानापरी जन कल्पिाती मोक्ष । परी तो प्रत्यक्ष नसे कोणा ॥ १ ॥
वासनेच्या क्षयें मोक्ष तो सांपडे । 'तत्त्वमसि' जोडे आत्महित ॥ २ ॥
त्वंपद तत्पद ऐक्य जैं होईल । 'असि' पदीं मूळ सांपडेल ॥ ३ ॥
बहिणी म्हणे वृत्ति होती जैं निश्चळ । तुटें तैं पडळ प्रपंचाचें ॥ ४ ॥

अभंग ४३८

श्रोत्र आणि त्वचा चक्षु जिव्हा घ्राण। ज्ञानेंद्रिनें जाण पांच ऐसीं ॥ १ ॥
याहुनी वेगळा आत्मा तो निश्चयें । अनुभवें पाहें मनामार्जी ॥ २ ॥
वाचा पाणि पाद शिश्न आणि गुद । कर्मेंद्रियें सिद्ध पांच ऐसीं ॥ ३ ॥
अंतःकरण मन बुद्धिचित्त चौथें । अहंकार येथें पांचवा तो ॥ ४ ॥
शब्द स्पर्श रूप रस गंध जाण । विषय दारुण पांच ते हे ॥ ५ ॥
बहिणी म्हणे ऐसा पंचाविसां शोध । तत्पदींचा बोध करीं मना ॥ ६ ॥

अभंग ४३९

पंच कोश आणि ताप जे त्रिविध । ईषणा प्रसिद्ध हारपल्या ॥ १ ॥
तयासी ब्राह्मण बोलिजेती सत्य । विचारोनी सत्य सांगितलें ॥ २ ॥
षडूर्मि आणिक षड्भाव देहींचे । विचारेंही साचे वोसंडीले ॥ ३ ॥
बहिणी म्हणे इच्छानिरास हा जेथ । ब्राह्मण तो सत्य ब्रह्मवेत्ता ॥ ४ ॥

अभंग ४४०

वाचे लक्ष याचा जया अंगीं बोध । 'सत्' शब्द स्वानंद सांपडला ॥ १ ॥
तोचि ब्रह्मनिष्ठ ब्राह्मण बोलिजे । विज्ञान सहजें देह त्याचे ॥ २ ॥
ज्ञप्ति अखंडता पूर्णता बाणली । समाधि लागली असंप्रज्ञ ॥ ३ ॥
बहिणी म्हणे चिन्ह हेंचि ब्राह्मणाचें । निश्चयें शास्त्राचें सांगितलें ॥ ४ ॥

अभंग ४४१

सत् शब्दीं समर्पी स्वधर्माचें फळ । होउनी अढळ ब्रह्मनिष्ठ ॥ १ ॥
तयासी ब्राह्मण म्हणों आम्ही शुद्ध । मोक्ष तो प्रसिद्ध भेटी होतां ॥ २ ॥
अहंकार अंगीं जयासी न साहे । कर्तेपणीं नये दुजेपण ॥ ३ ॥
बहिणी म्हणे ऐसे ब्राह्मग भेटतां । ब्रह्म सायुज्यता घरा आलें ॥ ४ ॥

अभंग ४४२

देव अंतरला योगही लोपला । भाव दुरावला प्राणियासी ॥ १ ॥
काय करावें तें संचित वोखटें । विषय गोमटे वाटताती ॥ २ ॥
नाम नये मुखीं नावडेचि भक्ति । जिवासी विरक्ति चिंता देते ॥ ३ ॥
बहिणी म्हणे संत साधु महानुभाव । नावडे तो ठाव पातक्यासी ॥ ४ ॥

अभंग ४४३

जडलेंसे चित्त विषयीं सर्वदा । नये ब्रह्मबोधा आत्मनिष्ठे ॥ १ ॥
पूर्वील संचित नाहीं शुद्ध ज्याचें । देह पातकाचे वोतीव ते ॥ २ ॥
अहंकार देहीं काम क्रोध लोभ । आवडे अशुभ कर्म ज्यासी ॥ ३ ॥
बहिणी म्हणे श्रेष्ठां न मानी प्रमाण । तेचि एक हीन वोळखावे ॥ ४ ॥

अभंग ४४४

अंधालागीं जेवीं उदयेला भानु । कोल्हिया चंदनू व्यर्थ जैसा ॥ १ ॥
ज्ञानहीन तेवीं आत्मा हा प्रत्यक्ष । नये मना साक्ष मूर्खपणें ॥ २ ॥
चंद्राचा प्रकाश कावळ्यांसी पाहें । वानरांसी काये वस्त्रें होतीं ॥ ३ ॥
बहिरियासी काय गीत तानमान । श्वानासी प्रमाण जयापरी ॥ ४ ॥
नपुंसका जेवीं पद्मिनी सुंदरा । प्राणाविण नरा भोग जैसा ॥ ५ ॥
बहिणी म्हणे तैसा सन्मार्ग मूढासी । बोधितां तयासी सिद्ध नाहीं ॥ ६ ॥

अभंग ४४५

नाहीं जया हेत प्रीति ते सुबुद्धि । वैराग्याचा विधि ठाउकी हे ॥ १ ॥
तया ज्ञानप्राप्ति न घडे सर्वथा । मोक्षाची ते कथा केवीं तेथें ॥ २ ॥

काय तो संदेह असे या अर्थासी । पाहिजे क्रियेसी अंगीं बळ ॥ ३ ॥
बहिणी म्हणे हेत धरी जैसा भक्त । तेणेंचि तो मुक्त होय भावें ॥ ४ ॥

अभंग ४४६

घृतासी तो संग अग्नीचा जालिया । मीठ घातलीया जलामाजीं ॥ १ ॥
संगाचा स्वभाव लागला जयासी । सामर्थ्य तेजासी सहज जाण ॥ २ ॥
लोखंड परिसा झगटलें जेव्हां । *माघासी तें किंवा वृक्षवल्ली ॥ ३ ॥
बहिणी म्हणे चंद्र पौर्णिमेसी द्रवें । सिंधूसी हेलावे सहज येती ॥ ४ ॥

अभंग ४४७

हिंगाचिया संगें कापूर नासला । लवणें विध्वंसिला क्षीरयोग ॥ १ ॥
म्हणोनियां संग करावा तोंवरी । जो हो सौख्य-कारी प्राणियासी ॥ २ ॥
केशरकाजळासी संगत जालीया । काजळाचा तया संग लागे ॥ ३ ॥
बहिणी म्हणे संग धरावा तो ऐसा । मोक्ष तो अपैसा होय जेणें ॥ ४ ॥

अभंग ४४८

चंदनाचा संग जालिया निंबासी । चंदनत्व त्यासी ठसावलें ॥ १ ॥
तैसा संतसंग कळला जाणिजे । विवेक हा कीजे मनामाजीं ॥ २ ॥
पुष्पाचे संगतीं तंतूचाही मान । तुलसीसंगें जाण मृत्तिकेतें ॥ ३ ॥
बहिणी म्हणे संग करीं रे नेटका । धरूनियां टेका आत्मनिष्ठा ॥ ४ ॥

अभंग ४४९

ब्रह्मत्वाची खूण जप गायत्रीचा । जो सर्व वेदाचा मूळमंत्र ॥ १ ॥
तयाहून परतें आहेसे सांगती । जाणावे ते मतिमंद हीन ॥ २ ॥
गुणसाम्य ऐसी म्हणती मूळमाया । गायत्री ते जया ब्रह्मरूप ॥ ३ ॥
अकार उकार मकाराचें बीज । ओंकाराचें निज उन्मनी हे ॥ ४ ॥
इजपासुनिया जाले वेदविद । गायत्री प्रसिद्ध वेदमाता ॥ ५ ॥
बहिणी म्हणे जया गायत्रीचा जप । तो ब्रह्मस्वरूप केवळ जाणा ॥ ६ ॥

---

*संत बहिणाबाईचे वेळीं 'माघ फाल्गुन वसंतऋतु' असा प्रघात असावा असें या चरणावरून मानणें प्राप्त आहे.

अभंग ४५०

वर्णाश्रम धर्म शुद्ध आचरावा । भगवंत धरावा एका भावें ॥ १ ॥
ऐसें जो न करी ब्राह्मणाचा तो धर्म । जाणावा अधम पापदेही ॥ २ ॥
आधीं स्नानसंध्या गायत्रीचा जप । करावा निष्पाप अष्टोत्तरशत ॥ ३ ॥
त्यावरी मग तर्पण करावें । धर्म हा स्वभावें विप्रालागीं ॥ ४ ॥
गीता रामनाम जपावें सादर । घेवोनी विचार प्रेमभावें ॥ ५ ॥
मग यथाविधि देवाचें पूजन । धूपदीप जाण मंत्रयुक्त ॥ ६ ॥
नैवेद्य वाढोनी वैश्वदेव कीजे । प्रांतींचें ठेविजे स्विष्टकृत ॥ ७ ॥
नैवेद्य करोनी स्विष्टकृत कीजे । शेवटींचें दीजे बलिदान ॥ ८ ॥
तये काळीं कोणी आला जो अतीत । जाणावा भगवंत देवरूप ॥ ९ ॥
आधीं पूजा त्याची मग इतरांची । त्याउपरी भुक्तिची पंक्ति कीजे ॥१०॥
ग्रासोग्रासीं देव आठवावा जाण । न करावें भोजन असाक्षी तें ॥११॥
बहिणी म्हणे येणें कर्मब्रह्मनिष्ठ । रोकडें वैकुंठ प्राप्त त्यासी ॥१२॥

अभंग ४५१

वेद तो जीवात्मा । वेद तो परमात्मा ।
ब्रह्मसुखमहिमा । ज्याचेनी हा ॥ १ ॥
वेद नव्हता जेव्हां ब्रह्मांड कैंचें तेव्हां ।
सुखदुःख भोगणें जीवा । कासया पाहें ॥ २ ॥
ओंकार ब्रह्मींचा बिंदु । तेथुनी उपजला वेदू ।
त्रिगुणेंसी वाढला भेदू । ब्रह्मांडाकारें ॥ ३ ॥
ऊर्ध्वमूळ अधोशाखा । प्रसवला वेद देखा ।
खांद्या पत्रपुष्प सर्वथा । निर्माण जाल्या ॥ ४ ॥
छंदपदजटाक्रम । अरण्य-ब्राह्मण जाण ।
विस्ताराला वेद आपण । ब्रह्मस्वरूप ॥ ५ ॥
कर्म तेंचि ब्रह्म जाण । ब्रह्म तेंचि कर्म आपण ।
कर्मब्रह्म नाहीं भिन्न । वेदार्थ बोले ॥ ६ ॥

तत्त्वार्थ वेदींचा अर्थु । वेदांताचा मथितार्थु ।
जेणें निरसे संसार भेदू । अद्वयबोधें ॥ ७ ॥
अद्वय ऐसें हें वचन । दुसरें नव्हेचि हें जाण ।
स्वसंवेद्य अवघा आपण । सर्वी सर्वत्र ॥ ८ ॥
भूतमात्रीं व्यापक । तोचि तूं वर्ततू देख ।
व्यतिरेकान्वयें सुख । अनुभवें पाहें ॥ ९ ॥
बहिणी म्हणे वेदान्वयें । ज्ञान तें निखळ लाहे ।
वरकड तें मलिन होये । अंधाचिये परी ॥१०॥

अभंग ४५२

कर्माआदि अंतीं मध्यें ब्रह्मभाव । जाणे तो अनुभव ज्ञानियाचा ॥१॥
ऐसिया स्थितीचे ब्राह्मण ते खरे । येर ते पामरें वोळखावे ॥२॥
ॐकार आदरीं तत्कारें समर्पी । सत्कारें स्वरूपीं ऐक्य करीं ॥३॥
बहिणी म्हणे तेही ब्रह्मची निर्भ्रांत । अनुभवोनी तथ्य लीन होय ॥४॥

१२. श्रीक्षेत्र पंढरी-श्रीपंढरीनाथपर

अभंग ४५३

ब्रह्मांड पंढरी हे आजी जाली खरी ।
मुखीं नाम घेतां हरि हरि ॥ १ ॥
सुख सुखावलें कोणा सांगूं गे माये ।
जिकडे पाहें तिकडे माझा हरि भरला आहे ॥ २ ॥
सरली भ्रांति; हारपला देहभाव ।
महामहासीही नुरे जेथें ठावाठाव ॥ ३ ॥
गेलें मीपण हारपला भावाभाव ।
बहिणी म्हणे देखियला पंढरीचा राव ॥ ४ ॥

अभंग ४५४

माझा दीननाथ दीनबंधु हरि ।
नांदे भीमातीरीं पंढरीये ॥ १ ॥
विटे नीट उभा समचरण साजिरे ।
पाऊलें गोंजिरीं सुकुमार ॥ २ ॥
वैजयंती माळा रुळतसे गळां ।
कांसेसी पिंवळा पीतांबर ॥ ३ ॥
भाळीं ऊर्ध्व पुंड्र कानीं कुंडलें गोमटीं ।
चंदनाची उटी सर्वांगासी ॥ ४ ॥
शिरीं टोप साजे रत्नांचा साजिरा ।
काढियेला तुरा मोतियांचा ॥ ५ ॥
शोभती दंतपंक्ति जैशा हिऱ्यांच्या ज्योति ।
बहिणी म्हणे तया ध्याती हृदयामाजीं ॥ ६ ॥

अभंग ४५५

जन्मोनियां जोडी जोडिली संसारीं । सांपडली तीरीं चंद्रभागे ॥ १ ॥
घन-श्याम मूर्ति सांवळी डोळस । उभी सावकाश विटेवरी ॥ २ ॥
नामरूपातीत चैतन्य शाश्वत । आत्मस्वरूपस्थित प्रगटली ॥ ३ ॥
वेदा अगोचर श्रुतीहूनिया पर । निर्गुण निर्विकार पहातो गे ॥ ४ ॥
अखंड चिद्घन दिसे सर्वसाक्षी । बहिणी तया लक्षी हृदयामाजीं ॥ ५ ॥

अभंग ४५६

लाचावलें मन नव्हे त्या वेगळें । देखिलें सांवळें परब्रह्म ॥ १ ॥
जाली तन्मयता हालेना पापणी । घेत असे धणी स्वरूपाची ॥ २ ॥
विसरलें मन आपलें आपण । पडोनि ठेलें शून्य मी-तूंपणा ॥ ३ ॥
नाठवे तें मीपण पडला विसरू । इंद्रियव्यापारू पारूषला ॥ ४ ॥
राहिलीं इंद्रियें अचेतन वृत्ति । मना आत्मस्थिति लागलीसे ॥ ५ ॥
लागल्या पैं वृत्ति खुंटली हे गति । बहिणी तें भोगिती आत्मसुख ॥ ६ ॥

अभंग ४५७

चालतां पाऊल पंढरीचे वाटे । ब्रह्मसुख भेटे रोकडेंचि ॥ १ ॥
पहातां ऐसें सुख नाहीं त्रिभुवनीं । तें पहावें नयनीं पंढरीसी ॥ २ ॥
गाता हरिनाम । वाजवितां टाळी । प्रेमाचे कल्लोळीं सुख वाटे ॥ ३ ॥
दिंडीचा गजर होतो जयजयकार । मृदंग सुस्वर वाजताती ॥ ४ ॥
हमामा टिपरी घालिती हुंबडी । होवोनिया उघडी विष्णुदास ॥ ५ ॥
बहिणी म्हणे ऐसा आनंद वाटेचा । कोण तो दैवाचा देखे डोळां ॥ ६ ॥

अभंग ४५८

चला झटझटा वोसंडुनी वाट । पंढरी मूळपीठ दूरी आहे ॥ १ ॥
सोडा आडकथा वोसंडा * मारग । वाट पांडुरंग पहातसे ॥ २ ॥
स्वहिताची जया असेल तांतडी । तेणें घडी घडी काळ साधा ॥ ३ ॥

* वाट

गेलिया दिवस पडेल अंधारी । हीना तैसी परी थार नाहीं ॥ ४ ॥
पडो देह राहो, धरावा निर्धार । पांडुरंगीं भाव सांडूं नये ॥ ५ ॥
बहिणी म्हणे आजी जावें वेळोवेळ । तरीच पर्वकाळ साधिजेल ॥ ६ ॥

अभंग ४५९

सर्वांगव्यापिनी भीमेचा महिमा । वर्णावया ब्रह्मा अनिर्वाच्य ॥ १ ॥
धन्य ते दैवाचे पंढरीचे लोक । घेती प्रेमसुख विठोबाचें ॥ २ ॥
भीमा-चंद्रभागासंगम जे ठायीं । वानावा तो काई महिमा तेथें ॥ ३ ॥
त्याहीवरी जेथें पंढरीचा देव । काय सांगूं भाव क्षेत्रमहिमा ॥ ४ ॥
तिहींचा संगम घडे जये ठायीं । सांगावा तो काई महिमा त्याचा ॥ ५ ॥
ऐसिया क्षेत्रींचा महिमा ऐकतां । पापाचिये वार्ता स्वप्नीं नाहीं ॥ ६ ॥
स्नानदान घडे देवाचें दर्शन । तेथें जन्ममरण काय करी ॥ ७ ॥
फिरे सुदर्शन सदा सर्वकाळ । काळ आणि वेळ कैंची तेथें ॥ ८ ॥
स्नानालागीं देव येताती मिळूनि । बैसुनी विमानीं मध्याह्नीसी ॥ ९ ॥
ऐसा क्षेत्रमहिमा कोण वर्णी सीमा । नकळे अधमा असोनिया ॥१०॥
धन्य पुंडलीक धन्य त्याचा भाव । क्षेत्राचा अनुभव वाढविला ॥११॥
बहिणी म्हणे पुण्य पाहिजे तें गांठीं । व्हावयातें भेटी विठोबाची ॥१२॥

अभंग ४६०

धन्य ते दैवाचें वारकरी साचे । अंकित विठोबाचे जन्मोजन्मीं ॥ १ ॥
ऐसियांची भेटी होतां हितगोष्टी । सुखाचिया कोटी हेळावती ॥ २ ॥
कोण सांगूं पुण्य पंढरीच्या लोकां । अखंड श्रीमुखा न्याहाळीती ॥ ३ ॥
चंद्रभागे स्नान देवाचें दर्शन । अखंड कीर्तन महाद्वारीं ॥ ४ ॥
करिती जयजयकार मिरवे दिंडीभार । गर्जे पैं अंबर नामघोषें ॥ ५ ॥
प्रपंचपरमार्थ अवघा सुखरूप । कळिकाळा मुख स्वप्नीं नाहीं ॥ ६ ॥
तुळसीवृंदावन पद्मरांगोळिया । कुंकुमाचे पाहा सडे द्वारीं ॥ ७ ॥
कामधाम अवघें जालें विठ्ठलरूप । पंढरीचे लोक विठ्ठल पैं ॥ ८ ॥

वोखदासी पाप न मिळे पाहतां । ब्रह्मसायुज्यता पंढरीये ॥ ९ ॥
जीवन्मुक्तदशा पंढरीं पाठणीं । ब्रह्म हें गोठणी विठ्ठलवेषें ॥१०॥
पंढरीवरून येती जाती जीव । मुक्तीचा निर्वाव पशुपक्ष्यां ॥११॥
बहिणी म्हणे आम्ही धन्य जालों सुखी । येतां नाम मुखीं पंढरीचें ॥१२॥

अभंग ४६१

पंढरीचें सुख काय सांगों आतां । जेथें चारी वाचा वोसरल्या ॥ १ ॥
जेथें पुंडलिकें केला रहिवास । धन्य त्याचा वंश मातापिता ॥ २ ॥
पंढरीचा महिमा कोण करी सीमा । वर्णावया ब्रह्मा अनिर्वाच्य ॥ ३ ॥
बहिणी म्हणे क्षेत्र पंढरीसारिखें । ऐसें हें न देखें भूमंडळीं ॥ ४ ॥

अभंग ४६२

उदंड ऐकिला उदंड गाईला । उदंड देखिला क्षेत्रमहिमा ॥ १ ॥
पंढरीसारिखें नाहीं क्षेत्र कोठें । जरी तें वैकुंठ दाखविलें ॥ २ ॥
ऐसी चंद्रभागा ऐसें भीमातीर । ऐसा विटेवर देव कोठें ॥ ३ ॥
ऐसें वाळुवंट ऐसी हरिकथा । ठाईं ठाईं देखा दिंडीभार ॥ ४ ॥
ऐसे हरिदास ऐसें प्रेमसुख । ऐसा नामघोष सांगा कोठें ॥ ५ ॥
बहिणी म्हणे आम्हां अनाथांकारण । पंढरी निर्माण केली देवें ॥ ६ ॥

अभंग ४६३

चोविसां मूर्तींसी आसन मुद्राध्यान । पांडुरंग जाण निर्गुणरूप ॥ १ ॥
ज्याचे पायीं जन्म देवा आणि तीर्था । मूर्ति ते तत्वतां विठोबाची॥ २ ॥
वेदां आणि शास्त्रां अकार हा मूळ । सर्वांचें समूळ पांडुरंग ॥ ३ ॥
विटेचा संकेत पांचवी अवस्था । ब्रह्मसायुज्यता शुद्धरूप ॥ ४ ॥
करीं हात दोन्ही खुणाची दाखवी । अनेक एकत्वीं पहा कैसें ॥ ५ ॥
बहिणी म्हणे तया लुब्धलें हें मन । धन्य जया खूण कळों आली ॥ ६ ॥

अभंग ४६४

तीर्थी तीर्थराव ती एक पंढरी । पाहतां पृथ्वीवरी आणिक नाहीं॥ १ ॥
धन्य ते दैवाचे घेती प्रेमसुख । सदा नामघोष मुखीं वसे ॥ २ ॥

भीमा चंद्रभागा दोहींचा संगम । नांदे मेघश्याम पांडुरंग ॥ ३ ॥
पुण्य पुष्पावती तीरीं वेणूनाद । सप्रेम गोविंद क्रीडा करी ॥ ४ ॥
बैसोनी विमानीं येती देव तिन्ही । काळ हा साधुनी मध्याह्नीसी ॥ ५ ॥
ब्रह्ममय क्षेत्र पंढरी पट्टण । म्हणोनी श्रेष्ठ जाण बहुतां गुणें ॥ ६ ॥
कर्मब्रह्मकाशी नामब्रह्म पंढरी । सर्व ब्रह्मगिरी खलुविद ॥ ७ ॥
पंढरीमाझारीं ब्रह्मत्रयवास । म्हणोन विशेष पंढरी हे ॥ ८ ॥
बहिणी म्हणे पंढरी सर्वांही वरिष्ठ । ऐशा श्रुती स्पष्ट बोलताती ॥ ९ ॥

अभंग ४६५

धन्य धन्य ते पंढरी । जेथें नांदतो श्रीहरि ॥ १ ॥
धन्य धन्य चंद्रभागा । जेथें वास पांडुरंगा ॥ २ ॥
धन्य धन्य ते पद्माळ । जेथें राहिले गोपाळ ॥ ३ ॥
धन्य धन्य वेणूनाद । जेथें क्रीडतसे गोविंद ॥ ४ ॥
धन्य धन्य वाळुवंट । जेथें उभा पायीं विट ॥ ५ ॥
धन्य धन्य पुंडलीक । हरि साधियेला देख ॥ ६ ॥
धन्य धन्य पुष्पावती । जेथें वृंदा हे श्रीपती ॥ ७ ॥
बहिणी म्हणे धन्य धन्य । पांडुरंगीं जे अनन्य ॥ ८ ॥

१३. (हरिभक्तमहिमा) पुंडलीकमाहात्म्य

अभंग ४६६

ऐका हरिभक्ताचा महिमा । केली पुंडलीकें थोर सीमा ।
गवसणी घातली व्योमा । पुरुषीं पुरुषोत्तमा साधिलें ॥ १ ॥
पुंडलिका ऐसा पतित । नसे त्रिभुवनीं अपवित्र ।
पितरांची मर्यादा न पाळित । गालिप्रदानें समर्पी ॥ २ ॥
पितरें जें सांगावें । तें पुंडलिकें न ऐकावें ।
शिव्यागाळीस द्यावें । आणि संपादावें पापासी ॥ ३ ॥
ज्या पितराचेनि हा संसारू । सुखाचे भोगिजे सुखतरु ।
त्या पितरांचे मांडिले चारु । ऐसा पुत्र निपजला ॥ ४ ॥
ऐसें करितां किती एक दिवशीं । असोनि चालिला वाराणशी ।
सर्वे कर्मभोग घेवुनी पुत्र विवशी । क्रमित वाट चालिला ॥ ५ ॥
तंव भाग्योदयकाळ आला । पापाचा संग्रह तुटला ।
उभयांचा भोग सरला । दिवस उदेला पुण्याचा ॥ ६ ॥
जेविं गाय सांपडे वाघा । ते हरि वळे पैं गा ।
अवचट धांवणें पावे वेगा । तेविं या उभयवर्गीं देव पावला ॥ ७ ॥
जेविं पाषाणीं फुटे झरा । कीं वांझ प्रसवली पुतरा ।
*तल्हातिं केस अंतरा । उपजला मोह पुंडलीका ॥ ८ ॥
देखोनि पवित्राचरण । पुंडलीक त्रास घेत मानून ।
म्हणे मी घोर पापी गहन । चुकलों भजन पितरांचें ॥ ९ ॥
कोण पाप होतें तटीं । पितृव्यांशीं केली आटाआटी ।
ऐसा कळवळोनी पोटीं । पाय कवटाळी पितरांचे ॥ १० ॥
म्हणे काय करावी वाराणशी । मातापितर हेचि माझी काशी ।
मुरडोनि आला मान देशासी । अटक वनासी प्रार्थिलें ॥ ११ ॥

---

* तळ हातीं (?)

समोंतीं बारा योजनें । देखोनि अंतीं दंडकारण्य ।
स्वर्नीं येती पक्षी जाण । न पडे कदा दृष्टीसी ॥१२॥
अत्यंत वृक्षाची दाटणी । झेपावल्या दिसती गगनीं ।
जेथें सूर्याचे दर्शनीं । मोकळीक असेचिना ॥१३॥
ऐसें भयानक वन । तेथें पुंडलीक राहिला जाण ।
पाहोनी सरोवराचें जीवन । केलें नामग्रहण चंद्रभागा ॥१४॥
तेथें आरंभिली सेवा । पुंडलिका उपजला भावा ।
मानित मातापिता दैवा । जडला सद्भावा चरणीं त्यांच्या ॥१५॥
ऐसे जाले कितीएक काळ । तंव देखिलें नारदें एके वेळ ।
म्हणे हा तो येथें प्रबल । कोण भक्तराव उदेला ॥१६॥
देखोनि पुंडलिकाची निष्ठा । जडली देहा पूर्ण काष्ठा ।
दृश्य सासनिया[1] अनिष्टा । नेणो हृदयस्था भेटी जाली ॥१७॥
देखोनिया भरतमुनि । जाला हर्षयुक्त अंतःकरणीं ।
थोर कौतुक वाटलें मनीं । अश्रु नयनीं लोटतां ॥१८॥
नारदें देखोनी निष्ठा । त्वरें गेला वैकुंठा ।
म्हणे नवल देखिलें भगवंता । हर्ष चित्तीं न समाये[2] ॥१९॥
सप्रेमें दाटला कंठ । बोलतां कांपती ओठ ।
नयनीं होत अश्रुपात । म्हणे भगवंत काय जालें ॥२०॥
देवें आलंगिला हृदयीं । नारदासी म्हणे सांग कांहीं ।
नवल वर्तलें लवलाहीं । तें गुज कांहीं सांग पां ॥२१॥
तंव नारद म्हणे नारायणा । मी गेलों होतों भ्रमणा ।
तेथें देखिलें नवल जाणा । त्या वचना ऐकावें ॥२२॥
मृत्युलोकाठायीं । दंडकारण्य नाम पाहीं ।
मानदेश अभिधानेंही । तेथें ठायीं देखिलें ॥२३॥

१ पूर्ण. २ मावत नाहीं.

भ्रमण करितां गेलों तेथें । तंव अवचितां देखिलें नवलातें ।
संतोष वाटला चित्तातें । तें तुजहृदयीं ठाउके ॥२४॥
तया अरण्यामाझारीं । द्विज एक पितृसेवा करी ।
त्याची देखोनियां भजन-कुसरी[1] । काय वानूं थोरी तयाची ॥२५॥
वायु उफराटा नेववेल । हें भूगोल पालथें घालवेल ।
अग्निप्रवेशही करवेल । परी तद्भक्ति-नवल सांगवेना ॥२६॥
विषाचे कवल घेववती । सहा समुद्र कोरडे करवती ।
परी तद्भक्तीची अपार शक्ति । तें चोज तुजप्रती काय सांगों ॥२७॥
वरकड[2] साधनें ते काय । कोण त्याचें नवल पाहें ।
साधनापरीस या पाहें । मज तो नव्हे साध्यता[3] ॥२८॥
त्याची भक्ति देवा पहातां । नेणें पावाल तादात्म्यता ।
कीं हें ब्रह्मसायुज्यता । आली तत्त्वतां रणांगणासी ॥२९॥
ऐकोनी भक्तीचें रहस्य । देवाचें उचंबळलें मानस ।
हातीं धरूनिया नारदास । गुप्त रूपेंसी निघाले ॥३०॥
सेजीं होती रुक्मिणी । तीसही साकळण[4] करूनी ।
गरुडासही सोडूनी । निघाले चक्रपाणि नारद ॥३१॥
पहा हा देवभक्तशिरोमणि । भक्तासाठीं चालिला चरणीं ।
उडी घातली वैकुंठाहुनी । आला क्षणीं मानदेशीं ॥३२॥
सवें नारदा माझारिया । वन उपवन दावितसे देवराया ।
अवचित देखिलें भक्तराया । तया पुंडलिकासी ॥३३॥
देवें देखोनी पुंडलीकासी । विस्मित झाला थोर मानसीं ।
पुंडलीक न देखेचि तयासी । चाड मानसीं धरेचिना ॥३४॥
मग नारद बोलिला मात । पुंडलिका आले रे भगवंत ।
जयासाठीं येवढें क्लेशार्थ । तो धांवत आला पाहें ॥३५॥

---

१ कौशल्य. २ इतर; बाकीचीं. ३ साधता (?) ४ नियंत्रण.

पुंडलीक जाला एकनिष्ठ । फिरोनी न करीच दीठ[1] ।
दिली भिरकावुनी वीट । तीवर वैकुंठ उभें ठेलें ॥३६॥
ठेवोनियां हात कटीं । ठाकलें ब्रह्म विटीं ।
नखाग्रीं लावुनी दृष्टि । ब्रह्म सृष्टि न्याहाळीत ॥३७॥
नेणो मुद्रा लागली खेचरी । तटस्थता लागली शरीरीं ।
दृष्टि ठेवुनी पुंडलिकावरी । जाला अंगभरी श्रीविठ्ठल ॥३८॥
जयाच्या अंतरीं प्रवेशे देव । तयासी पुसीं संसाराचा ठाव ।
व्यापकपणें नांदे स्वयमेव । देखोन सद्भाव भक्तीचा ॥३९॥
पुंडलिकाची देखोन भक्ति । धांवोनि आला वैकुंठपति ।
पुंडलिकाची निजस्थिति । प्रवेशला चित्तीं हरि त्याचे ॥४०॥
देखोन पुंडलिकाचा भावो । वास केला तया ठावो ।
वाहविला कीर्तीचा महिमा वो । पंढरी नाम स्थापियलें ॥४१॥
येरीकडे कैकुंठभुवनीं । उठोनी पाहे जंव रुक्मिणी ।
तंव न दिसे चक्रपाणि । थोर चिंतनीं पडियेली ॥४२॥
गरुडासी जंव पाहे । तंव तो द्वारींच उभा आहे ।
मग म्हणे कटकटा[2] माये । काय झालें कळेना ॥४३॥
कोणीकडे निजें केलें । नेणो कोणाचें धावणें कादिलें ।
ऐसें कोण सांकडें पडिलें । मौनेंच गेले श्रीपति ॥४४॥
गरुडासी म्हणे रुक्मिणी । आज विपरीत गमतें गा मनीं ।
न पुसतां गेले चक्रपाणि । भक्तशिरोमणी कोण भेटला ॥४५॥
तंव जाला हाहाकार । देव मिळाले सवळ[3] ।
म्हणती थोर जालें नवल । नेणो गोपाळ कोठें गेले ॥४६॥
नित्य दर्शना पडिलें[4] पाणी । उदास झाली वैकुंठभुवनी ।
जैसी विधवा अलंकारोनी । कोण जनीं मंडिता ॥४७॥

---

१ दृष्टि, नजर. २ हाय! हाय! ३ तत्काळ. ४ वाया जाऊं लागलें

देव करिताती रुदन । रुक्मिणी आक्रंदती गहन ।
थोर प्रळय मांडिला जाण । न लगे मार्ग भगवंताचा ॥४८॥
तंव अकस्मात नारदमुनि । रुक्मिणीनें देखिला नयनीं ।
पुसती जाली तयालागुनी । दीनवाणी जगन्माता ॥४९॥
वैकुंठींचे सकळ देव । हाहाकृत देखिला भाव ।
मग सांगितला निर्वाह[१] । चिंता न करा म्हणतसे ॥५०॥
मृत्युलोकाचे ठायीं । पुण्यशील देश पाहीं ।
पुंडलीक नामें द्विजदेही । करी निर्वाण[२] अनुष्ठान ॥ ५१ ॥
महा वृक्षांची दाटणी । अग्रें झेपावती गगनीं ।
रवि पहातां नयनीं । सर्वकाळ अंधारू ॥ ५२ ॥
ऐसिया वनाचे ठायीं । पुंढलीक ब्राह्मण पाहीं ।
पितृसेवा निर्वाही[३] । चंद्रभागासरोवरीं ॥ ५३ ॥
त्याचा पहावया भाव । गेला वैकुंठींचा राव ।
देखोनि भक्तिभाव । देवाधिदेव रहिवासले ॥ ५४ ॥
देखोन पुंडलीकाची निष्ठा । नेणो चांगली पूर्ण काष्ठा[४] ।
उणें आणुनी वैकुंठा । रहिवासले देखा वैकुंठपति ॥ ५५ ॥
ऐकोनी नारदाची मात । धांवोनि आले देव तेथें ।
विटीं देखोनि भगवंत । मौन मांडित राहिले ॥ ५६ ॥
श्रुतिशास्त्रश्रवण । करिती ब्रह्मादिक गण ।
परी तो नारायण । अणुमात्र वदेना ॥ ५७ ॥
मग म्हणती रे कटकटा । कोणी देखिली पुंडलीकनिष्ठा ।
उभें केलें वैकुंठा । चमत्कार मोठा भक्तीचा ॥ ५८ ॥
नाना उग्र साधनें । एक साधिती प्राणपानें ।
ब्रह्मांडीं नेला आत्मा जाणें । तेथेंही नारायण साधेना ॥ ५९ ॥

---

१ खरी स्थिति. २ कठिण. ३ खरी करून दाखवी. ४ मर्यादा.

या वेगळीं अनेक । करिती साधनें सोसून दुःख ।
परि भगवंत न सांपडे देख । तो कोणें सुखें रातला ॥६०॥
ऐसा करितां विचार । ज्ञानें निवडितां सारासार ।
तंव सांपडला भक्तीचा आगर । सेवा थोर पितरांची ॥६१॥
मग म्हणती हा भक्तराणा । जाणे ब्रह्मप्राप्तीच्या खुणा ।
प्रत्यक्ष साधिला वैकुंठराणा । खिळून वदन उभा केला ॥६२॥
पहा तें मूळ दंडकारण्य । त्याही वरतें ब्रह्मारण्य ।
तीर तरी चंद्रभागा जाण । देखोनि मन आनंदे ॥६३॥
ऐसियावरी हा भक्तराणा उदेला दिसे रवि जाणा ।
देवें जाणुनी पुंडलीक खुणा । रहिवास जाणा केला सुखें ॥६४॥
ऐसा जाणोनी अंतर्भाव । देवेंही केला निर्वाह ।
ठेविलें पंढरपूर नांव । वसविलें गांव पुंडलीकाचें ॥६५॥
रुक्मिणीसहवर्तमान । आले समस्त ऋषिगण ।
दुजें केलें वैकुंठभुवन । केलें नामग्रहण भूवैकुंठ ॥६६॥
ऐसी चंद्रभागा ऐसें भीमातीर । ऐसें वाळूवंट पुंडलीक भक्तवीर ।
ऐसे देव ऐसें नगर । जयजयकार कोठें महाद्वारीं ॥६७॥
ऐशा पताका ऐशीं निशाणें । शंखभेरी वाजती गहन ।
ढोल ढमामे तुरे जाणे । टाळ मृदंग वाजती ॥६८॥
घरोघरीं तुळसीवृंदावन । पद्मांकित रांगोळी जाण ।
कुंकुमार्चित सडे गहन । त्रिकाळ जाण पूजा करिती ॥६९॥
धन्य धन्य तेथींचे लोक । नगर नागरीक देख ।
पतंग भृंग पशुपक्षादिक । तरुवर धन्य झाले ॥७०॥
क्षेत्रावरून जाती येती । हो का नर-पशु-पक्षि-याति ।
पंचक्रोशीमाजीं जे सांपडती । त्यासी अधोगति नसेचि ॥७१॥

या पंढरीचा महिमा ऐकतां । नासे कोटी ब्रह्महत्या ।
या पंढरीस वास करितां । चिंता तयासी कासयाची ॥७२॥
ऐसी कथा ऐसें निरूपण । या पंढरीचें करितां श्रवण ।
तेणें बेचाळीस कूळ होय उद्धरण । जन्ममरण चुकलें त्या ॥७३॥
इतुका पुंडलीकाचा महिमा । वाढला भक्तिरसप्रेमा ।
थोर केली भक्तीची सीमा । पुरुषीं पुरुषोत्तमा साधिलें ॥७४॥
बहिणीचा निजभाव । जाला पंढरीसी निर्वाह ।
पांडुरंगीं जडला भाव । जाला ठाव निजपदीं ॥७५॥

---

१४. पतिव्रताधर्मपर

अभंग ४६७

पतिव्रता धर्म ऐका गे साजणी। धन्य ज्या गर्तिणी[१] पुण्यशील ॥ १ ॥
येणेंचि श्रवणें मुक्ति होय जीवा। पतीविण देवा नाठविती ॥ २ ॥
आपणां आपण ओळखिलें जिनें। धन्य तेचि जाणें पतिव्रता ॥ ३ ॥
प्रपंच परमार्थ चालवी समान। तिनेंच गगन झेलियेलें ॥ ४ ॥
कर्म तेंचि ब्रह्म ब्रह्म तेंचि कर्म। ऐसें जिनें वर्म जाणियेलें ॥ ५ ॥
अखंडित ध्यास भगवंताचा चित्ता। तेचि पतिव्रता तिन्ही लोकां ॥ ६ ॥
रागद्वेष मनीं जाणिवेचा[२] फुंग[३]। न धरिजे संग अधर्माचा ॥ ७ ॥
इंद्रियाच्या वृत्ति विधीनें सांवरी। न दिसे अंतरीं द्वैतभाव ॥ ८ ॥
साधुसंतसेवा पतीचें वचन। पाळी तेचि धन्य पतिव्रता ॥ ९ ॥
शांतिक्षमादया पाळी भूतकृपा। जाणोनी स्वरूपा पतीचिया ॥ १० ॥
पतीचें वचन अमृतासमान। धन्य तिचा जन्म मातापिता ॥ ११ ॥
बहिणी म्हणे तिनें जिंतिला[४] संसार। वैकुंठींचा थार[५] केला तिनें ॥ १२ ॥

अभंग ४६८

परपुरुषाचें[६] काय सांगों सुख। हरे सर्व दुःख संसाराचें ॥ १ ॥
म्हणोनिया संग धरावा तयाचा। सकळ सुखाचा सुखदाता ॥ २ ॥
परपुरुषाचें देखतां चरण। उपरमे[७] मन सुखावोनी ॥ ३ ॥
परपुरुषाचें देखतां स्वरूप। कोटि सूर्यदीप हारपती ॥ ४ ॥
परपुरुषाचें सुख लाधे जरी। उतरोनी करीं सीस[८] घ्यावें ॥ ५ ॥
बहिणी म्हणे काय न कळे पुण्य केलें। सुख हें लाधलें परपुरुषाचें ॥ ६ ॥

---

१ कुलस्त्रिया. २ ज्ञानाचा. ३ अभिमान. ४ जिंकला. ५ आश्रय.
६ परमेश्वराचें. ७ तुष्ट होई. ८ मस्तक.

अभंग ४६९

पतीचिया बोला सर्वस्वें उदार । न भंगे उत्तर जीव जातां ॥ १ ॥
धन्य ती संसारीं जाति गोत-कूळ । वैकुंठींचें मूळ तियेलागीं ॥ २ ॥
कायावाचा मनें पतीसी शरण । खेळे ब्रह्मज्ञान तिचे द्वारीं ॥ ३ ॥
पापपुण्य काहीं न विचारितां मनीं । पतीच्या वचनीं जीव देई ॥ ४ ॥
विधीचें भजन अखंड शेजारीं । जैसी ते कामारी[१] दासी पाहें ॥ ५ ॥
बहिणी म्हणे तिनें उभयही कुळें । तारियेलीं बळें पतिधर्में ॥ ६ ॥

अभंग ४७०

ऐका गे साजणी स्वहिताच्या कोणी । सांगतां हें मनीं धरा बाई ॥ १ ॥
आपुल्या संसारा कांहीं हित करा । सांगताहें धरा मनोभावें ॥ २ ॥
पाहिजे तें पुण्य सुकृताचे कोडी[२] । तेव्हां लागे गोडी परपुरुषीं ॥ ३ ॥
परपुरुषीं रातली[३] स्वप्रेमें मातली । तिची काय बोली येर[४] आतां ॥ ४ ॥
स्वसुखें रातली जनांत नाहली । निघूनियां गेली लोकाचारीं ॥ ५ ॥
क्रियानष्टधर्म आचरूं लागली । वाळीसी टाकिली गणगोतीं ॥ ६ ॥
न कळे याति-कुळ-नांवरूप कोण । गेली पैं रिघोन त्याजसवें ॥ ७ ॥
तियेचेनि नांवें फोडावी[५] घागरी । नाहीं ते संसारीं बहिणी म्हणे ॥ ८ ॥

अभंग ४७१

ऐसी कोण आहे उदार जीवाची । गोडी घेत याची मनोभावें ॥ १ ॥
आपुलेनि हातें घरा लावी आगी । मग सुख भोगी संगें त्याच्या ॥ २ ॥
जनवाद लोक बोलती अपार । न खंडी निर्धार संग त्याचा ॥ ३ ॥
बहिणी म्हणे कायावाचामनें प्राण । परपुरुषालागोन रातलीसे ॥ ४ ॥

अभंग ४७२

सांडियेली लाज लौकिकव्यवहार । मांडियेले चार परपुरुषीं ॥ १ ॥
आतां आम्हांसवें काय जनां चाड । कासयाची भीड धरूं बाई ॥ २ ॥

---

१ सेवक. २ वीस ही संख्या. ३ रममाण झाली. ४ दुसरी. ५ घागर फोडावी, म्हणजे मेली असें समजावें.

लोकलाज शंका सारिला पडदा । परपुरुषीं सदा रळी[1] करूं ॥ ३ ॥
मान-अपमाना नाहीं आम्हां काज । एकांताचें गुज सेवूं बाई ॥ ४ ॥
बहिणी म्हणे तोंड नलगे दावावें । ऐसें केलें देवें काय करूं ॥ ५ ॥

अभंग ४७३

धन्य त्रिभुवनीं वंद्य पतिव्रता । जी निजहिता प्रवर्तली ॥ १ ॥
ऐसियाची भेटी होतांचि लौकरी । पापाची बोहरी[2] होय तेणें ॥ २ ॥
स्वपति जिनें वोळखिला चित्तीं । धन्य ती जगतीं त्रिभुवनीं ॥ ३ ॥
श्रवणीं तोचि ऐके मननीं तोचि देखे । निजध्यास सुखें घेत असे ॥ ४ ॥
अणुमात्र वृत्ति नव्हे तिची भिन्न । सदा समाधान स्वामिसुखें ॥ ५ ॥
दृश्यत्व तिमिरा सारोनियां मागें । सदा स्वामिसंगें उभी शेजीं ॥ ६ ॥
स्वामीचें बोलणें खुणाचि जाणणें । मौनेंचि करणें विहित कर्म ॥ ७ ॥
बोलतां तें मौन आकारा ना शून्य । गुण ना निर्गुण वर्ततसे ॥ ८ ॥
अद्वैतानिराळें ब्रह्मांडावेगळें । ते सुखसोहाळे भोगीतसे ॥ ९ ॥
जीवनाचें जीवन असंगीं समाधान । त्रिपुटी विलक्षण नांदतसे ॥१०॥
ज्ञेय-ज्ञप्तिज्ञान[3] राहिले संपोन । निजानंदघन होउनी ठेलें ॥११॥
होउनी ठेली वृत्ति अवघी पारूषली[4] । तेथें कोण बोली बोलूं आतां ॥१२॥
ऐसी स्थिति जया स्त्रीसी वा पुरुषा । धन्य तेचि देखा पतिव्रता ॥१३॥
बहिणी म्हणे धन्या तेचि जन्मा आली । कीर्ति विस्तारली त्रिभुवनीं ॥१४॥

---

१ लडिवाळपणानें धरलेला हट्ट; विनोद. २ नाश. ३ ज्ञेय, जाणावयास योग्य, (ज्ञप्ति) = ज्ञाता, जाणता. ४ नष्ट झाली.